Bending the Rules

Bending the Rules

Procedural Politicking in the Bureaucracy

RACHEL AUGUSTINE POTTER

The University of Chicago Press
Chicago and London

The University of Chicago Press, Chicago 60637
The University of Chicago Press, Ltd., London
© 2019 by The University of Chicago
Published 2019
Printed in the United States of America

28 27 26 25 24 23 22 21 20 19   1 2 3 4 5

ISBN-13: 978-0-226-62160-9 (cloth)
ISBN-13: 978-0-226-62174-6 (paper)
ISBN-13: 978-0-226-62188-3 (e-book)
DOI: https://doi.org/10.7208/chicago/9780226621883.001.0001

Library of Congress Cataloging-in-Publication Data

Names: Potter, Rachel Augustine, author.
Title: Bending the rules : procedural politicking in the bureaucracy / Rachel Augus-
    tine Potter.
Description: Chicago : The University of Chicago Press, 2019. | Includes biblio-
    graphical references and index.
Identifiers: LCCN 2018051858 | ISBN 9780226621609 (cloth : alk. paper) | ISBN
    9780226621746 (pbk. : alk. paper) | ISBN 9780226621883 (e-book)
Subjects: LCSH: Administrative procedure—United States. | Administrative
    procedure—Political aspects—United States. | Administrative agencies—
    United States—Rules and practice.
Classification: LCC KF5411 .P68 2019 | DDC 342.73/06—dc23
LC record available at https://lccn.loc.gov/2018051858

♾ This paper meets the requirements of ANSI/NISO z39.48-1992
(Permanence of Paper).

For Team Potter
PBKP, HCP & DAP

Contents

Acknowledgments

I am so very glad to be done writing this book. It truly has been a labor of love and—as is often the case with long projects—sometimes a cross to bear. I once heard an author describe his experience of writing a book along the lines of "words just flying onto the page." That has not been my experience; instead, what you are reading is the accumulation of numerous long nights, myriad weekend hours, and too many cups of coffee to count. My hope is that all of this writing and rewriting, thinking and rethinking, editing and reediting, makes for a better-reasoned and more enjoyable final product for you, the reader.

I would be remiss if I did not alert you, dear reader, of my own bias in writing this book. From 2005 to 2007, I worked as a policy analyst at the White House Office of Information and Regulatory Affairs, an institution that figures prominently in the book's analysis. In this role, I became steeped in the rulemaking process and interacted with dozens of officials in the Executive Office of the President and bureaucrats in a host of federal agencies. Through this experience, I became deeply convinced of the talent and competence of career civil servants and political appointees across the federal bureaucracy. Those who view bureaucrats as paper pushers or slackers may well be put off, but I cannot help but see these individuals as smart and strategic; that belief shines through clearly in the pages that follow.

With that disclaimer out of the way, I turn to the task of giving credit where it is due. Many people have shaped this into a better project and saved it from being too solitary an endeavor. The project began at the University of Michigan, where I benefited tremendously from the counsel of Jowei Chen, Rick Hall, Ken Kollman, and Chuck Shipan. Chuck, in particular, has provided feedback on multiple drafts, offered career advice, and been an all-star mentor and human being. My colleagues at the University of Virginia have been unfailingly supportive in reading chapters and offering advice about the publishing process. I have been lucky to work with Jeff Jenkins, David Klein, Jon Kropko, Gabi Kruks-Wisner, David Leblang, Anne Meng, Sid Milkis, and Craig Volden, each of whom provided feedback on how to improve this book.

Outside of my home institutions, I have benefited from the generosity of many friends and colleagues in political science and beyond. Graeme Boushey, Greg Huber, George Krause, Molly Reynolds, Janna Rezaee, and Alan Wiseman all read portions of this book and provided useful feedback. Chuck Myers and Holly Smith at the University of Chicago Press have been both encouraging and patient. I am also thankful for the contributions of Madhura Bhat, Julia Gray, Andrew Kerner, Alison Roth-Kerner, the Augustines, and the Potters. Seminar audiences at Emory University, Georgetown University, Princeton University, Texas A&M University, Vanderbilt University, the University of Houston, and the University of Texas at Austin all asked incisive questions and helped me to think through different aspects of the project. Portions of the project were also presented at the National Capital Area Political Science Association American Politics Workshop at George Washington University, the "Separation of Powers Conference" at the University of Georgia, and various association conferences. Additionally, the undergraduate students in my Introduction to Public Administration course in the fall of 2016 read chapter 2 and gave feedback on how to make it more accessible.

In the early stages of the project, I received financial support from the Horowitz Foundation for Social Policy and later on from the Bankard Fund for Political Economy at UVA. I also benefited from the work of an army of research assistants who helped assemble the data for this book; for their service, I am indebted to Bennie Ashton, Kim Ganczak, Nick Jacobs, Erica Liao, Kal Munis, Steven Riley, Aïta Seck, Ilana Shapiro, Ricky Williams, and Connor Wood. Jason MacDonald generously offered his data on limitation riders, which informs the analysis in chapter 2.

Last, but certainly not least, this book is dedicated to my three most favorite people on this planet, each of whom weathered the storm of this book with remarkable aplomb. My husband, Phil, has been my devoted partner and best friend going on twenty years. Given his dry sense of humor and penchant for sarcasm, "cheerleader" seems ill fitting, but I can think of no better description of his unflagging enthusiasm for this book. My daughters, Hazel and Dorothy, have each contributed in their own way to the completion of this project. Hazel offered well-timed hugs and constructive criticism (page numbers are important, after all). Dorothy's impending arrival compelled the completion of the last chapters, and her subsequent debut has made our family complete. Team Potter inspires me to be a better wife, mother, scholar, and person each and every day. For that—and so much more—I am endlessly grateful.

Abbreviations

ACA	Patient Protection and Affordable Care Act
ACUS	Administrative Conference of the United States
AMS	Agricultural Marketing Service
ANPRM	Advance Notice of Proposed Rulemaking
APA	Administrative Procedure Act
APC	American Pizza Community
APHIS	Animal and Plant Health Inspection Service
CFR	*Code of Federal Regulations*
CMS	Centers for Medicare and Medicaid Services
CRP	Center for Responsive Politics
DOI	Department of the Interior
DOL	Department of Labor
DOT	Department of Transportation
ED	Department of Education
EPA	Environmental Protection Agency
FAA	Federal Aviation Administration
FDA	Food and Drug Administration
FMCSA	Federal Motor Carrier Safety Administration
FR	*Federal Register*
FSMA	Food Safety and Modernization Act
FTE	full-time equivalent
HEA	Higher Education Act
HHS	Department of Health and Human Services
HOS	hours of service
IFR	interim final rule

MC	member of Congress
NCLB	No Child Left Behind
NHTSA	National Highway Traffic Safety Administration
NOAA	National Oceanic and Atmospheric Administration
NRA	National Restaurant Association
NSF	National Science Foundation
OCC	Office of the Comptroller of the Currency
OESE	Office of Elementary and Secondary Education
OIRA	Office of Information and Regulatory Affairs
OMB	Office of Management and Budget
OPM	Office of Personnel Management
OSHA	Occupational Safety and Health Administration
RIA	regulatory impact analysis
RIN	Regulatory Identification Number
SSA	Social Security Administration
UA	*Unified Agenda*
USDA	United States Department of Agriculture
VA	Department of Veterans Affairs
WOTUS	Waters of the United States

1

The Power of Procedure

Contraception—who has access to it and how it is paid for—is contested ground in the ongoing culture wars in the United States. As of 2018, contraception is legally considered a "preventative service," and in most health insurance plans, women can obtain it without a co-pay or any out-of-pocket fees. When this so-called contraceptive mandate was first announced in August 2011, it ignited a firestorm; the president of Catholic University opined that the policy would lead religious organizations to "abandon their commitment to serve poor people of all faiths" and that the rule impinged on individual freedoms.[1] These positions were supported by numerous religious organizations and businesses, and over the next two years, these groups initiated more than sixty lawsuits against the mandate.[2] Meanwhile, organizations on the left celebrated the policy change, with the president of Planned Parenthood describing the policy as a "historic victory for women's health."[3]

Many assume, perhaps reasonably so, that such an important policy change originated in the halls of Congress. Indeed, the mandate is often incorrectly attributed to the Affordable Care Act (ACA, or "Obamacare"),[4] President Obama's landmark health-care program. However, while the ACA clocks in at more than 2,400 pages and addresses dozens of topics, including the requirement that insurers cover preventative services free of charge, it is mum on the payment status of contraception (i.e., whether contraception should be considered a preventative service and be provided free of charge).

1. Garvey (2011).
2. Morgan (2013).
3. Rice (2011).
4. Pub. L. No. 111-148.

The contraceptive mandate actually stems from a policy decision made by bureaucrats at the Department of Health and Human Services (HHS), a federal agency.[5] In August 2011, more than a year after the passage of the ACA, HHS drew on that legal authority to issue a discretionary but legally binding rule stating that contraception should be considered a preventative service.[6]

This example underscores a common misconception about how law is made in the United States. Schoolchildren are taught that elected legislators hold hearings, deliberate, and vote on bills, which are then sent to the president for his (someday her) signature. This is not inaccurate; many of the major policy changes that have occurred in the past twenty years—from the creation of Obamacare, to the passage of the Patriot Act, to the regulation of banks in the wake of the 2008 financial crisis—have been accomplished, at least in part, through the choreographed actions of Congress and the president.

But this is not the only way that law is made; in fact, it is not even the way the *majority* of new law is created in the United States today. Unelected bureaucrats—people who work at HHS or the Environmental Protection Agency (EPA), to name two among scores of agencies—routinely create, and subsequently implement, rules that carry the same force and effect as laws passed by Congress. By some estimates, more than 90 percent of American law is created by administrative rules issued by federal agencies.[7] In 2014 alone, federal agencies issued more than 3,500 legally binding rules, far outstripping the 224 new laws created by Congress and the president (and even those laws are typically implemented through rulemaking).[8]

Like laws, bureaucratic rules or regulations—I use the terms interchangeably throughout the book—are substantively important. As the contraceptive mandate rule demonstrates, rules have broad policy reach and meaning-

5. The policy decision, which came in the form of a rulemaking, was actually jointly issued by HHS, along with the Department of Labor and the Department of Treasury. I focus on HHS here, since it was the lead agency on the rule and the focal point of the backlash against the policy.

6. The agency's rule included an exemption for certain religious employers. The religious exemption proved to be the sticking point of the rule, as many opponents felt that the exception was too narrowly defined. HHS has subsequently relaxed the policy.

7. Warren (2011).

8. The judiciary also creates a body of case law through court decisions. That body of law is overshadowed by laws produced by the legislative process, although scholars debate the societal impact of policy changes made from the bench (see Rosenberg 2008). Lawmaking figures in this paragraph are drawn from the *Congressional Record*'s "Final Résumé of Congressional Activity" for 2014. Rulemaking counts are from the *Federal Register*.

fully affect the daily lives of citizens. In recent years rules have also triggered the following policy changes:[9]

- In 1996, the Food and Drug Administration (FDA) published a rule that limited the advertising and promotion of cigarettes by manufacturers. Among other major changes, the rule prohibited cigarette sales to people younger than the age of eighteen and limited the extent to which tobacco companies could promote their products through public events (e.g., sporting events, concerts) or materials (e.g., T-shirts).[10]
- In 2000, the Agricultural Marketing Service (AMS) established national standards for the labeling of agricultural products that are marketed as "organic." These regulations created an accreditation program for state and private certifying entities and set certification standards for farms and handling operations. At the time, the program was described as the "strongest and most comprehensive organic standard in the world."[11]
- In 2007, the Office of Surface Mining in the Department of Interior proposed a rule that allowed mountaintop coal mining. Before the rule's issuance, the legal status of this mining practice was dubious, so the rule accelerated the use of mountaintop mining.
- In 2008, the Department of Health and Human Services promulgated a so-called medical conscience rule that required recipients of federal funds to allow doctors and nurses to abstain from participating in procedures (e.g., abortions) if those procedures were at odds with their religious convictions.
- In 2009, the EPA issued a regulatory finding that greenhouse gases endangered public health.[12] This finding laid the groundwork for a series of subsequent rules designed to limit or reduce greenhouse gas emissions. These rules constitute the largest organized response to climate change at the federal level.
- In 2011, the Office of Postsecondary Education in the Department of Education wrote a "gainful employment" rule that set benchmark standards for colleges and universities to meet in order to continue participating in the federal student aid program. The standards required programs to

9. Rules can also address new and challenging policy problems. As of this writing, the Federal Aviation Administration was working on a series of rules to set boundaries for both commercial and recreational drone use, and the Food and Drug Administration was drafting regulations that establish standards for the production and sale of electronic cigarettes.

10. The Supreme Court overturned this rule in the seminal case *FDA v. Brown & Williamson Tobacco Corp.* (529 U.S. 120 (2000)). See Derthick (2011) and Kessler (2001) for fascinating accounts of the politics of tobacco in the 1990s and this FDA rule in particular.

11. US Department of Agriculture (2000).

12. The EPA issued this finding in response to the Supreme Court's ruling in *Massachusetts v. Environmental Protection Agency* (549 U.S. 497 (2007)).

meet minimum thresholds, such as a base debt-to-income ratio for their graduates. The intent of the rule was to remove the bad apples from the federal student aid program, particularly for-profit and vocational schools that had been charging students high rates but delivering little in terms of educational and professional outcomes.[13]

• In 2015, the Employee Benefits Security Administration within the Department of Labor (DOL) proposed a rule that addressed conflicts of interest for financial advisers. The proposed rule aimed to redress a loss in retirement savings of nearly $17 billion a year, resulting from the fact that some brokers who did not have a fiduciary responsibility to their clients selected investments that were in their own pecuniary interest. These self-serving investments cost clients more in fees than did other potential investments that performed as well or better.

Of course, these are just a small subset of the policy changes that were generated through rulemaking. Each of them was also controversial and netted front-page headlines; indeed, several were even challenged and subsequently overturned in court.[14] However, just as the bulk of laws passed by Congress lack substantive policy heft—instead tweaking existing programs, dealing with symbolic issues, or commemorating relatively trivial dates such as World Plumbing Day[15]—the majority of rules issued by federal agencies deal with the mundane matters of the administrative state. For instance, in 2001 the AMS, the same agency that created the National Organic Program the year before, used rulemaking to set new standards for the size of holes in Swiss cheese.[16] More recently, in 2007, the Office of Personnel Management (OPM) issued a rule that increased the amount that federal agencies reimbursed civilian employees for uniform purchases from $400 to $800 per year. While rules such as these are banal in the grander policy schematic, the point remains that, like laws, rules can fulfill a multitude of policy needs.

There are other parallels between lawmaking and rulemaking. Lawmaking is widely understood to be a political activity, meaning that in Harold Lasswell's famous words it deals with "who gets what, when, and how." Accord-

---

13. This rule was partially vacated by the DC district court in *Association of Private Colleges and Universities v. Duncan* (No. 11-1314 (D.D.C. 2012)), leading the agency to restart the rulemaking anew. I discuss this rule in more detail in chapter 2.

14. Further, some of these rules later became the target of the Trump administration's regulatory rollback program. As I discuss later in the book, the Trump administration likely constitutes a distinct regulatory regime from the one under study.

15. World Plumbing Day was created by an act of Congress. It is celebrated on March 11.

16. For what it is worth, the new standards established that the cheese "eyes" should be between 3/8 and 13/16 of an inch in diameter to qualify as Swiss cheese.

ingly, scholars in the positive political science tradition have devoted considerable effort to understanding what motivates legislative actors, who has power within this process, what the strategic incentives of these actors are at each stage, and, ultimately, how laws are made (or not made).[17] Traditionally, rulemaking was considered a rote administrative activity,[18] with observers often describing it as a way to "fill up the details" of laws.[19] This created a perception that policy changes made through rulemaking were both neutral and unimportant. In recent years, however, scholars have increasingly come to view rulemaking in the same vein as lawmaking: as a decidedly political activity.[20]

The argument in this book builds from this emergent view that rulemaking is inherently political. It is political not just because it deals with politically important topics, but also because the bureaucrats who manage the process behave in politically strategic ways when creating new rules. Indeed, this is a book about how the regulatory sausage is made. Agency bureaucrats inevitably have preferences involving the policies that are created through the rulemaking process. These preferences arise from a host of concerns, including those related to career advancement, job satisfaction, program quality, and even policy itself. However, bureaucrats are not free to implement their preferred policies unimpeded. Because rulemaking occurs in a separation-of-powers system, each of the three constitutional branches—the president, Congress, and the courts—can get involved in the process, often at the bidding of affected interest groups or other constituents. Once involved, these overseers can (and often do) redirect agency rulemaking efforts or sanction agencies that have overstepped bounds, real or perceived.

However, rather than capitulating to the demands of the political branches, the argument I make in this book is that bureaucrats can use their position as both policy proposers and process managers to their advantage. That is, working within a set of established constraints, bureaucrats can use administrative tools to strategically and systematically insulate their rulemaking proposals from political scrutiny and interference. Scholars typically home in on bureaucrats' advantage at the policy proposal stage; while this is

17. For discussions on each of these points, see Beckmann (2010); Cameron (2000); Cox and McCubbins (2005); Binder (2003); Krehbiel (2010); and Mayhew (1974, 2005).

18. This perception follows from Stewart's (1975) "transmission belt" theory of bureaucracy, which posits that agencies merely carry out the statutory directives laid out by Congress and do not exercise their own political judgments.

19. This phrase originated with Justice Marshall's decision in *Wayman v. Southard* (23 U.S. 1 (1825)), which dealt with the legality of legislative delegation to the other branches.

20. See, for example, Gersen and O'Connell (2008, 2009); Nou (2013); Nou and Stiglitz (2016); O'Connell (2008, 2011); and Tiller and Spiller (1999).

undoubtedly important, my argument instead focuses on the process, specifically how bureaucrats manage the procedures associated with rulemaking.

Rulemaking procedures are typically cast as a way to constrain bureaucratic behavior; by forcing agencies to follow a set process, bureaucrats—theoretically speaking—have less room to maneuver than they might otherwise. However, procedures are implemented by the very bureaucrats whose behavior they are designed to constrain. Further, the expert bureaucrats who run the administrative process have superior insight into how rulemaking procedures tend to play out and can use this information to steer policy making. This enables bureaucrats to deploy procedures to their advantage in what I refer to as *procedural politicking*, or using procedures in strategic ways so as to insulate policies that are at risk of political interventions and ensure that bureaucrat-preferred policies endure.

Importantly, I do not take up the question of when and why bureaucrats choose to undertake the regulatory process in the first place—numerous scholars have already addressed that question.[21] Rather, I consider what happens once that decision has been made and, more specifically, how procedural choices influence the course of a rulemaking. Ultimately, my goal is to encourage scholars and observers to think about how bureaucratic power is exercised in this policy-making venue.

Understanding Rulemaking

Before proceeding further, it is worth a detour to clarify just what a rule is—and what it is not. According to the Administrative Procedure Act (APA),[22] the primary law governing the rulemaking process, a rule is a statement of agency policy that is designed to "implement, interpret, or prescribe law or policy" and that has general or particular applicability and future effect. Rules are distinct from adjudicative actions, which deal with individual case deci-

21. For instance, Potter and Shipan (2018) argue that agencies adjust the volume of their rulemaking activity in light of the political environment. See also Boushey and McGrath (2015). Other scholars make the case that agencies can strategically pursue venues other than rulemaking to achieve policy gains. To take one example, Melnick (2014) argues that the Office of Civil Rights within the Department of Education has often used guidance documents (and other nonbinding policy instruments such as "Dear Colleague" letters) instead of rulemaking to make important public policy changes with respect to race and gender policies under Title IX in higher education. While these policy instruments are not legally binding, regulated parties often comply as if they were. Raso (2015) also considers how agencies trade off between rules and guidance documents.

22. Pub. L. No. 79-404.

sions, in that they are policies that apply uniformly to similarly situated individuals.[23] The aggregate body of law that is created through the rulemaking process is referred to as the *Code of Federal Regulations* (CFR).

To create a new rule, agencies must typically follow a process known as notice-and-comment, which requires that affected parties be given prior notice of a rule change and be afforded an opportunity to submit written comments on the change.[24] This form of rulemaking, also known as informal rulemaking, is the most common way that agencies make changes to the CFR.[25] Generally speaking, the process includes the publication of a proposed rule in the *Federal Register*, a comment period during which the public can participate, and the subsequent publication of a binding final rule in the *Federal Register*. The rule generally takes effect after a waiting period (usually thirty days after the final rule is published).

In studying this process, academic scholarship crosses several disciplinary boundaries, including economics, political science, law, and public administration. This interdisciplinarity has led to a rich but disjointed body of research on the regulatory process. Broadly speaking, research on bureaucracy and rulemaking takes one of two approaches, focusing either on external actors and how they can exert political influence over an agency or on internal actors and how meaningfully they deliberate when making policy decisions.

The external perspective on bureaucratic politics is often premised on a principal-agent framework. Borrowed from economics, this framework was developed to explain the dilemma an employer (the principal) faces with respect to her employee (the agent). The principal and the agent are assumed to have different preferences, and so there are a number of intrinsic compli-

23. A hypothetical example helps illustrate the difference between rulemaking and case adjudication. In May 2008, the Social Security Administration (SSA) revised its regulations regarding Ticket to Work, a program that allows disabled beneficiaries to return to work and still remain on the disability rolls (73 FR 29323, May 20, 2008). In that rulemaking, SSA expanded the program to include all adult beneficiaries with disabilities who were classified as "medical improvement expected" (MIE); previously, the program had been limited to MIE beneficiaries only after they had completed their regularly scheduled disability review. Expanding the program could, theoretically, have been accomplished through individual case adjudication; SSA could have granted individuals entrance to the program on a case-by-case basis.

24. Like any bureaucratic process, however, there are numerous exceptions. For example, agencies can also publish a prerule (i.e., an Advance Notice of Proposed Rulemaking) or hold hearings in conjunction with the public comment period. I cover these procedural exceptions in more detail in chapter 2.

25. The alternative, formal rulemaking, is rarely used. It is a cumbersome process, conducted in an adversarial and trial-like manner, with an agency "judge" who calls witnesses in a series of hearings. See Kerwin and Furlong (2011).

cations. Because the principal is unable to provide a complete-enough contract to stipulate all the conditions that the agent might possibly encounter
and how the agent should behave in those circumstances, she gives the agent
discretion—which can be misused. The agent may also misrepresent himself
at the point of being hired (adverse selection) or change his behavior after
securing the contract (moral hazard).

In the context of rulemaking, the legislature is typically conceived of as
the principal (although the president and the courts are sometimes given this
role) and the bureaucratic agency as the agent.[26] The fundamental problem
is that the principal wants the agent to produce rules (which in turn produce
policy outcomes) that align with her preferences. The principal must delegate this function as a result of limits on both her capacity and her expertise.
However, there is an information asymmetry; she can observe outcomes only
in terms of the rules the agency publishes, and not the facts on the ground
that led the agency to make that choice. More specifically, the principal cannot obtain this information without substantial investigation (which requires
resources) and may not be able to acquire it at all.[27]

Scholars have identified institutional mechanisms that a principal can implement to solve this "political control" problem and to incentivize the agent
to adhere to the principal's preferences. Most notably, a series of seminal
articles by Mathew McCubbins, Roger Noll, and Barry Weingast (colloquially known as "McNollgast") from 1987 and 1989 argues that by establishing
a process that an agency must follow before reaching a policy decision—
otherwise known as an administrative procedure—political principals can
constrain agency decision making.[28] Rulemaking is considered the prototypical administrative procedure; by requiring notice-and-comment, the presi-

26. The model is often applied to questions of delegation, where the principal must decide
which tasks to give to the agent (e.g., Bawn 1995; Epstein and O'Halloran 1999; Huber and
Shipan 2002). However, with respect to rulemaking, delegation has often already occurred. As I
discuss in the next chapter, there is often a considerable time gap (sometimes spanning decades)
between when a legislative action occurs and when an agency issues a rule based on that statutory authority (Wiseman and Wright 2015). Accordingly, I focus on applying the framework
to questions of oversight and whether the agency is properly using the authority it has been
granted.

27. Put another way, the agency has acquired policy expertise that is not shared by Congress
or the president; for more on how agents deal with information problems, see Gailmard and
Patty (2013).

28. Other administrative procedures include advisory committees (Doherty 2013; Moffitt
2010) and reporting requirements (Doherty and Selin 2014). Of course, the president and Congress have other tools to influence the bureaucracy aside from administrative procedures. For

dent and Congress are assured that they will be given advance warning of an agency's intended policy change. Additionally, these principals need not monitor the process directly but can rely on vigilant interest groups to sound a "fire alarm" and alert them if intervention is necessary.[29] In this way, principals can stop a rule in its tracks when needed rather than being presented with a noxious final rule as a fait accompli.

The idea that external principals successfully steer the administrative process has been extraordinarily durable.[30] Yet this approach ignores the agency's role in responding to these outside political pressures. The rulemaking process affords principals ample opportunity to intervene in agency decisions, but it is not all driven from the top down. Agencies have considerable powers of their own in the process. Instead of treating this relationship as rigidly hierarchical, the relationship is likely a more dynamic one wherein principals institute processes and agencies strategically respond to those processes.[31] This reconception of the process is particularly appropriate in the context of

---

instance, the president can staff the agency with presidential appointees (Lewis 2008) or central-ize oversight of the agency into the Executive Office of the President (Moe 1985).

29. The notion of fire-alarm oversight originated with McCubbins and Schwartz (1984). This type of oversight relies on outside parties (usually interest groups) to pull a fire alarm and alert overseers to agency infractions. When compared with more traditional forms of routin-ized oversight like oversight hearings (which they dub "police patrols"), fire-alarm oversight is believed to be less costly for overseers and may even be more effective at detecting infractions (Aberbach 1990; Horn 1995).

30. In spite of the framework's deep roots, its application has both theoretical and empirical inconsistencies. On the theoretical side, Wiseman and Wright (2015) point out several logical inconsistencies in McNollgast's original argument (McCubbins, Noll, and Weingast 1987), par-ticularly that *deck stacking* and *autopilot*, the mechanisms by which procedures facilitate control, conflict with how the courts have interpreted agency legal obligations and rights under notice-and-comment. Their work provides an important contribution in that it meaningfully brings in the role of the courts. On the empirical side, the evidence confirming external political influence over agencies is mixed. Some studies have shown that when the preferences of political princi-pals change, agencies increase or reduce their outputs accordingly (e.g., Olson 1996; Ringquist 1995; Shipan 2004; Weingast and Moran 1983; Wood 1988; Wood and Waterman 1991), providing broad support for the idea that principals maintain some level of influence over agencies. How-ever, while a statistically significant effect may suggest that there exists some level of influence, there is no sense of how much control is enough to determine which actors effectively dictate the course of public policy. In perhaps the only direct test of McNollgast's argument, Balla and Wright (2001) find no evidence to support the idea that the groups that are supposedly favored by the administrative process actually receive preferential treatment, which suggests that proce-dures do not necessarily advantage principals.

31. For more on dynamic principal-agent models more generally, see Krause (1999); and Moe (2006).

notice-and-comment, where the APA's basic setup has been in place for more than seventy years, enabling bureaucrats to learn and adapt to the process's nuances, loopholes, and incentive structure.

In contrast to the external perspective on notice-and-comment taken in the political science and economics literatures, public administration and legal scholars tend to take a more bottom-up, agency-centric approach. This perspective digs into how agencies manage their administrative functions and analyzes the normative implications of these activities.

This manifests most concretely in an attempt to understand whether agencies meaningfully deliberate and represent the public interest when making regulatory policies. A repeated finding is that there is an imbalance in the volume of public comments that agencies receive from business and other moneyed interests compared to public interest groups and citizens.[32] Many have also pointed out that that these moneyed and organized groups tend to enjoy privileged access to agencies at earlier stages in the process, even before a proposed rule is put out for comment.[33] This creates an impression that the regulatory process is closed to outsiders, leading to investigations of whether agencies actually take this feedback into account in their final decisions. There is no consensus on that point; while some find that group comments are of no consequence for the agency's final policy decision, others find that there is an effect but that it holds only in certain contexts.[34]

Taken together, concerns about a participatory imbalance and lack of agency responsiveness to comments have led many observers to dismiss notice-and-comment as fundamentally undemocratic.[35] Perhaps, most famously Elliott (1992) described the process as "kabuki theater," wherein agencies conduct all of the real business offstage and the drama on the public stage is just window dressing as agencies go through the motions.

Yet studies like these that view the rulemaking process up close rarely consider the broader political environment in which agencies operate and how that environment might affect an agency's willingness to deliberate (and to

32. See Golden (1998); Yackee (2006); Yackee and Yackee (2006); and Wagner, Barnes, and Peters (2011).

33. Chubb (1983); Furlong and Kerwin (2005); Golden (1998); Yackee (2006); Yackee and Yackee (2006); Wagner, Barnes, and Peters (2011).

34. On the former, see Magat, Krupnick, and Harrington (1986); and Nixon, Howard, and DeWitt (2002). On the latter, see Golden (1998); and Yackee (2006).

35. See Bernstein (1955); Lowi (1969); Wagner, Barnes, and Peters (2011). Meanwhile, others have considered how to engage citizens more meaningfully in the process (Mendelson 2011; Farina et al. 2011).

do so publicly).[36] Additionally, many (though not all) of these studies assume that agencies passively accept feedback from stakeholders rather than actively (and strategically) inviting feedback and shaping its content.

Moving beyond rulemaking, other scholars have cast agencies and bureaucrats in a more strategic role. For example, Moffitt (2010) argues that the FDA strategically consults its advisory committees (i.e., standing groups of outside experts), effectively spreading a drug's risk from the agency to a broader group of stakeholders and also burnishing the agency's reputation. Similarly, Huber (2007) suggests that bureaucrats at the Occupational Safety and Health Administration (OSHA) practice "strategic neutrality" when it comes to enforcement policy. At high levels, OSHA makes strategic policy choices about which industries to target for enforcement actions, while lower-level leaders insist that these decisions be implemented in a consistent and seemingly neutral manner. The net result is that agency is able to build political support and accomplish agency leaders' strategic ends while maintaining a reputation for professionalism and competence. Though not focused on rulemaking per se, studies like Moffitt's and Huber's advance the perception that bureaucrats are strategic actors in an ongoing dynamic game. Yet from a design perspective, this approach often yields a narrow focus on the inner workings of one agency.[37] This deep dive is often necessary to gain empirical and theoretical traction, but it invariably draws on the particular cultural and professional norms of the agency under study, raising questions about the broader generalizability of such theories to other agencies.

Both the external and the internal perspectives raise important theoretical considerations about the politics of rulemaking. External actors can and do impose constraints on what agencies do. Internally, agencies follow their own set of processes and norms and can exercise considerable autonomy. The theory I develop in this book bridges these perspectives. I acknowledge that the infrastructure surrounding notice-and-comment was created and is overseen by actors outside the agency, but I also consider how bureaucrats strategically respond to the incentives that the process induces. This allows

36. A handful of studies have drawn out the effects of the political process on agency rulemaking decisions (see, e.g., O'Connell 2008; Potter and Shipan 2018; and Yackee and Yackee 2009).

37. Additionally, the same agencies appear time and again as the foci of bureaucratic case studies. For example, the FDA is also studied by Carpenter (2010); Moffitt (2014); and Olson (1996). OSHA is also studied by Kim (2007); Schmidt (2002); Scholz (1991); Scholz, Twombly, and Headrick (1991); and Shapiro (2007).

me to identify systematic patterns of behavior in the regulatory process that persist across the administrative state.

Overview of the Argument

Studies of political institutions typically identify a set of fixed rules and explore how strategic actors respond and adapt to changes in those conditions. I adopt that approach here, treating notice-and-comment as an institution in its own right and assuming that its strictures are externally imposed. This book tackles three questions: (1) What are bureaucrats' incentives in the rulemaking process? (2) How do bureaucrats strategically manage the process in light of those incentives? (3) What are the broader implications of this behavior for democracy and policy making by the bureaucracy?

Rulemaking is a time- and resource-intensive endeavor for agencies. Agencies devote months, even years, to developing a rule, including time spent gathering information, conducting research, drafting and redrafting a policy, consulting with stakeholders, and managing and responding to public comments (which can number in the millions).[38] Some rules require detailed technical assessments, such as cost-benefit analysis, and others require sign-off by the Office of Information and Regulatory Affairs (OIRA), the White House clearinghouse for agency rules. The time it takes to complete all of these tasks is difficult to ascertain, since the point at which the agency first put pen to paper is not necessarily documented. Nonetheless, West (2004) finds that the average length of the proposal development period for the forty-two rules in his study was more than five years. Given that the time from the publication of the proposed rule to the publication of the final rule alone averages more than a year, it is clear that rules require a significant investment of the agency's time and resources.

Rules are not created in a vacuum but rather in the context of political oversight in a separation-of-powers system. And there are numerous points in the process of rule development that political intervention—from the president or OIRA, the courts, or congressional overseers—can stall a rule or gut it altogether. However, agencies, or more specifically the bureaucrats that work within them, are not passive observers of this political exchange. Because the outcome of the rulemaking process affects so many aspects of bureaucrats' livelihoods, from their career prospects to concerns over policy and implementability, they can insulate policies that are under development

---

38. Nou (2013) and West (2009) both discuss the labor involved in producing a new regulation.

from political intervention.[39] Of course, since political overseers are some-times supportive of agencies and their rules, insulation is not always nec-essary. Rather, it is when rules are most vulnerable to political interference because overseers are predisposed against them that bureaucratic insulation is warranted.

When it comes to rulemaking, bureaucrats are the "first movers," mean-ing that they have the opportunity to initiate regulatory proposals. In doing so, they often have considerable latitude in the particulars of the policy they advance. An obvious way that agencies can make their regulatory proposals "stick" is by proposing regulatory policies that are tolerable to those political overseers who have the ability to overturn them. While making policy con-cessions is a tried-and-true strategy,[40] it may be unattractive from the agency's perspective, since it may yield a policy that does not align with other policy goals of the agency or the policy preferences of bureaucrats themselves. Yet agencies have another path to strategically insulate their rulemaking without sacrificing their preferred outcome: procedural politicking. An agency's pro-cedural powers include things like control over how a proposal is written or whether the agency consults its advisory board beforehand.

Some examples of HHS's use of procedural politicking shed light on how such tools can be useful to an agency. Agencies can frame their rulemaking proposals in terms that are more acceptable in the current political discourse, or they can avoid the use of certain terms that may be politically charged. In the HHS contraception rule discussed in the introduction to this chapter, HHS staff were careful to frame the issue in medical terms, as a change that was necessary for women's health and well-being.[41] In an op-ed piece published in *USA Today* Secretary Kathleen Sebelius of the HHS equated the policy with vaccinations for children, cancer screenings for adults, and wellness visits for seniors.[42] In the press materials and the rule text itself, the agency employed the more neutral (and medical sounding) term "contraception," avoiding the more loaded term "birth control." These tactics, while nuanced, helped to shape the way the public—and political overseers—perceived the rule.

---

39. O'Connell (2008, 966) summarizes this position as follows: "Agencies presumably want at least some of their rules to 'stick,' likely because of the rules' economic, political, or career benefits. In other words, agencies want their rules not to be withdrawn before final enactment, not to be rescinded after promulgation, not to face hostile [OIRA] or congressional oversight, and not to be struck down by the courts."

40. See, e.g., Cameron (2000) for a discussion of how a first-mover can propose policy in order to have it accepted by a veto player.

41. In contrast, the opposition framed the issue as one of religious freedom.

42. Sebelius (2012).

After a rule is drafted, it must be legitimated through notice-and-comment. Agencies again have considerable discretion in managing this part of the process, and rarely do two rules receive the same procedural treatment at this stage. Rather, for each rule an agency makes decisions about how much stakeholder outreach to conduct (and how much of this will be done publicly versus privately), and when to release various documents, among numerous other choices. Manipulating these procedural choices enables agencies to protect their rules when the political climate is hostile.

Again, reflecting on the contraceptive mandate clarifies the role of procedures at this stage of the process. In crafting the contraceptive mandate, HHS was careful to consult with many stakeholders outside the agency, including the renowned Institute of Medicine (IOM) and the agency's advisory committee. This consultation was consciously designed to transpire in the public eye; the advisory committee's meetings were open to the public and the IOM produced a report that was made publicly available (and was widely reported on by the media). Highly visible consultation of this nature is a procedural choice, and in this case it helped to legitimize the agency's decision in the public's eyes and thereby insulate the policy from principals.

Procedural powers mean that agencies have considerable influence over how the rulemaking process is managed, and that influence helps them achieve independent political objectives. While political oversight of the rulemaking process can (and does) occur, these managerial powers make oversight more difficult and, therefore, less frequent. As a result, unelected bureaucrats have substantial leverage over the regulatory policies that become binding law, much more than our current understanding gives them credit for. As with all political actors in our system of checks and balances, bureaucrats do not operate unchecked, but they are a powerful political force in the American system.

The Approach

In making the argument that bureaucrats can strategically exercise autonomy in a highly constrained policy-making environment, I do not tell the story of one rule or one agency. Rather, the focus is on how bureaucrats in a host of agencies scattered across the federal government systematically respond to the incentives created by a procedure-bound policy-making process. In the chapters that follow, I trace the arc of the rulemaking process from when an agency first begins working on a rule to when it completes that regulatory action. I rely on both case studies and statistical analyses to make my case. I also draw from interviews with more than a dozen agency regulatory personnel and interest group officials. All nonessential statistical details are relegated to appendixes or to footnotes, where interested readers may find them and others are unencumbered. My hope is not that any one individual case or test will definitively prove my theory, but rather that the preponderance of evidence will persuade readers of the argument.

The theoretical and empirical focus of this book is intentionally circumscribed: I focus on agencies within the executive branch over the twenty-year period from 1995 to 2014.[43] I do this for two reasons. First, the time period of this study was a period of relative stasis in the political and legal landscape surrounding rulemaking. The rulemaking process has evolved over time. In the 1970s and 1980s several landmark court rulings and the establishment of centralized regulatory review by the White House led agencies to reinterpret their regulatory duties.[44] In contrast, during the time period of this study, there were very few—if any—of these watershed moments.[45] Additionally, early in his administration, President Clinton issued an executive order that altered how centralized regulatory review was managed. In prior presidential administrations all rules were reviewed, but from Clinton's order onward only the most important rules were subject to review. Put differently, this period constitutes a distinct regulatory regime, where the rules and expectations of the regulatory game were clear to all of the parties involved. This regime was therefore different from the earlier period before Clinton's order and, as I discuss in the concluding chapter, may differ from the years that immediately followed its close.

Second, rulemaking by independent agencies is fundamentally different from rulemaking by executive branch agencies, and pooling the two types together would mask many important differences. Independent agencies

43. Where possible, I distinguish rules that are substantively important (e.g., contraception) from those that are less so (e.g., Swiss cheese holes).

44. Inter alia, *Chevron USA, Inc. v. Natural Resources Defense Council, Inc.* (467 U.S. 837 (1984)), *Motor Vehicles Manufacturers Association v. State Farm Mutual Automobile Insurance Corp.* (463 U.S. 29 (1983)), and *Vermont Yankee Nuclear Power Corp. v. Natural Resources Defense Council, Inc.* (435 U.S. 519 (1978)). I discuss the role of landmark cases in chapter 2.

45. A possible exception during this time period is *United States v. Mead Corp.* (533 U.S. 218 (2001)). In that case, the Supreme Court ruled that court deference to agencies should be reserved for instances where the agency issued a rulemaking, and not necessarily for other administrative actions such as tariff decisions. Some have suggested that in the wake of *Mead*, the benefits to agencies of issuing a rule increased (compared to other less-deferential agency actions), leading to an overall increase in the volume of regulatory actions produced (see, e.g., O'Connell 2008). However, because my analyses are conditional on the agency choosing to write a rule (i.e., I do not try to explain why agencies decide to issue rules at the outset), this change does not affect my analysis.

are largely free from the strictures of presidential oversight, which alters the
political context by removing one of the principals that agencies face. Specifically, while executive agencies are subject to centralized regulatory review,
independent agencies are not.[46] Additionally, many independent agencies
like the Federal Communications Commission have a board structure and
publicly vote on draft regulations. This process has no parallel in executive
branch agencies and affects the way that these agencies draft regulations
internally.[47]

The net result of these design choices is that this study provides a complete snapshot of agency management of the rulemaking process over a finite
but contemporary period of time. During this time, rules accomplished important policy objectives but were subject to a set of relatively fixed political
institutions. This allows for an exploration of how agencies respond to proxi-
mate changes in the political environment, such as changes in partisan control of Congress or the presidency. Understanding this regime also establishes
a baseline against which future regulatory reforms can be judged.

Defining Bureaucrats and Agencies

In discussing the politics of rulemaking I frequently use the terms "bureaucrat" and "agency" to describe, respectively, the actor and the institution responsible for the creation of rules. These are catchall terms that apply generically across the large swaths of rules and units of the administrative state, but
it is worth clarifying exactly what these labels mean in practice.

No one person is responsible for the creation of a rule. As I explain
in more detail in the next chapter, rules are typically drafted by teams of
people drawn from many different units within an agency. The creation of
a single rule can involve program personnel, legal representatives from the
general counsel's office, budget staff, economists, and paperwork specialists,
among many others. Most of these personnel are "careerists," or civil servants who spend the bulk of their professional lives working in the federal
bureaucracy. Some of the officials involved in the rulemaking process may be
political appointees, or individuals who serve "at the pleasure of" the presi-

---

46. OIRA review does not extend beyond the executive branch, although in recent years several bills have been introduced in Congress to extend review to independent agencies. However,
to date, none of these bills has gained any real traction.

47. See Rothenberg and Sweeten (2015) for a summary of the FCC's unique voting system.
See also Bolton (2015).

dent. Among this elite group, only the very upper echelon is confirmed by the Senate.[48]

The term "bureaucrat," then, applies broadly to both career civil servants and political appointees. While the former group is almost always involved in some aspects of creating a rule, the latter group tends to engage intermittently, and then only on higher-level policy issues. From the outside looking in, it is difficult to disentangle whether careerists (e.g., staff economists, program officials) or political appointees (e.g., deputy secretary, secretary) are responsible for particular decisions. Most often it is a combination of many voices reaching consensus on a policy, with the balance of power tipped in careerists' direction for less substantively important rules and in appointees' direction for more important rules. "Bureaucrat," then, refers broadly to the consensus voice of individuals working on the rule, and where possible, I identify whether those individuals are careerists or appointees.

The term "agency" has many different uses in discussions about bureaucracy. Often it used to refer to a Cabinet-level department such as the DOL or an organization that is in the executive branch but not a part of the Cabinet, such as the EPA. At other times, the same term is applied to smaller subunits or bureaus that fall under the umbrella of those larger organizations, such as OSHA within the DOL or the Office of Air and Radiation (OAR) within the EPA.[49] For the sake of clarity, in this book I use the term "agency" to refer generically to an organizational unit of government. Where greater clarity is important, I refer to the lower-level unit (OSHA or OAR in this example) as the bureau and the higher-level unit (DOL or EPA) as the department.[50]

Contribution

Bending the Rules, the title of this book, is a phrase used to suggest that a set of rules is being adapted in order to make a goal easier to accomplish on one occasion. The rules in this case are the procedures associated with the notice-and-comment rulemaking process, and, I argue, they are adapted

48. David Lewis (2008) provides an in-depth description of the modern personnel system in the federal bureaucracy, highlighting the differing roles of careerists and appointees. See especially chapter 2 of his book.

49. Selin (2015) describes differences in structural independence across these lower-level units. She refers to these units as bureaus.

50. Technically, the EPA is not a department, as that term is reserved for organizations that are in the president's cabinet. However, because this distinction does not matter for my argument, I gloss over such technicalities here.

so as to ensure that the proposed rules sponsored by bureaucrats survive to become binding law. The maneuvering this requires means that bureaucrats must be strategic and exercise discretion. These are not new ideas; as one scholar succinctly states, "Substantial agency autonomy is a fact of regulatory life."[51] Indeed, Carpenter (2001) develops a theory of bureaucratic autonomy that is rooted in the notion that autonomy is a central aspiration of bureaucrats.[52] Using a historical case approach, he shows how autonomy is built, not given, on the basis of the efforts of bureaucratic leaders to enhance the agency's reputation. Where his argument is based on the entrepreneurialism of individual managers, the contribution that this book makes is in identifying a mechanism—procedures—by which bureaucrats can translate their autonomy into concrete policy gains. Additionally, because my empirical arguments rests on analyses of approximately eleven thousand rules from 150 bureaus over twenty years, I am able to speak to how this mechanism is employed across the administrative state under different political conditions.

Understanding the persistence of bureaucratic autonomy is important because so much attention is often directed at explaining limits placed on bureaucrats by the political system. In other words, the external perspective discussed previously receives the lion's share of both academic and popular attention. Yet procedures are a reliable way that bureaucrats can carve out autonomy in the face of such limits. While the substantive focus of my argument is on rulemaking, procedures are the bread and butter of bureaucratic agencies. Therefore, the logic of procedural politicking can naturally be extended to other procedure-laden contexts to show how those in charge of administering the process secure preferred outcomes. Within the bureaucracy, such extensions naturally include government contracting, regulatory enforcement, and personnel hiring. They also include policy decisions at the state and local level, as well as policy making in other governmental systems. In other words, bureaucrats may be able to bend the rules in these other procedural venues to steer the process in their preferred direction. In the words of Max Weber, the father of the study of the modern bureaucracy, "Bureaucratic domination means fundamentally domination through knowledge."[53] Procedural politicking draws from this insight that knowledge of procedures—and how to manipulate them strategically—is an essential source of bureaucratic power.

51. Croley (2003, 832).

52. See also Huber's (2007) account of how OSHA bureaucrats exercise their duties in a politically savvy manner while maintaining a veneer of administrative neutrality.

53. As quoted in Swedberg and Agevall (2005, 19).

THE POWER OF PROCEDURE

Procedural politicking comes with normative consequences. As previously discussed, very few people are familiar with the particulars of how a new rule is made. As one former agency official put it, most people have a better chance of being struck by lightning than of understanding the rulemaking process.[54] One study notes that this may even extend within the Washington Beltway: "Even lawyers and people who work for the federal government tend not to understand the rulemaking process unless they have been personally involved in some way."[55] Those who do understand and engage with rulemaking tend to have an institutionalized stake in the outcome of the process and the resources to back up their convictions. When bureaucrats deploy key procedures that restrict participation, obfuscate, and render their work less visible, they may reinforce the already-existing disparity between the average citizen and these moneyed interests. Seen in this light, procedural politicking helps to explain why the rulemaking process is widely perceived to be an insiders' game.

Road Map for the Book

The arc of this book tracks the stages of the rulemaking process. That is, I show how a strategically minded agency responds to separation-of-powers constraints imposed at each stage of the process.

In the next chapter, I describe the nature and the process of rulemaking. The rules governing rulemaking are arcane; indeed, their very arcaneness is central to my theory. But because the argument I make rests in part on the ability of agencies to use their procedural prerogatives to their advantage, it is important for readers to have a basic understanding of the process itself. This chapter briefly explains that process, highlighting key areas of agency discretion. I also explain the different oversight mechanisms that the president, Congress, and the courts have over rulemaking.

Chapter 3 presents the theory and explains agencies' managerial advantages. I demonstrate that, from the agency's perspective, writing a rule is a significant investment, presenting important opportunity costs and staking the agency's reputation. As a result, agencies make sure that the rules they write represent their preferred (albeit constrained) policy. Fortunately, from the agency's perspective, they have tools that help them protect their investments. These include the power to propose a policy—a power that is well understood by political scientists—as well as procedural power. Because inter-

---

54. Interview with former agency general counsel, Dec. 2016.
55. Farina et al. (2011, 9).

ventions by the president, Congress, or the courts are costly to the agency, I argue that agencies use their procedural powers strategically to avoid political sanctions and secure policy gains. The chapter concludes with a set of testable hypotheses, derived from the broader theory, that offer expectations about how agencies will strategically manage procedures relating to proposed rule writing, public consultation, and timing.

The next three chapters delve into the ways that agencies use these procedural tools strategically. Chapter 4 tackles the writing of proposed rule, investigating how agencies can draft a proposal in a way that effectively insulates it from political oversight. I begin by introducing the *Regulatory Proposals Dataset*, a new dataset of approximately eleven thousand rules from 150 agencies, as well as the measures that I use to separate the most important rules from the least important ones. Using these data, I then explore how agencies manipulate the accessibility of a rule as a tool of procedural politicking. Relying on tools of text analysis, I show that bureaucrats write longer and less readable rules when political principals are at ideological odds with the agency and when interest groups serve as more active monitors.

Chapter 5 picks up at the next stage of the rulemaking process: public consultation. Here I show how the feedback that an agency receives from key stakeholders can either enhance or detract from a rule's prospects. Anticipating this, agencies craft their consultation strategies with key external constituencies in mind. Focusing on the public comment period, I show empirically how agencies extend or limit public consultation opportunities in response to the political environment. This analysis highlights the important role that outside audiences, and an agency's core interest groups in particular, play in the procedural politicking game.

In chapter 6, I look at timing, specifically how it is employed as a procedural politicking tool at the final rule stage. I argue that agencies sometimes speed up the publication of a final rule—and other times slow it down—so as to ensure that the rule is not released in a political environment that may lead it to be overturned. Additionally, in this chapter I consider—and ultimately rule out—some alternate explanations for the observed patterns of regulatory pacing. Observers often bemoan the sluggish place of rulemaking; this chapter offers a decidedly political explanation for regulatory delay.

In chapter 7, I show in a case study how a multitude of procedural tools functioned in the context of a single, high-profile rule. This approach allows me to draw a direct connection between the procedural machinations undergirding a rulemaking and the final policy outcome. The rule in question was issued by the FDA under the Obama administration and required chain restaurants and other retail food establishments to display nutritional informa-

THE POWER OF PROCEDURE

tion on their in-store menus. The so-called menu labeling rule was difficult for the FDA to tackle, and I explain how the agency used the tools introduced in the previous chapters to steer the process in its preferred direction. Because much of what happens in rulemaking occurs behind the agency's closed doors, I draw on interviews with bureaucrats and interest group officials, as well as on primary source documents to illustrate these mechanisms.

The evidence demonstrates that bureaucrats do not neutrally implement the administrative process. Rather, they use their political acumen and procedural prerogatives to insulate policies from political interference. Chapter 8 draws out the public policy implications of this bureaucratic power. I consider how political polarization is likely to affect procedural politicking in the longer term and also whether, normatively speaking, citizens should be concerned that unelected bureaucrats have such an outsized influence over the direction of public policy in the United States. I conclude by considering how the lessons learned about the importance of bureaucrats' incentives and capabilities speak to a number of regulatory reform proposals that have been floated in recent years.

Summary

The contraceptive mandate rule that began this chapter was controversial; some spectators described it as a rallying call for a "war on religion." Given the extent of the backlash (and under a court mandate), HHS under the Obama administration expanded the religious exceptions in the rule to include several groups that the 2011 version had excluded. Since, presumably, the intent of the policy was to expand women's access to contraception, this watered down the policy considerably. When the new Trump administration came into office with a decidedly different agenda focused on deregulation, they also took aim at the rule and attempted to further relax the rule's religious and moral opt-out provisions. However, to date, the courts have blocked Trump's efforts to roll back the rule—largely on procedural grounds. That is, the courts have kept the Obama-era rule intact because the new administration has not followed the appropriate procedures in attempting to roll the rule back.[56]

The post-promulgation politics of the contraception rule highlight three key features of my argument. First, while rules are not immortal, the policies created through rulemaking are hard to undo. Second, as the court's rebuff

56. See *State of California v. Health and Human Services*, Case No. 17-cv-05783-HSG (N.D. Cal., Dec. 21, 2017).

of the Trump administration demonstrates, a nuanced understanding of procedures is critical to successfully managing the process. Third, and perhaps most significant, rules make important and durable policy changes. Stepping back, it is clear that regardless of how the squabbling over exceptions is resolved, HHS successfully moved the policy needle on contraception. The conversation is now not whether employers have to pay for contraception—they do, and by all accounts, they will continue to have to do so. Instead, the conversation centers on which employers can be excluded from this general requirement. In the broadest sense, the contraception rule has successfully changed contraception policy on the ground; according to a study in *Health Affairs*, as a result of HHS's policy, in 2015 women spent 50 percent less out-of-pocket on birth-control pills, saving an estimated $1.4 billion per year.[57] The rest of this book aims to develop a more nuanced understanding of how an agency like HHS was able to secure this victory and to unpack the broader implications of such strategic behavior. Let's get started.

57. Becker and Polsky (2015).

2

The Nuts and Bolts of Notice-and-Comment

Before he was president of Princeton University or the United States, Woodrow Wilson was a public administration scholar. His foundational essay "The Study of Administration," published in 1887, contains many insights that scholars today still reflect upon.[1] Perhaps no comment he made was more prescient than a statement that must have seemed mundane at the time: "There is scarcely a single duty of government which was once simple which is not now complex." What Wilson was observing at the time was the modernization of government precipitated by the close of Reconstruction and the rapid industrialization that characterized the Gilded Age. If Wilson was amazed at the size of government in 1887, he could have scarcely imagined the size and scale of the administrative state today. And much of what the government does in the United States today is accomplished through regulatory action.

In the broadest terms, rules constrain, limit, or otherwise direct the behavior of individuals or firms.[2] The notice-and-comment process to create a new rule is complex; and in keeping with Wilson's observation, it has become ever more so as it has evolved over time. It is also relatively opaque to outsiders.

The purpose of this chapter is to acquaint readers with this complex and opaque process and also to explain how this process fits into our broader separation-of-powers system. There are three key points that the reader

---

1. To wit, according to Google Scholar the piece has been cited nearly four thousand times since its publication.

2. Rules can be deregulatory too, meaning that agencies can issue rules that repeal existing regulatory requirements.

should take away from this chapter. First, the centrality of regulation to pub-lic policy has evolved over time; whereas at the beginning of the twentieth century administrative rules were little more than a historical footnote, today they are a critically important form of lawmaking. Second, creating a new regulation involves numerous steps and dozens of people. As a result, from an agency's perspective, the process is very resource intensive, and bureaucrats have incentives to lock in policy early on and avoid making changes as the process progresses. Third, each of the three constitutional branches has the authority to overturn, or veto, agency rules as they are being made. Although vetoes are rarely employed, they are costly for agencies in terms of reputa-tion and lost resources and, accordingly, remain a credible threat. As a result, bureaucrats anticipate when such actions might occur and make efforts—specifically using procedural means—to avoid inviting such consequences.

A Brief History of Rulemaking

Like Wilson, the Founding Fathers did not envision an administrative state that remotely resembles what we have today. The Constitution makes only passing reference to an administrative arm in the executive branch. The fact that the federal bureaucracy has grown to encompass more than four million employees and thousands of rules each year would have been unfathomable. And the idea that agencies today can create binding law through rulemaking would likely have been anathema.[3]

It is not known when the first legally binding agency rule was written.[4] However, it is most likely a creature of the late nineteenth or early twentieth century, with the creation of federal agencies that had the power to regulate the economy, such as the Interstate Commerce Commission (created in 1887) and the Federal Trade Commission (created in 1914). Throughout this pe-riod, the federal bureaucracy was largely clerical in nature.[5] Most citizens' interactions with the federal government revolved around the Post Office,[6]

3. Scholars today still debate whether administrative rulemaking is consistent with con-stitutional principles. This debate goes under the heading of the "nondelegation doctrine" and centers on whether the Constitution grants Congress the authority to delegate legislative function to the executive branch. For competing perspectives on this doctrine, see Schoenbrod (2008) and Posner and Vermeule (2002).

4. Kerwin and Furlong (2011, 8) suggest that there were some instances of delegation of rule-writing powers from Congress to the president as early as 1796, although such efforts did not resemble rulemaking as we understand it today.

5. Carpenter (2001).

6. Rogowski (2015).

and early rulemaking efforts did not garner much interest. For example, in 1911 the Supreme Court heard a case about a US Department of Agriculture rule that levied a fine against a rancher whose sheep had grazed in a national park without a permit, and the rule was upheld without much fanfare.[7]

Two historical trends contributed to the advent of rulemaking as a noteworthy policy tool. First, the rapid growth of government in the early 1930s resulting from the New Deal meant that the federal government began to take on tasks that had previously been assigned to the states or had been relegated to the private sector. At the same time, the federal bureaucracy was becoming increasingly professionalized, a development attributable to the decline of patronage and the expansion of Progressive reforms such as the merit system.[8]

The confluence of these trends meant that bureaucratic agencies were increasingly charged with making policy decisions that applied to broad groups of people rather than particular individuals. Historically, individual case adjudication (i.e., deciding each case separately on its own merits) had been an attractive way to deal with such issues. However, the growth in demand, combined with the Weberian ideal of dispensing with cases in a consistent and routine manner, meant that the idea of creating a general rule was ever more desirable. By the mid-1930s, all manner of agencies were writing rules, although the process that they followed was haphazard and idiosyncratic. Around this time, Congress passed the Federal Register Act, which established a centralized repository where agencies were required to publish documents having "general applicability and legal effect."[9] Although this created a publishing routine for agency documents, legislators recognized that the process of creating these policies still remained unstandardized.

For much of the following decade (and in the middle of World War II), Congress debated how to routinize the administrative process. These debates were heated and cut to the heart of whether New Deal programs—which required considerable agency action, including rulemaking, to be properly implemented—would endure. In an effort to hamstring President Franklin Roosevelt's program, Republicans pushed to circumscribe agency policy making. Meanwhile, Democrats advocated keeping agencies as unencum-

---

7. See *United States v. Grimaud* (220 U.S. 506, 509 (1911)); and Strauss (1996, 751).

8. The Pendleton Act established a merit-based civil service system, meaning that bureaucrats were to be selected on the basis of their qualifications rather than their political affiliation. Although the law was passed in 1883, its uptake was slow. Positions were converted to the merit system on a case-by-case basis, meaning that by 1897, approximately 50 percent of positions were covered; by 1932, nearly 80 percent of the federal civil workforce was merit based (Lewis 2008, 19).

9. Pub. L. No. 74-220, § 5.

bered as possible. Following FDR's death in 1945, the Democrats capitu-
lated, and the Administrative Procedure Act (APA) was passed the following
year "without a recorded vote and with no indication of dissent" (Gellhorn
1986, 232).[10]

The law was brief—a mere nine pages—with a little under a page devoted
to rulemaking. Yet those words accomplished two critical goals. First, the APA
instituted procedural rights for individuals, laying out that individuals should
be allowed to petition agencies to create, amend, or revoke regulations; establishing that they should be given notice of proposed rule changes and the opportunity to comment; and explaining how they could pursue judicial review
of agency actions. Second, the APA instituted a set of procedures that agencies must follow in creating a new rule. These procedures were intentionally
minimal, designed to give agencies maximum flexibility.[11]

The new regime required agencies to do three basic things. First, they had
to publish notice of a proposed rulemaking in the *Federal Register* that stated
the statutory authority under which the rule was issued and that provided a
description of the subjects and issues involved.[12] Second, the agency had to
provide interested persons an opportunity to participate in writing. Unless
otherwise required in statute, the agency could determine whether parties
should also be given the opportunity to participate orally. Third, the agency
was required to state the effective date of the rule, which under the normal
course of business should be no less than thirty days from the publication of
the final rule.

Following the passage of the APA, agency rulemaking became more frequent, although adjudication was still a far more common way for agencies
to make policy decisions.[13] Rules tended not to be controversial. The political
branches rarely engaged with the process. Strauss (1996, 753) explains: "Rulemaking was an ordinary agency activity. The dominant understanding was
that agency action was 'expert,' intended to operate at some remove from
politics; and both Congress and the White House tended not to get involved."

10. However, this should not be interpreted as consensus on the APA's policy dictates; Shepherd (1996, 1560) explains that "the APA passed only with much grumbling" and that many
parties were dissatisfied with the compromise achieved. For a positive political theory account
of why the Democrats changed course, see McCubbins, Noll, and Weingast (1999).

11. Scalia (1989).

12. See § 4 of the APA (Pub. L. No. 79-404) for the statutory language regarding rulemaking
procedures. Under the so-called good cause exception, the APA allowed agencies to waive the
notice and public procedure requirements when the agency deemed these requirements to be
"impracticable, unnecessary, or contrary to the public interest."

13. Mashaw (1994).

Rulemaking took on a more central, and controversial, role in the 1960s and 1970s. Public opinion about the need for government regulation of health, safety, and the environment coalesced during this period, and rulemaking was a natural vehicle for agencies (and government more broadly) to employ. For example, in the face of mounting evidence about the health risks associated with smoking tobacco, in the 1960s the Federal Trade Commission used the rulemaking process to require cigarette manufacturers to add warning labels to cigarette packaging and to put limits on cigarette advertising.[14] Similarly, during the Rights Revolution in the 1970s, the EPA used rulemaking to tackle arsenic standards in drinking water.

The courts, however, aggressively checked agency advances in this period, expanding standing to include all affected parties, requiring agencies to engage extensively with stakeholders, and frequently striking down agency rules.[15] Bressman (2007, 1761) notes that "the goal [of the courts] was no longer simply to promote fairness and rationality in line with traditional due process or rule-of-law values. It was to promote participation so that decision-making would reflect the preferences of all involved."[16] Leading administrative scholars during this period lamented that agencies actively avoided issuing rules because of the courts' aggressive stance, relying instead on case-by-case adjudication decisions.[17] The result was a perceived lack of consistency and fairness in agency decision making.

The 1980s ushered in a new era for rulemaking. The precipitating event was an executive order issued by President Reagan in 1981,[18] which established centralized review of regulations by the Office of Information and Regulatory Affairs (OIRA).[19] Housed within the White House Office of Man-

14. Fritschler (1969).

15. The president was not much help to agencies either. Writing in 1971, Noll explained that "although the president could exercise authority over regulatory agencies, there is little evidence that he makes much of an attempt to do so" (36).

16. Courts were very demanding when reviewing agency rationales and assessing whether the agency had considered other options during this period. Melnick (1983, 11) argues that, combined with the courts' willingness to "second-guess agencies on their readings of statutes and evidence," judicial meddling in the EPA's implementation of the Clean Air Act during this period has resulted in long-term, deleterious consequences for clean air policy in the United States.

17. Davis (1969); Mashaw and Harfst (1986).

18. Exec. Order No. 12,291, Feb. 17, 1981; 46 FR 13193.

19. To be sure, the institution of OIRA was not the first attempt by the president to gain control over agency rulemaking. Earlier presidents experimented with weaker forms of regulatory oversight. For example, President Ford issued an executive order (Exec. Order No. 11,821, Nov. 29, 1974; 39 FR 41501) that required agencies to draft inflation-impact statements for new major rules. The Council on Wage and Price Stability, a unit within the White House, would

agement and Budget (OMB), OIRA was given the authority to review executive branch agencies' draft regulations before they entered the public realm.
This was a major change in how agencies drafted rules, as now the president
(or, more aptly, OIRA) had an institutionalized role in shaping agency rules.
I discuss OIRA review in detail later in this chapter, but suffice it to say that
contemporary scholars were quick to recognize this paradigm shift,[20] and
many observers worried that OIRA review would stifle agencies' ability to
write rules quickly, or at all.

However, OIRA review was not the only major change during this period.
Several major court decisions cemented the regime shift. Most notably, in
1984, the Supreme Court ruled in the well-known *Chevron v. Natural Resources Defense Council* case that, unless Congress has explicitly stated otherwise, courts should defer to agency expertise in determining the correct
course of action.[21] Other important cases shielded agencies from pressures
to repeal rules for purely political reasons,[22] and also limited the ability of
courts to impose rulemaking procedures on an agency.[23] The net result of
these actions was that, at least from a legal perspective, the scales were tilted
in the agency's favor.

Today, the APA remains the backbone for the rulemaking process, although numerous procedural requirements have been layered on top by
Congress and the president. For instance, by executive order, presidents now
require agencies to conduct formal cost-benefit analyses for certain rules be-

---

then comment on these statements. See Tozzi (2011) for a review of these predecessor organizations. When Bill Clinton was elected in 1992, many speculated that the new Democratic
president would dispense with OIRA, as it was a creature of his Republican forerunners. Instead,
Clinton issued Executive Order 12,866, which expanded and cemented OIRA's powers, simultaneously reducing the office's workload, by requiring the office to only review "significant" rules
(Exec. Order No. 12,866, Oct. 4, 1993; 58 FR 51735). Although Presidents Bush and Obama both
issued executive orders relating to OIRA, the basic framework instituted by Reagan and tweaked
by Clinton remained intact throughout the study period.

20. See, for example, Moe (1985).

21. See *Chevron USA, Inc. v. Natural Resources Defense Council, Inc.* (467 U.S. 837 (1984)).
Courts applying *Chevron* deference employ a two-step test. First, the court must assess whether
in making its decision the agency violated the clear intent of the statute in question. If the agency
passes the first step, in the second step the court assesses whether the agency's decision was
reasonable in light of the discretion afforded by Congress. If the court finds the agency's application reasonable, the agency's decision is typically upheld. In practice, in cases where the
Chevron standard is applied, courts frequently side with the agency (Eskridge and Baer 2007;
Hume 2009).

22. *Motor Vehicles Manufacturers Association v. State Farm*, 463 U.S. 29 (1983).

23. *Vermont Yankee Nuclear Power Corp. v. Natural Resources Defense Council, Inc.*, 435 U.S.
519 (1978).

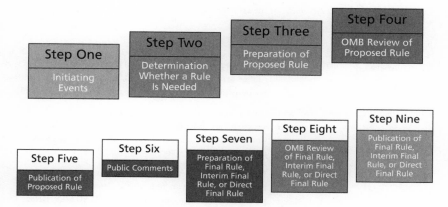

FIGURE 2.1. Map of the notice-and-comment rulemaking process
Note: Adapted from the Reg Map (http://www.reginfo.gov/public/reginfo/Regmap), a cooperative effort of the US General Services Administration and ICF Consulting. See the Reg Map for considerably more detail on what happens during each stage of the process, as well as the legal requirements associated with each step.

fore submitting them to OIRA for review. In addition, the Small Business Regulatory Enforcement Fairness Act requires agencies to provide an assessment of whether each rule will have an adverse impact on small businesses.[24] Other requirements target specific agencies or specific types of rules. For instance, under the Higher Education Act of 1992,[25] the Department of Education must conduct regulatory negotiation with stakeholders for all substantive rules that are issued under that law's authority.[26]

The Rulemaking Process Today

Creating a rule through notice-and-comment is intricate. The average bureau issues about twenty-three proposed and twenty-six final rules each year.[27] This means that, at any given point, a bureau likely has several ongoing rulemakings, with each rule at a different stage in the development process. Figure 2.1 illustrates the typical course that a developing rule follows. Although there are many steps, the process is anchored around two points: the issuance

24. SBREFA, Pub. L. No. 104-121.

25. Pub. L. No. 102-325.

26. Negotiated rulemaking, or "regneg," is a modification of notice-and-comment that requires the agency to negotiate the proposed and final rules with a set of preselected stakeholders. Regneg was popular in the 1990s, but it has fallen out of vogue in recent years. Nevertheless, some scholars still see promise in this form of rulemaking (Kerwin and Furlong 2011). See also Coglianese (1997); and Harter (1982).

27. Figures from the *Unified Agenda*. See section A of the data appendix for details.

TABLE 2.1. Reasons an agency might initiate a rule

Reason	Department or bureau	Example
Agency initiative[a]	ED/OPE	*Gainful-employment rule.* Established benchmark standards for colleges to receive federal student aid. Intended to weed out predatory for-profit colleges from the program. Finalized in 2011.
Statutory mandate	DOT/FMCSA	*Hours of service rule.* Set weekly time limits for truckers to work so as to reduce driver fatigue. Required under the Interstate Commerce Commission Termination Act of 1995. First round of rulemaking finalized in 2003.[b]
Lawsuit	DHS/ICE	*Optional practical training (OPT) visa extension rule.* Offered a visa extension program for foreign students in science, technology, engineering, or mathematics (STEM) fields. DHS finalized the first OPT STEM rule in 2008. However, after the Washington Alliance of Technology Workers sued the agency and won,[c] DHS was compelled to issue a new proposed rule in 2015. Finalized in 2016.
Petition	HHS/FDA	*Tobacco sales and advertising rule.* Prohibited tobacco sales to minors under age 18 and limited sales promotion efforts by tobacco companies. Requested by a petition from the Coalition on Smoking OR Health. Finalized in 1996.
OMB prompt letter	DOT/NHTSA	*Frontal offset crash test proposed rule.* Considered a standard for vehicle crash tests that focused on the vehicle's front end and were designed to protect occupants' feet and legs. Spurred by an OIRA prompt letter in 2001, NHTSA published a comment solicitation (ANPRM) in 2004. Withdrawn in 2005.

[a]Agencies may also issue rules as the result of required reviews. For example, OMB often asks agencies to conduct "retrospective reviews" to eliminate unnecessary regulations from the books or to fix ineffective rules. Additionally, agencies may issue rules at the suggestion of other actors, such as peer agencies or federal advisory committees. I consider both of these to be subsets of agency-initiated requirements because it is ultimately up to the agency to take up such suggestions.
[b]For more on the history of this rule, see chapter 3.
[c]See *Washington Alliance of Technology Workers v. U.S. Department of Homeland Security* (D.D.C. 2015). DHS lost the case on a procedural technicality; the court found that the agency had inappropriately used the good cause exemption to issue an interim final rule in 2008.

of a proposed rule (step 5) and, subsequently, a final rule (step 9). In the sections that follow, I provide a brief sketch of what transpires during each of these stages.[28]

28. Of course, there are many additional steps and many possible exceptions that an agency may take. For example, an agency may skip the proposed rule altogether and issue a direct final rule, which takes effect shortly after publication. Direct final rules are intended as a way for agencies to make administrative or noncontroversial regulatory changes. Agencies will often

DECIDING TO WRITE A RULE

The impetus for a new rule can come from many sources. As table 2.1 shows, rules can be driven by actors outside the agency, such as when an interest group files a lawsuit (which results in a court mandate to write a rule),[29] or when it writes a formal petition asking the agency to take some sort of regulatory action. Political overseers can also push the agency to initiate a rulemaking. For instance, Congress can include language in a statute that directs an agency to write a rule on a specific topic, or the president (or OMB) can ask agency leaders to draft a proposal to accomplish a key administration goal. At other times, a rule is initiated by the agency itself to address a policy need. Such a discretionary rule (or a "homegrown rule," as one agency official described them to me) is drafted on the basis of the agency's existing legal authority (e.g., broad authority granted to the agency in its originating statute or subsequent amendments). Although scholars occasionally attempt to disentangle discretionary rules from mandatory ones,[30] the distinction is blurry in practice, since even a mandatory rule requested by Congress, for example, may include discretionary elements (i.e., provisions that were in no way intended by the enacting legislative coalition or stated in the statutory language).

GETTING IT RIGHT THE FIRST TIME

Proposal development is a critical point in the life of a rule. While the policy the agency offers in the proposed rule can be tweaked later on in the life of the rule, doing so may come at a price. Most critically, there may be legal consequences if the agency switches course on the policy direction of a rule late in the process, because courts can vacate a rule if the agency did not provide adequate notice.[31] Additionally, the agency may take a reputational hit if, say, it

---

repeal direct final rules if they receive even one adverse comment about the rule. See Kerwin and Furlong (2011) and Lubbers (2012) for other procedural exceptions.

29. Agencies do not always defend themselves in lawsuits from interest groups but sometimes settle the case out of court. These settlements often involve the agency agreeing to draft a rule favorable to the group in question. According to a 2013 report by the US Chamber of Commerce, these "sue and settle" regulations have become more frequent in recent years.

30. For instance, West and Raso (2013, 504) conduct a study of 878 agency rules, where agency rule writers were asked to evaluate whether a rule they had written could be classified as either mandatory or discretionary. They find that 60 percent of the rules in their sample (and 53 percent of significant rules) were initiated on the basis of the agency's discretion rather than a statutory mandate.

31. See note 49 in this chapter for a discussion of the relevant legal principles.

proposes something that is considered infeasible or insufficiently researched or if the proposal contains factual errors. Similarly, OIRA is more likely to veto a rule that is of low quality or is internally inconsistent. As a result, when writing a proposed rule agencies face tremendous pressure to "get it right the first time" (West 2004, 2009) and tend to propose policies that are, at least from the agency's perspective, in near-final form.[32]

Irrespective of how the rulemaking was initiated, the act of drafting a proposed rule, though slightly different for each agency, tends to follow a well-worn path. The process begins when an agency leader or program manager puts together a small rule-writing team. This team usually includes individuals from the program office, but it can also include staff economists, representatives from other program offices or from the general counsel's office, or, occasionally, even political leadership.[33]

This team may decide that research is needed to establish a rationale for the agency's proposed policy course. This research can involve conducting a review of the relevant academic, policy, or technical literature, or it can involve conducting original research. If original research is warranted, the agency can do it internally or contract with an outside vendor to complete a study. Depending on the policy domain and the scope of the draft rule, the proposal may be subject to a host of analytical requirements, such as cost-benefit analysis or analyses assessing the impacts on tribes, civil rights, federalism, children, the environment, or paperwork, to name a few. Such analyses, and cost-benefit analysis in particular, can be extremely sophisticated and run into the hundreds of pages.[34]

The team may also decide that additional consultation with stakeholders is necessary. If this is the case, the agency may opt to publish an Advance Notice of Proposed Rulemaking (ANPRM). An ANPRM, which occurs prior to the publication of a proposed rule, is a notice in the *Federal Register* that invites comments from the public on the direction of policy and the types of

---

32. Many scholars have critiqued agencies for issuing proposed rules that are treated as if they were final rules (Chubb 1983; Elliott 1992; Heinzerling 2014; Wagner 2010; Wagner, Barnes, and Peters 2011; West 2004, 2009). The chief complaint associated with this behavior is that agencies become reluctant to make changes as the result of comments submitted during the public comment period.

33. Interview with EPA official, May 2013; interview with FDA official, May 2013; interview with DOT official, May 2016.

34. West (2009, 580) explains that "important [proposed rules] are often accompanied by lengthy discussions (sometimes in excess of 100 pages) that may examine alternative courses of action and that may cite thousands of pages of supporting evidence."

data the agency should consider in preparing a proposed rule. ANPRMs are optional, and because they are not required, they remain infrequently used.

Alternatively, the agency may take a less formal route and hold "listening meetings" in which select groups are invited to come and present information to the agency. Generally speaking, outreach during these early stages tends to be "informal and idiosyncratic" (West 2009, 577). That said, a growing amount of evidence suggests that agencies engage in significant amounts of informal information gathering with interest groups during the early stages of drafting a proposed rule.[35] For instance, drawing on a series of case studies of energy-related bureaucracies and interest groups, Chubb (1983) finds that most interest group influence comes informally, before a proposed rule is put forward for public comment. He interviews more than seventy officials working in energy policy in the late 1970s and reports that agencies developed cozy relationships with industry groups and came to rely on the expertise they provide. This, in turn, led to frequent consultation *before* a proposed rule went out for comment. Chubb summarizes his interviews as follows: "With two exceptions, every group with sufficient experience to comment explained that petroleum regulation was influenced in the early, formative stages, and that once proposed regulations reached the *Federal Register* they could not be changed. At that point, as several oil company representatives put it 'regulations are cast in cement'" (142).[36]

Once the draft policy is complete from the program office's perspective, it goes through the agency's internal clearance process. This is often quite contentious, as different units within the same agency can have a stake in the policy and a very different take on how it should look. Things that the program office decided on months earlier can be reopened and redecided at this stage.

What should be clear is that the drafting of a proposed rule can be an extremely time-intensive process, often taking years to complete.[37] It is difficult to systematically assess how much time agencies spend drafting their proposed rules, since there is no requirement for agencies to record the first time someone within the agency put pen to paper (not to mention began to consider) a particular rulemaking project. In one study, West (2004) finds that the average length of the proposal development period for forty-two rules in his study was more than five years.

35. Furlong and Kerwin (2005); Golden (1998); Yackee (2006); Yackee and Yackee (2006); Wagner, Barnes, and Peters (2011).
36. A recent report by the Administrative Conference of the United States (Sferra-Bonistalli 2014) actually encourages agencies to conduct outreach when drafting a proposed rule, so long as the agency is transparent and avoids perceptions of favoritism or bias.
37. Nou (2013); West (2009).

In his memoir about the FDA's struggle for tobacco regulation in the 1990s, former FDA Commissioner David Kessler (2001) recounts how the agency spent years gathering data on the tobacco industry and formulating the agency's approach to regulating cigarettes. Kessler launched a team that included law enforcement investigators, scientists, press specialists, librarians, lawyers, and policy experts. Investigators traveled the country interviewing industry informants, lawyers scoured industry documents, scientists in the lab evaluated the nicotine content of all manner of cigarettes, and policy analysts conducted site visits of the major cigarette manufacturers. Although he was the head of the agency, Kessler personally directed the team and played an integral role in the development of the proposed rule. Although the rule was eventually overturned by the Supreme Court,[38] the proposal itself was a tour de force.

CLEARING THE (FIRST) OIRA HURDLE

After the draft proposed rule has cleared the agency's internal processes, OIRA has the opportunity to review it.[39] Under Executive Order 12,866, the primary executive order governing OIRA review, OIRA can review any rule that is "significant," meaning that the rule has a large economic impact or important policy ramifications.[40] Specifically, under the order, a rule is significant if it will do any of the following:

1. Have an annual effect on the economy of $100 million or more or adversely affect in a material way the economy, a sector of the economy, productivity, competition, jobs, the environment, public health or safety, or State, local, or tribal governments or communities;
2. Create a serious inconsistency or otherwise interfere with an action taken or planned by another agency;
3. Materially alter the budgetary impact of entitlements, grants, user fees, or loan programs or the rights and obligations of recipients thereof; or

---

38. See *FDA v. Brown & Williamson Tobacco Corp.*, 529 U.S. 120 (2000).

39. With a handful of exceptions, OIRA's purview is limited to executive branch agencies. For example, OIRA reviews rules that are written by some agencies that are informally considered "independent," such as the Social Security Administration and the Pension Benefit Guaranty Corporation. However, these agencies are the exception rather than the rule. The vast majority of independent agencies are exempt from OIRA review.

40. Prior to this issuance of this executive order, OIRA reviewed all rules drafted by agencies under its jurisdiction. Following the release of the order in 1993, review was limited to just those rules that OIRA deemed significant.

4. Raise novel legal or policy issues arising out of legal mandates, the President's priorities, or the principles set forth in this Executive order.

Of course, OIRA—not the agency—determines whether a rule is significant, meaning that OIRA has considerable latitude in determining which draft rules it reviews. While many observers focus on OIRA's review of economically significant rules (those that exceed the $100 million threshold), OIRA makes liberal use of the fourth pillar ("novel legal or policy issues") to bring rules in for review.[41]

If OIRA declines to review a proposed rule, the agency can send the document directly to the *Federal Register* for publication. However, if a rule is brought in for review, OIRA has ninety days to complete its work.[42] In practice, review time varies considerably, with rules that represent administration priorities receiving expedited review and those on which the agency and OIRA disagree taking much longer.[43]

OIRA's review is intended to make sure that the agency's proposed policy adheres to good governance principles, is consistent with administration priorities, and does not conflict with other programs managed by the federal government. Its review can focus on the technical aspects of a rule, such as the assumptions undergirding a cost-benefit analysis or how a new program might work with an existing program at another agency, or on the broader policy implications of a rule, such as whether the rule sets a precedent or establishes rights for certain groups.

OIRA's review process is opaque from the outside, although leaked documents and anecdotal accounts indicate that reviews can be quite contentious. Recounting her time as an EPA official, law professor Lisa Heinzerling (2014, 314) explains OIRA's role as follows: "OIRA decided what to review, offered line-by-line edits of regulatory proposals, convened meetings with outside parties, mediated disputes among the agencies, decided whether an agency's cost-benefit analysis was up to snuff, and more." The relationship she describes between OIRA and the EPA during the Obama administration was a contentious one: OIRA micromanaged the EPA's actions and lacked transparency and accountability. However, former OIRA Administrator Cass

41. See Heinzerling (2014) for an argument that OIRA abuses this authority.

42. Again, this speaks to the contemporary arrangement under Executive Order 12,866. Prior to that order, OIRA had sixty days to review major proposed rules, thirty days for major final rules, and ten days for nonmajor rules.

43. See Bolton, Potter, and Thrower (2016) for consideration of factors affecting the duration of OIRA review. During the Obama administration review times exceeded the ninety allotted days with much greater frequency than in previous administrations.

Sunstein (2013a) paints a much more cooperative and collaborative picture of the relationship between OIRA and the agencies. The discrepancy in the two accounts may stem from the authors' vantage points; OIRA officials may see asking probing questions about agency proposals and analyses as part of their core responsibility, as well as their value-added. Meanwhile, the agency officials who create these documents may view these same questions from OIRA as hostile or invasive rather than as a valuable part of the process.

Ultimately, however, review concludes with a simple decision: approve (or, in the lingo of OIRA desk officers, "clear the rule") or veto the rule, which I discuss in more detail later in this chapter. If a proposed rule is cleared by OIRA, it is then sent to the *Federal Register* for publication.

THE PUBLIC COMMENT PERIOD

At the point of a proposed rule's publication in the *Federal Register*, the public comment period begins and members of the public have the opportunity to weigh in on the agency's proposal. This public consultation must include a set time during which members of the public can submit written comments to the agency. There is considerable variation at this stage, with regard to both the length of the public comment period (see chapter 5) and the number of comments agencies receive. Often agencies will receive no comments or only a very small number of comments. On the other end of the spectrum, agencies sometimes receive more comments than they know what to do with; for instance, in 2012 the EPA received more than two million public comments on a controversial greenhouse gas proposed rule. Finally, at this stage, agencies may choose to do additional outreach by holding hearings or public forums.

While a rule is out for public comment, the agency is generally discouraged from communicating directly with outside parties about the rule, including interest groups, the media, and members of Congress.[44] This is referred to as ex parte communication, meaning "off-the-record, private communications between agency decision-makers and other persons concerning the substance of the agency's proposed rule" (Lubbers 2012, 303). In the case that outside contact occurs (usually for reasons outside of the agency's control), the agency is supposed to generate a record of it, explain the nature of the

---

44. Such restrictions are usually not written in law but rather are a matter of written agency policy or regulations. See Sferra-Bonistalli (2014).

contact, and include it in the public (and court-reviewable) docket.[45] This restriction remains in effect until the final rule is published.

Critics of the notice-and-comment process view the public comment period with skepticism. Their central critique is that if agencies are indeed issuing proposed rules in near-final form, then the comments that agencies receive during this period serve little deliberative function.[46] However, the comments do enter the rulemaking record, which means that agencies must respond to them in writing in the preamble to the final rule.[47] Comments also lay down a marker that may be useful for judicial review of the rule at a later point. If a regulated party fails to raise pertinent issues to the agency during the rulemaking process, it may be waiving its right to judicial review later on. Indeed, groups may not even expect that agencies make the changes they request in the final rule; instead, groups may be preserving the option to bring suit in the future.[48]

THE FINAL RULE

The final rule stage is an important milestone for the agency, as it puts the end goal—binding regulation—in sight. Finalization requires the agency to review the public comments. Sometimes this is a trivial exercise (since there may be no comments); at other times it is a substantial undertaking. Returning to the example of the FDA's tobacco regulation, the agency rented a warehouse just to process the 710,000 comments submitted by the public. Kessler (2001, 337) describes a frenetic scene: "Dozens of people, many of them temps, worked in two shifts from eight in the morning to eleven at night. The

45. The practice varies by agency, however. For instance, several of the interviews that I conducted for this research covered ongoing agency rules and were included in the agency's public docket for those rules.

46. Elliott (1992); Shapiro (1988); Wagner (2010).

47. Shapiro (1988, 47–48) notes that this dialogue requirement is likely a consequence of the courts' midcentury tendency to encourage agencies to engage in pluralism: "One way to insure that someone has really listened is to require that he respond to everything that is said to him. He must listen in order to respond even if he doesn't believe it is worth listening because he knows everything already. The courts came to say that a rule maker had to respond to every significant comment submitted to the agency. . . . With rulemaking records in front of them, judges could see whether the agency had replied to each comment and thus whether the agency had really granted meaningful access—had really listened—to every group." As a result agencies began to keep detailed records of their decision-making processes and to lay out as much of their logic as possible in the final rule.

48. See Schmidt (2002).

first group registered the responses and entered data into computer banks. The stacks of paper were then rushed to a second group, where each individual comment was read and categorized into one of hundreds of topics. . . . Finally, the responses were sped to a third team of professional FDA staff for careful analysis." The FDA's breakneck pace and scrupulousness in comment processing are not typical, but the case demonstrates that agencies do sometimes take the process of addressing comments seriously. To speed processing, many agencies hire contractors to manage high volumes of public comments and rely on plagiarism detection software to identify duplicates.

After reviewing the public's feedback, the agency decides whether to make any changes to the policy it laid out in the proposed rule. This is not an exercise in averaging; the agency does not weigh the balance of the comments and what the majority of commenters want. Instead, the agency selects what it believes to be the best final policy, although it must explain in the preamble to the final rule the types of comments it received and why it chose to adopt or reject the commenters' suggestions. Importantly, the agency must not introduce changes at the final rule stage if those changes were not adequately foreshadowed at the proposed rule stage or in the comments received.[49] This requirement, again, puts the onus on "getting it right the first time" (West 2004, 2009).

After sending the draft final rule through the agency's internal clearance

---

49. See Kannan (1996). This is a doctrine known as logical outgrowth, meaning that the final rule must derive in a reasonable way from the proposed rule. If an agency violates this principle, the rule can be challenged in the courts and overturned on the grounds that it is arbitrary and capricious. For instance, a 2014 court ruling overturned a final rule issued by the Department of Health and Human Services on the grounds that the agency changed the meaning of a key part of the rule at the final rule stage. The rule pertained to the calculation of the reimbursement rate for Medicare Part E (treatment of disproportionately low-income patients). The proposed rule (2003) would have excluded certain patients from the numerator of the formula, whereas the final rule (2004) took the exact opposite stance and included those patients in the numerator. The change had considerable financial implications for regulated parties. In overturning the final rule, the federal district court noted that this was not a harmless error on the agency's part:

> We ask ourselves, would a reasonable member of the regulated class—even a good lawyer—anticipate that such a volte-face with enormous financial implications would follow the Secretary's proposed rule. Indeed, such a lawyer might well advise a hospital client not to comment opposing such a possible change for fear of giving the Secretary the very idea. . . . the Secretary's final rule was not a logical outgrowth of the proposed rule. (*Allina Health Services v. Sebelius* (D.C. Cir. 2014))

In other words, the court vacated the rule because commenters had not been given adequate notice and the opportunity to comment on the new numerator.

process, OIRA again has an opportunity to review the draft rule. If OIRA selects the rule for review, it has another ninety-day period to conduct its review, and all the stipulations about the review at the proposed rule stage apply here. Subject to OIRA's clearance, the final rule is published in the *Federal Register*.

At this point, the agency has succeeded in creating new law, but the rule still has to take effect. Rules become legally binding for regulated parties after a waiting period; often this window is short (e.g., thirty days), but it can occasionally be quite long (e.g., one year from publication). During this interim period, the agency is sometimes forced to extend the effective date of the rule, further putting off the culmination of this long process. Implementation delays can be a way for the agency to buy time—to deal with an external demand (e.g., a request from key congressional overseers) or an internal one (e.g., an unforeseen issue with respect to the enforcement timeline). Regardless, delaying the effective date leaves open the possibility of backsliding, suggesting to relevant parties that some unknown event may still upset all the effort that has gone into a rulemaking.[50]

A final rule taking effect signifies that the rulemaking process is over—at last. The road has likely been long and winding; the agency may have spent years or even decades promulgating the rule. But the battle is not over; political overseers—or principals in the language of political science—have been monitoring the rule all along the journey, and struggles often continue long after the rule takes on legal effect.

Political Oversight of Rulemaking

The overview of the rulemaking process provided to this point has been relatively straightforward, charting an uninterrupted course from idea to fully realized regulatory policy. In practice, the path can be full of obstacles. Technical issues can interfere with the agency's ability to complete a rule or to complete it in a timely fashion; it is not easy determining the optimal number of particles per million for an air pollutant or deciding whether ten or eleven hours is the upward limit on a trucker's ability to drive continuously. Even more challenging problems can arise from the political sphere.

---

50. From a legal perspective, the ability of an agency to indefinitely delay a regulation that has been finalized but not taken effect is murky. Nonetheless, incoming presidents often direct agencies to temporarily delay the effective date of final rules that have not yet taken effect. As with all implementation delays, agencies are supposed to go through notice-and-comment for these "crack of dawn" suspensions (Congressional Research Service 2018).

Because rules can deal with politically important and high-stakes topics, it is not surprising that all three branches of government play a role in overseeing their creation. Through OIRA, the president has a direct hand in the regulatory process, reviewing draft agency rules before they are public knowledge. Congressional and judicial actors do not get privileged ex ante access to agency rules. Rather, much of the oversight from these branches is facilitated by interest groups.[51] While members of Congress (MCs) may occasionally discover that the agency is pursuing policy counter to their preferences on their own (in what McCubbins and Schwartz term "police patrols"), more often they rely on outside monitors, such as interest groups, to "sound the fire alarm" when necessary. Similarly, vigilant interest groups bring cases to the court in search of judicial relief. As a result of these institutional differences, oversight by each branch is exercised through different means and at different points in the process.

Not only does each branch oversee the rulemaking process; each also is capable of "vetoing" an agency rule. Table 2.2 lists the different ways that each branch can turn back an agency rule. I address each tool in detail in the sections that follow. It is important to note at the outset that regulatory vetoes are relatively infrequent events. However, just because they are rare does not mean that they are unimportant. In fact, as I argue in the next chapter, one of the primary reasons for their paucity is that agencies anticipate when they might be used and attempt to head them off by procedural and other means.

Of course, vetoes are not the only way that the political branches influence agency rules. They exist alongside all the usual carrots and sticks that political actors have at their disposal. Presidents can staff agencies with loyal appointees and use the power of their office to persuade bureaucrats to follow presidential preferences.[52] Presidents can also fire appointees who do not

51. Clearly, interest groups are a critical link between agency rules and the probability of oversight. Yet interest group complaints (or, however rare, issuances of praise) must be received by some other party in order to effect change. Complaints on their own do not amount to much. Although issues are often brought directly to the agency's attention, absent the possibility of oversight, groups must rely on the agency's goodwill to see requested changes implemented. However, political oversight means that groups are not limited to persuading the agency to "do the right thing"; they can also prevail upon the agency's political principals to pressure the agency to make their preferred decision. Put differently, interest groups are an important connector between agencies and the probability of political oversight occurring. However, groups on their own do not have the power to sanction agencies directly or to stop an adverse rule from proceeding. Rather, when groups are dissatisfied with the direction of an agency rule, they must bring their concerns to the attention of a political principal.

52. Lewis (2008); Neustadt (1960).

TABLE 2.2. Pathways to the regulatory veto

Actor	Tool	Description
President	OIRA review	OIRA reviews a draft agency rule (proposed or final) and rejects the rule or puts pressure on the agency to withdraw the rule.
Congress	Passage of law overwriting rule	Congress passes a law that overwrites the agency's rule and the president signs it.
Congress	Nullification under the Congressional Review Act	Both chambers pass a resolution of disapproval for a major final rule and the president signs the resolution.
Congress	Limitation rider	Congress attaches a rider to a "must-pass" appropriations bill preventing the agency from completing a rule (proposed or final) or from using appropriated funds to implement a final rule.
Courts	Judicial review	Court vacates a final rule or remands the rule to the agency for further consideration.

heed their wishes or slash agency budgets in retribution. Members of Congress can also try to convince agency leaders to mold the rule to their own preferences.[53] If persuasion fails, Congress can punish the agency in myriad ways, including cutting the agency's budget, dragging agency heads to testify in front of a hostile committee, reducing the agency's discretion by writing more specific statutes or stripping the agency of its authority, strengthening administrative procedures, enhancing the power of the courts to review the agency's actions, or increasing monitoring.[54] Finally, courts can curb an

53. Often this can take the form of members of Congress writing letters to agencies to "back channel" their policy preferences vis-à-vis a specific rule (Lowande 2018; Ritchie 2018). However, it is rare for agencies to provide detailed policy responses to members about rules under development. Recall that if the proposed rule has already been published, most agencies follow strict ex parte rules, which prevent them from consulting with those outside of the agency—and this extends to Congress.

54. Each of these forms of agency oversight has received considerable attention in the literature. On hearings, for example, Marvel and McGrath (2016) identify pernicious consequences of repeated oversight hearings, including decreased agency morale. On authority stripping, Fritschler (1969) describes how in the early 1960s Congress took away the Federal Trade Commission's oversight of cigarette advertising in response to the agency's perceived power grab in regulating cigarettes. On court review, see McCann, Shipan, and Wang (2017), who suggest that the level of judicial review that particular agencies and programs receive is the result of strategic calculations by congressional actors. Last, on enhanced monitoring, see, e.g., Carpenter (1996); Epstein and O'Halloran (1999); Huber and Shipan (2002); McGrath (2013); McCubbins, Noll, and Weingast (1987); and Shipan (1997).

agency's authority by revoking the agency's jurisdiction over a particular policy area.[55]

Decades of research in political science demonstrates that these conventional oversight tools powerfully shape bureaucratic action. I focus on the ability of the three branches to veto an agency's rule because it is targeted at specific rules and because vetoes are extremely costly for agencies.

THE PRESIDENTIAL VETO

The public holds the president, as chief executive, responsible for the performance of the executive branch. Many observers assume that since the president is in charge, agencies move in lockstep with presidential preferences. Yet these relationships are rife with principal-agent problems. Presidency scholar Richard Neustadt (1960) famously described Cabinet agency heads as the president's "natural enemies," and President Nixon extended this distrust from presidential appointees to the thousands of civil servants working in the agencies, stating, "They're bastards who are here to screw us."[56] More recently, President Trump's complaints about the "deep state" and unreliable bureaucrats echo this same sentiment. Presidents attempt to solve this principal-agent problem institutionally, by selecting loyal appointees to lead agencies, and for regulations, through centralized review by OIRA.

Since its inception, OIRA has been controversial. Despite its tiny size,[57] the office is highly influential and has been described as both the "cockpit of the regulatory state" (Sunstein 2013b) and the "killing ground" for agency rules (Shapiro 2011). The controversies surrounding OIRA often focus on a perceived lack of transparency surrounding review and the expansive nature of the office's review powers.[58] Ultimately, however, OIRA review matters be-

55. Congress and the courts can also enact deadlines (through statutes or court orders, respectively) to compel agencies to issue a rule by a specific date. However, agencies routinely miss these deadlines (Gersen and O'Connell 2008; Lavertu and Yackee 2012).

56. As quoted in Waterman, Rouse, and Wright (2004, 53).

57. Although its staff size has waxed and waned across time, since the mid-1990s OIRA has maintained approximately sixty policy analysts, who are called desk officers. The office is led by one Senate-confirmed political appointee, the OIRA administrator, but the majority of the staff are career civil servants who serve regardless of which party holds the White House. Most of the staff have backgrounds in economics and policy analysis.

58. OIRA's authority is broad and relatively amorphous, a fact that is often noted with chagrin by agency personnel. Heinzerling (2014, 325) describes the review process as opaque and "ad hoc and chaotic rather than predictable and ordered."

cause it can compel an agency to change a draft rule or result in the rule being vetoed.

OIRA reviews approximately 30 percent of executive branch rules, although some agencies are "audited" at higher rates than others.[59] This review power is doubly dangerous for agencies, because OIRA gets two "bites" at agency rules: once at the draft proposed rule stage and once at the draft final rule stage. Importantly, this is an ex ante review power, meaning that, at both stages, OIRA review occurs before the rule reaches the public domain.

Regulatory vetoes by OIRA come in two forms. Most directly, OIRA can "return" the rule to the agency for further consideration (a euphemism for rejecting the rule). Although this veto power has existed since OIRA was first created in 1981, the tool took on a more prominent role at the start of the George W. Bush administration. At that point, OIRA, under the leadership of Administrator John Graham, began publicly posting "return letters" to its website. These letters, which recount in some detail the reason(s) that OIRA found the rule to be deficient, serve to publicly shame the agency. Their high visibility virtually ensures that they are rare events; between 2001 and 2014, only twenty-seven return letters were issued.[60]

Return letters, however, are not the only avenue for a presidential veto of an agency's proposed rule. In cases where OIRA credibly threatens to return a proposed rule to the agency, the agency can voluntarily "withdraw" the rule from consideration before OIRA officially returns the rule. Indeed, according to former OIRA Administrator Cass Sunstein (2013a, 1847), "because many rules are withdrawn and many change as a result of OIRA review, it is misleading to focus on the number of return letters as a measure of OIRA's impact."[61]

As illustrated in figure 2.2, when OIRA vetoes are calculated to include both withdrawals and formal returns, vetoes are actually a relatively common occurrence. Based on the number of rules reviewed by OIRA each year, considering vetoes in this manner results in an average annual veto rate of

59. Acs and Cameron (2013).

60. Return letters are available on OIRA's website, at http://www.reginfo.gov/public/do/eoReturnLetters.

61. Withdrawals essentially function as a quiet veto of the agency's proposal; OIRA stops the rulemaking process from proceeding, and the agency does not have to endure the humiliation of a return letter. Although this strategy is less conspicuous than a return, withdrawals are taken seriously. For instance, one observer suggested that under President Obama, OIRA encouraged agencies to withdraw rules in order to "unceremoniously dispose of long-overdue OIRA reviews involving important safeguards that are vigorously opposed by industry" (Goodwin 2013).

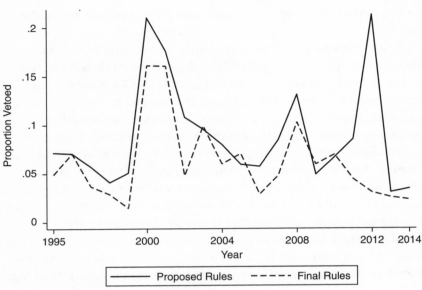

FIGURE 2.2. OIRA vetoes of agency rules, 1995–2014
Note: Data compiled by the author from OIRA records (available at http://www.reginfo.gov).

8.8 percent for proposed rules. Empirically speaking, vetoes at the final rule stage are rarer, with a veto rate of approximately 6.1 percent.[62] While the veto rate for individual agencies varies from this average, the overall veto rate of 6 percent to 8 percent of rules produced means that agencies must take OIRA review seriously.

THE CONGRESSIONAL VETO

Congressional oversight of agency rules is much more fragmented than presidential oversight. It is safe to say that members rarely, if ever, scour the pages of the *Federal Register* to keep up with what agencies are doing. Rather, they tend to learn about problematic agency rules from constituents, interest groups, the media, one another, and sometimes the agencies themselves. The result of this system of oversight is that individual MCs learn about problematic rules in an ad hoc fashion and after they have become public.

62. The difference between proposed and final veto rates is likely explained by the fact that most of the final rules were already reviewed and approved by OIRA at the proposed rule stage (so if OIRA was going to veto the rule, it would have already done so). Also, it may be more politically costly for OIRA to intervene and overturn a rule at the final rule stage than at the proposed rule stage.

Additionally, oversight is not limited to members of congressional oversight committees, since members whose constituents may be disproportionately affected by the rule can become involved. This means that coalitions of engaged members vary from rule to rule.[63]

Members of Congress who wish to disrupt a rule have at least three potential options: passing a new law that overwrites or otherwise prohibits the agency's rule, nullifying the rule through powers enumerated in the Congressional Review Act (CRA), or attaching a limitation rider, which blocks the rule, to an appropriations bill (see table 2.2).[64] Each of these paths achieves the same end (a veto), yet each path presents different challenges for members of Congress and has different implications for the agency on the receiving end.

There is very little empirical data on the frequency with which regulatory vetoes are issued through new legislation. Anecdotally, it appears that MCs frequently introduce bills aimed at stopping agencies from completing certain rules.[65] Yet it is unclear how many of these bills actually become law or whether their introduction is merely a form of constituency work or credit claiming for MCs.[66] For instance, at least six bills that would have thwarted the FDA's proposed rule on menu labeling (see chapter 7) were introduced in the 112th through the 114th Congresses. None of those bills received meaningful consideration.

The second congressional veto option, the CRA, is very similar to the power to annul a rule through passage of a new law. To use the CRA, both

---

63. Fragmented and overlapping oversight jurisdiction is a problem that is endemic to congressional oversight of agencies and is not specific to rulemaking. Clinton, Lewis, and Selin (2014) argue that this fragmentation tilts influence away from Congress and toward the White House.

64. Berry (2016, 2) argues that another avenue for congressional oversight of the bureaucracy is via a distinct form of legislative veto, or "statutes that authorize either or both house of Congress, or specific committees, to approve, disapprove, or defer certain executive actions." Although the Supreme Court struck down the ability of one chamber to unilaterally veto a presidential action in *Immigration and Naturalization Service v. Chadha* (462 U.S. 919 (1983)), Berry makes the case that the legislative veto is still alive and well today, albeit in a modified form (e.g., requiring committee approval of a study). Following this logic, the legislative veto can be used as another tactic—in addition to those identified in table 2.2—that members of Congress can use to affect regulatory policies.

65. Bills may also be used to signal congressional discontent on an issue, in a manner similar to Clark's (2009) argument about "court curbing" bills introduced by members of Congress to keep the court in line. Clark argues that such bills can be an informative signal to the courts about public opinion on a particular issue. "Agency curbing" bills may serve a similar function in that they inform agencies about public opinion and the political salience of particular rules.

66. See Fiorina (1989); and Mayhew (1974).

chambers must pass a joint resolution, which then must be signed by the president. Invoking the CRA has the advantage that the resolution is given expedited consideration, which reduces the internal hurdles in Congress.[67] However, the requirement for presidential agreement means that either there must be a sympathetic president (more common when the administration has changed) or the chambers have sufficient votes to overturn a veto. It is unsurprising, then, that the CRA was successfully deployed exactly once during the twenty years covered in this study;[68] in 2001 Congress overturned a final rule from the Occupational Safety and Health Administration (OSHA) that enacted broad ergonomics standards for workplaces. The rule was issued at the tail end of the Clinton administration and overturned by a Republican Congress at the commencement of the Bush administration. The rule itself was extremely controversial and is considered an atypical rulemaking case.[69] However, as Copeland and Beth (2008) point out, if Congress can overcome its collective action problem and actually deploy the CRA, it comes with an additional punch: it prevents the agency from issuing the rule (or a "substantially similar" version of the rule) at any point in the future.[70]

Finally, regulatory limitation riders are the most accessible way for MCs to veto an agency's rule. As MacDonald (2010) explains, these riders are attached to appropriations bills and bar agencies from spending money to issue or implement specific regulations. Because appropriations bills are considered "must pass" legislation, from an MC's perspective this is close to a unilateral veto power, because the president would have to veto the entire appropriations package in order to block the rider.[71] Figure 2.3 shows the

67. See Reynolds (2017) for a discussion of the role of expedited procedures in moving measures through Congress.

68. However, this was not from a lack of trying. As Rosenberg (2008) reports, forty-seven resolutions of disapproval relating to thirty-five rules were introduced under the CRA from 1996 to 2008. Although only one passed, three were approved by one chamber and not the other. Beginning in 2017, three years after the close of the time period under study here, the Trump administration worked with a unified Republican Congress to use the CRA much more frequently, overturning numerous regulations from the Obama administration. As I discuss in chapter 8, increased reliance on the CRA may represent a change in norms and a shift to a new regulatory regime.

69. The rule covered approximately 102 million workers in 6 million workplaces, at an estimated annual compliance cost of roughly $4.5 billion; see Shapiro (2007).

70. Copeland and Beth (2008) also note that the CRA is a useful tool for a new Congress because it grants the opportunity to overturn last-minute rules issued during the waning days of the previous Congress (or administration).

71. Consistent with this explanation, MacDonald (2013) finds that riders are more commonly used under divided government.

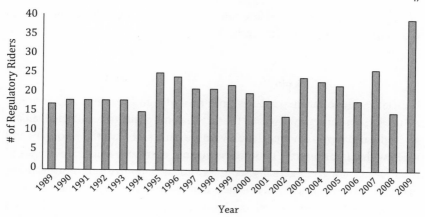

FIGURE 2.3. Regulatory limitation riders, 1989–2009
Note: Bars indicate the number of congressional regulatory vetoes issued via limitation riders in fiscal years 1989–2009. This combines riders issued for proposed rules, final rules, and "preemptive" vetoes for rules that have yet to be proposed. Data are from MacDonald (2010).

annual incidence of regulatory limitation riders using MacDonald's (2010) dataset. The figure demonstrates that limitation riders are used to veto agency rules with some regularity, although they are less common than OIRA vetoes and still negligible when compared to the overall volume of agency rules issued in a given year.[72]

Notably, each congressional veto option requires collective action by Congress; passing a bill overwriting a rule, using the CRA, or enacting a limitation rider all require members to work together to gain needed floor time and to obtain sufficient votes. Additionally, the president must actively assent for any of these items to pass,[73] although, as previously indicated, the president may be less of an obstacle when a regulatory rider is but one piece of a broader legislative package. Given the well-documented collective action problems associated with passage of any law,[74] and the plethora of items

72. Plotting limitation riders in this way masks a key nuance of these data. These riders are often used preemptively to prevent agencies from issuing rules in new areas. For example, of the 512 riders in MacDonald's dataset, 22 (4.3 percent) were issued to prevent agencies from writing rules to implement the Kyoto Protocol. These vetoes occurred even though no agency had started working on a rule to implement the treaty.

73. But presidents do not always assent. For instance, in 2016 President Obama vetoed a joint resolution under the CRA that the Congress had passed. The resolution would have nullified a controversial rule from the Department of Labor that required financial advisers to act in best interests of clients saving for retirement.

74. Cox and McCubbins (1993, 2005); Krehbiel (2010).

competing for congressional attention, it is not surprising that congressional vetoes of agency rules are relatively rare.

THE JUDICIAL VETO

Judicial review of agency rules is both sporadic and reactive. The sporadic nature of judicial review owes to the fact that, for a rule to be litigated, an aggrieved party has to find legal fault with the rule and have the resources and wherewithal to bring suit. This means that not every rule can be litigated, and in fact, very few rules actually see the inside of a courtroom. For example, between 1995 and 2014 the EPA issued an average of sixty-one final rules each year. During that same period, the DC Circuit court heard about eight cases (annually) involving that agency, and the Supreme Court heard even fewer: an average of less than one case per year.[75] Even then, the EPA is an outlier in the sense that its rules are among the most litigated of any agency, so other agencies are even less likely to have their rules dragged into court.

Review by the courts is also reactive, because it tends to occur after a rule has been promulgated. Generally, judicial review must occur during a defined time window, although the precise timing of that window depends on at least two factors. One is a legal principle known as finality, which states that parties cannot bring suit until the agency has made a "final agency action," meaning that the party must wait until the agency has finished deliberating and issued a final rule.[76] A second factor is ripeness, which means that the case is ready for judicial review and would not require the court to engage in extensive hypothetical or abstract arguments (e.g., speculating about the consequences of a final rule). The ripeness standard is intended to promote efficient use of judicial resources.[77] Historically, ripeness meant that a rule

75. Of the appellate court cases involving the EPA, more than three-quarters pertained to rulemaking. Supreme Court data are from the Supreme Court database (Spaeth et al. 2016); appellate figures and rule figures are from my analysis of circuit court cases and *Unified Agenda* data.

76. Of course, as with all things involving rulemaking, there are exceptions. For instance, agencies can be sued at the proposed rule stage for "unreasonable delay" in issuing a rule for which there was a reasonable expectation of completion. This can occur, for example, if Congress issued a statutory deadline for the agency to issue a proposed rule and the agency missed that deadline (Kerwin and Furlong 2011; Lubbers 2012).

77. In the words of Justice John Harlan, "The basic rationale [of ripeness] is to prevent the courts, through avoidance of premature adjudication, from entangling themselves in abstract disagreements over administrative policies, and also to protect the agencies from judicial interference until an administrative decision has been formalized and its effects felt in a concrete way by the challenging parties" (*Abbott Laboratories v. Gardner*, 387 U.S. 136 (1967)). In this pivotal

had to have taken effect—and parties have suffered harm as a result—for the courts to hear a case. More recently, however, Congress has taken to including explicit statutory language to allow for preenforcement review of agency regulations issued under the statute's authority. These statutory provisions mean that .parties must bring suit before an allotted amount of time has passed and that judicial review is no longer allowed once enforcement of the regulation has begun.

If a rule does make it to court, the APA instructs judges to "hold unlawful and set aside agency [rulemaking] action" that is arbitrary and capricious.[78] Exactly what constitutes an "arbitrary and capricious" rule depends on the case at hand, and judges have considerable discretion.[79] For instance, in 2012, the DC district court struck down a high-profile Department of Education (ED) rule regulating institutional eligibility for federal student aid programs. The rule would have required higher education institutions receiving student aid to meet benchmark standards relating to postgraduation employment and debt statistics for their students. The intent of the so-called gainful-employment rule was to crack down on for-profit colleges that saddled students with debt while providing them with very little by way of job prospects. When the Association of Private Colleges and Universities sued ED over the rule, the court struck it down on the grounds that even though the department had the right to regulate in this area, one of the benchmarks the agency had set was not selected on the basis of sound reasoning. In remanding the rule to the agency, the judge explained why he found the rule to be arbitrary: "No expert study or industry standard suggested that the [benchmark] rate

---

case, the Supreme Court allowed an FDA rule to be litigated before the rule had taken effect (and in the absence of explicit statutory language allowing preenforcement review). The Court found that the case was ripe because drug makers (the regulated industry) would have suffered immediate and direct harm and because the case involved a purely legal question, which would not have been alleviated or altered by deferring review. For a deeper explanation of ripeness, see Lubbers (2012, 405–22).

78. Pub. L. No. 79-404, § 10.

79. A key question is whether courts will apply the hard-look doctrine, a principle that requires judges to take a "searching and careful" look of the rulemaking record and, given that evidence, evaluate whether the agency reached a reasonable decision in the final rule. See *Citizens to Preserve Overton Park v. Volpe* (401 U.S. 402 (1971)). A hard look requires an evaluation of three components of the agency's decision making: appropriateness of the legal standard the agency used, reasonableness of the application of that legal standard (e.g., consideration of relevant factors, reasonable alternatives), and justification of the agency's decision. This is a demanding standard for agencies to meet, and it forces the agency to focus on creating a detailed rulemaking record. As a result, hard look is often criticized for contributing to regulatory ossification and delay.

selected by the Department would appropriately measure whether a particular program adequately prepared its students. Instead, the Department simply explained that the chosen rate would identify the worst-performing quarter of programs. That this explanation could be used to justify any rate at all demonstrates its *arbitrariness*."[80] This particular overturn focused on the lack of evidence supporting the agency's position. Another judge reviewing the same case may have overturned the case on different grounds.

While this example highlights a case where the agency's rule was overturned, judges more often defer to agency expertise. The normative rationale for judicial deference is straightforward: agencies are subject-matter experts, and they are accountable to democratically elected principals. Judges are, by their nature, generalists who lack the requisite area expertise; therefore, when a question before the court is ambiguous, judges should give agencies the benefit of the doubt. Often deference is tied to the aforementioned *Chevron* doctrine. In this Supreme Court case, the justices unanimously upheld the Environmental Protection Agency's interpretation of the Clean Air Act on "the principle that the courts will accept an agency's reasonable interpretation of the ambiguous terms of a statute that the agency administers."[81] While *Chevron* deference is by far the best-known deference doctrine, there are other deference standards that courts can apply.[82] Together these doctrines have established a general norm for judicial deference to agencies.

However, despite this norm, agencies are not always victorious before the courts. Agencies sometimes win and sometimes lose, but regardless of the outcome these cases are costly to litigate, and bureaucrats would prefer to avoid judicial review altogether. Figure 2.4 shows the annual proportion of cases in the DC Circuit court—the appellate court that hears the vast majority of cases involving federal agencies—where agencies won out. While the proportion of agency successes varies by year and by agency, overall, agencies won an annual average of 55.4 percent of cases that went before this court.

80. *Association of Private Colleges and Universities v. Duncan*, No. 11-1314 (D.D.C. 2012), p. 31 (emphasis added).

81. Scalia (1989, 511).

82. For instance, the *Curtiss-Wright* standard (*United States v. Curtiss-Wright Export Corp.*, 299 U.S. 304 (1936)), which applies to executive interpretations of foreign affairs and national security decisions, affords agencies a high level of deference. Meanwhile, the *Skidmore* standard (*Skidmore v. Swift & Co.*, 323 U.S. 134 (1944)) is a considerably less deferential standard that courts can apply while still granting the agency deference. Together, the different deference standards form a "continuum of deference" (from very deferential to not very deferential) that reviewing courts can apply to cases involving agency decision making. See Eskridge and Baer (2007).

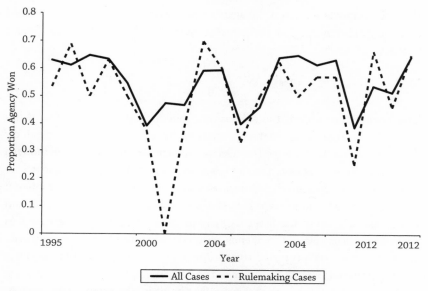

FIGURE 2.4. Agency win rate in DC Circuit court cases, 1995–2014
Note: Data compiled by the author.

And when it comes to cases involving rulemaking, agencies do a little worse; they were successful only about half the time (50.1 percent). These results largely comport with studies of the Supreme Court, where scholars find that deference is not a given.[83]

As these figures demonstrate, there are no guarantees for rules when it comes to the court. An agency can never be sure which of its rules will end up before the court. When a rule does fall before the courts, it is not a sure bet that the agency's interpretation will be granted deference. In a survey of agency rule drafters, most were reluctant to agree that the application of judicial deference by the courts was "reasonably predictable."[84] In the end, then, judicial review is something of a wild card for agencies, and it is difficult for bureaucrats to appropriately factor the courts into their planning when crafting a new rule. However, the specter of judicial review does under-

83. In a study of more than one thousand Supreme Court cases involving agencies, Eskridge and Baer (2007) find that agencies have a slightly higher win rate before the high court (68.8 percent).

84. In the survey, 107 agency rule drafters responded to the prompt "Please evaluate the following statement: The level of deference (Chevron, Skidmore, no deference, etc.) that courts will apply to a particular agency statutory interpretation is reasonably predictable." The responses were as follows: strongly agree, 3; agree, 25; agree somewhat, 49; and disagree or strongly disagree, 23. See Walker (2014) for further details.

score the importance, from the agency's perspective, of preparing a detailed and comprehensive rulemaking record so as to withstand potential legal challenges.[85]

Summary

This chapter introduced the rulemaking process and explained how it has evolved over time. In the scope of American history, rulemaking as a vehicle for important policy change is a relatively recent development. The modern period of rulemaking began in the 1980s, and the institutional infrastructure has been in a period of relative stasis since the mid-1990s. Under the current regime, writing an important rule consumes considerable agency time and resources. Because of the investment required in producing a new rule, as well as concerns relating to agency reputation and the legal basis, agencies attempt to produce proposed rules in near-final status rather than publicly adjusting rules as they move through the process.

Agencies do not, however, have a free hand in the rulemaking process. Political oversight of rulemaking is alive and well, but it operates differently for each of the three branches. Through OIRA, the president has a direct veto over the creation of each new rule. OIRA can return a rule to an agency or, more commonly, require the agency to make changes to a draft rule. This action occurs before a draft rule ever makes it to the pages of the *Federal Register*. Congress and the courts get involved in the process later. Congressional actors tend to engage after the publication of a proposed or final rule and can use tools ranging from legislative overrides to legislative prohibition on agency rules. When courts hear cases involving rulemaking, it is typically after the final rule is published. Court tools range from remanding the rule to the agency to invalidating it altogether. The point is that each actor has the ability to undo an agency rule, yet regulatory vetoes are rare events. OIRA approves most rules. Congress is rarely concerned and has to overcome considerable collective action problems to block a rule. The courts hear relatively few rulemaking cases, and when they do, they uphold the agency's position slightly more often than not.

So just how effective, then, is political oversight of rulemaking? Less effective even than the veto rate of regulations might suggest. One key insight of this chapter is that the basic steps that agencies must follow when creat-

---

85. According to Vogel (2012, 260), "90% of the scientific factual data prepared by the EPA are to enable the agency's decisions to withstand judicial review." See also Wagner (2012).

ing a new rule are numerous but variable. This variability means that the timing and exact nature of the particular procedures are left to the agency's discretion. In the next chapter, I pick up with a consideration of how this procedural discretion intersects with an agency's ability to anticipate political oversight and how this politicking can shift the balance of political power between political overseers and agencies.

3

Rulemaking as a Strategic Enterprise

If you let me write the procedures and I let you write the substance, I'll [beat] you every time.

FORMER REP. JOHN DINGELL[1]

Representative John Dingell (D-MI) served in the US House of Representatives for nearly sixty years and currently holds the record as the longest-serving member of Congress in history. As the epigraph to this chapter illustrates, Dingell knew how the game was played. He knew that rather than attacking a difficult policy head-on, it is often easier to sidetrack a bill by referring it to an outside commission for additional study or by calling for a vote to table the measure, a procedural maneuver that "effectively defeats a proposal without rendering a clear judgment on its substance" (Oleszek 1996, 12). Skilled legislators like Dingell also resort to procedural means to get difficult or controversial items passed through the chamber. For instance, the budget reconciliation process allows savvy legislators to circumvent the sixty votes needed to overcome a filibuster in the Senate.[2]

Yet when it comes to the bureaucracy, procedures have traditionally been understood as a mechanism for political overseers to constrain what bureaucrats do, since these overseers establish procedures at the outset. This logic is fundamentally shortsighted. Because bureaucrats implement and manage these procedures, they can take on a life of their own and can be employed strategically, much as they are in Congress. As George Krause (1999) puts it, influence is a "two-way street." And in the realm of rulemaking, procedures can be an avenue for bureaucratic influence and power that exists separately from the power to propose and implement policy.

1. Quoted in Oleszek (1996, 12).

2. Reconciliation procedures have been used to pass several major policy reforms, including welfare reform in 1996, the 2001 and 2003 Bush tax cuts, and the Affordable Care Act in 2010. See Reynolds (2017) for a careful accounting of the politics of the reconciliation process.

This chapter lays out a theory of—and develops testable hypotheses around—how and when agencies engage in procedural politicking. The argument is built on the assumption that bureaucrats have an incentive to see the policies they propose in their rulemakings succeed. However, as chapter 2 explained, rulemaking is a constrained policy-making venue; the president, Congress, and the courts all have tools to veto a rule or otherwise punish an agency. While proposing a policy that would satisfy all overseers is one way (and sometimes a necessary one) that an agency can ensure a rule does not provoke oversight consequences, compromise is often suboptimal from the agency's perspective. Another option, often more appealing to agencies, is the strategic use of procedures to insulate a rule from oversight. This approach can alleviate the need to make significant policy concessions.

I focus on three distinct phases of the rulemaking process: drafting, consultation, and timing. The procedures associated with these phases are most likely to be employed strategically—that is, in ways that raise monitoring costs for principals or that persuade principals of the agency's position— precisely when agencies expect that their principals might punitively deploy tools from the oversight toolbox. The interest groups that monitor an agency can also be critical to an agency's procedural strategy, as groups can be more or less supportive of an agency's goals—and, accordingly, more or less willing to pressure principals into providing oversight. By relying on procedural politicking at moments when the political environment is particularly inhospitable, agencies can enhance a rule's prospects of surviving to become legally binding. Rather than a purely administrative activity,[3] the portrait that emerges in this chapter is one of rulemaking procedures as carefully crafted political strategy.

The Strategic Enterprise

Some rulemaking projects succeed while others fail. By "succeed," I mean that a proposed rule that the agency has invested in by conducting research, engaging with stakeholders, and drafting goes on to become a binding final rule.[4] Failure, however, is also a possibility. When this happens, all the resources that went into those activities are essentially squandered. And failure can come short of a regulatory veto (i.e., an overturn of a rule by the Office of Information and Regulatory Affairs [OIRA], by Congress, or by the courts).

3. Stewart (1975).
4. A separate question, of course, is whether the rule goes on to accomplish its intended policy goal.

For example, unforeseen political events may compel an agency to make undesirable changes to a policy. Bureaucrats then spend additional time and effort on revisions and are left to implement a less than desirable policy.

Success in rulemaking is important to the agency's broader policy agenda. Given the time, research, and effort involved in completing a rulemaking, the choice to initiate a new rulemaking project is a commitment. Once an agency has made that commitment, other opportunities are essentially foreclosed. This is not a hypothetical concern; nearly all agencies face a backlog in rulemaking, with an ever-increasing list of policy fixes and improvements on the regulatory to-do list.[5] This point was made concretely during the course of an interview for this project. While sitting in the office of one agency's regulatory director, I noticed a whiteboard listing approximately thirty ongoing rulemaking projects at the agency, along with the stage of completion for each. Should any one of those projects be held up—by, say, a request for information from Congress or a particularly difficult review from OIRA—the time and resources the agency would devote in responding would draw directly from another project on that same board. In other words, regulatory projects present opportunity costs, because time the agency invests in issuing one rule comes at the direct expense of others.

The success of a rulemaking project can also enhance an organization's reputation, whereas failure can detract from it. The concept of organizational reputation has gained increased attention in recent years, with scholars agreeing that, for the most part, agencies strive to develop and maintain reputations for competence and superior performance.[6] Concerns over reputation can shape the level of autonomy granted to an agency and also the administrative choices that agencies make.[7] A rulemaking failure, in contrast, has the potential to damage the agency's autonomy, as Congress and the president

5. See Kerwin and Furlong (2011).

6. Carpenter's (2001) work is perhaps the most widely known on this point. Using a historical approach, he argues that agencies can build support coalitions with key interest group allies and establish reputations for reliability and efficacy. The agency can then capitalize on its positive reputation to achieve greater autonomy. See also Carpenter (2010); Carpenter and Krause (2012); and MacDonald and Franko (2007).

7. For instance, Moffitt (2010) argues that concerns about reputation guide the Food and Drug Administration's decisions about advisory committee consultation. By engaging externally and having outsiders acknowledge a drug's risks, the FDA can "demonstrate that any failure associated with the policy is inherent to the policy itself and not attributable to (lack of) agency expertise." Similarly, Carpenter (2002) demonstrates that reputation-based concerns affect the timing of new drug application approvals at the FDA. See also Maor, Gilad, and Bloom (2013).

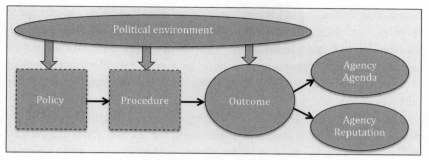

FIGURE 3.1. The influence of rulemaking choices on an agency's agenda and reputation

may be less willing to delegate activities to an agency with a poor reputation in the future. Agencies deal with the same OIRA desk officers, members of Congress, congressional committees, judges, and journalists again and again, meaning that the problem can compound since these actors may scrutinize the agency's actions more closely after regulatory setbacks.

Figure 3.1 illustrates the theoretical logic linking concerns about an agency's agenda and reputation to choices made during the rulemaking process (dashed squares represent agency choices). The entire rulemaking process occurs within the context of the broader political environment, which influences an agency's choices about policy and procedures, as well as the eventual outcome of the process. That outcome can be success or failure (or something in between), and it can have consequences both for an agency's ability to accomplish its policy agenda and for its organizational reputation. However, agencies are not merely observers of the outcome of their rules. Instead, taking into account the political environment at a given point in time, they can make strategic choices that make particular outcomes more or less likely. Accordingly, the figure also highlights that the final outcome is the product of both the policy contained in the rulemaking proposal and the procedures used to manage the rulemaking process. I now consider each of these factors in greater detail.

THE POLITICAL ENVIRONMENT

Agencies operate within a political context, and as figure 3.1 shows, this environment not only influences the actions that the agency takes but also affects the outcome of the rulemaking process itself. Broadly construed, the political environment includes the three constitutional branches—the president, Congress, and the courts—as well as a constellation of interest groups that have a stake in the agency's regulatory actions.[8] As the previous chapter made clear, each of the constitutional actors has the authority to issue a regulatory veto or to otherwise sanction an agency for a perceived overstep of its authority. Agencies therefore have good reason to take the preferences of these actors seriously and to factor them into their decisions about policy and procedure.

Interests groups—by which I mean organized entities that include businesses and public interest groups—also influence the political environment. Although they do not hold the same formal powers to reward and sanction agencies as do the political branches, these stakeholders can increase an issue's salience in the eyes of those that do hold formal oversight power. In other words, while interest groups have very little power to directly sanction agencies, they can pressure political overseers to either exert or withhold their influence. This pressure augments a rule's prospects for success if groups are aligned with the agency's purposes; when powerful groups support the agency's regulatory agenda, they can help to convince skeptical political overseers. Alternately, group influence can work against the agency; when powerful groups oppose the agency, they can encourage political principals to open their oversight toolbox—and possibly deploy a regulatory veto. As McCubbins and Schwartz (1984) famously described it, interest groups can pull "fire alarms" and activate oversight.

Because agencies work in different policy areas, the constellation of interest groups they deal with varies.[9] For example, the Environmental Protection Agency (EPA) is situated between business interests that strive to reduce the regulatory burden the agency imposes on industry and environmental groups that aim to increase protections for the natural environment. The balance of power between these opposing interests has shifted across time. In the 1970s, during the heyday of the environmental movement (and when the EPA was first created), environmental groups enjoyed considerable po-

8. The political environment can be expanded further to include other actors such as the media or narrowed to focus on particular actors who have interests relevant to the agency (e.g., individual members of Congress, particular interest groups). The focus on the president, Congress, the courts, and interest groups, which are consistently present, allows me to make a general argument that holds across a large swath of agencies.

9. The stakeholder groups in an agency's orbit are truly diverse. For instance, the Occupational Safety and Health Administration balances the demands of both labor and management interests, and the Centers for Medicare and Medicaid Services' stakeholders include health-care providers, insurers, patient advocacy groups, and the states. The differences in interest group constituencies may affect an agency's strategic choices (see, e.g., Gormley 1983); future work exploring these relationships is certainly welcome.

litical clout.[10] Over time, the power of business groups in comparison to that of environmental groups has increased. Meanwhile, other agencies, like the National Science Foundation (NSF), have a narrower regulatory reach, with policies that affect a more unified group of stakeholders—in the NSF's case mostly universities and research institutions.[11] Regardless, agencies are keenly aware of the powerful interest groups in their operating space (and, if relevant, whether the balance of power among groups has shifted), as well as how groups are predisposed to respond to particular policies. Accordingly, agencies adjust their approach to both policy and procedures on the basis of whether group involvement in their rulemaking is likely to improve or diminish a rule's prospects for success. Put differently, agencies condition their strategies according to the responses they anticipate from relevant interests.[12]

Of course, the political environment is not a constant. Sometimes agencies operate in an environment where there is broad political support for their mission and the types of rules they are advancing. Far more common, however, one—or more—of an agency's political principals is skeptical of the agency and what it is trying to accomplish. When this occurs, the machinations of disaffected interest groups may prove particularly effective, as they can fall on sympathetic ears. Accordingly, agencies must make policy and procedural choices with extreme care. For instance, President Obama was ideologically in step with the EPA and worked closely with that agency to issue regulations aimed at reducing climate change.[13] However, when Republicans gained control of the House in 2010, their Tea Party–infused agenda focused on eliminating "job-killing regulations," among which EPA regulations were a prime target. Indeed, the chair of the House Energy and Commerce Committee went so far as to promise Administrator Lisa Jackson of the EPA that she would be called to testify before Congress so often that she should reserve

10. See Moe (1989).

11. See chapter 5 of Wilson (1989) for a typology of agencies according to the mix of groups that are affected by the agency's dealings.

12. This should not be read as an argument that agencies have complete information about how relevant interest groups would respond to different policy proposals. Rather, my point is that bureaucrats have informed priors about group preferences that enable them to anticipate, if imperfectly, how groups might respond.

13. Throughout the book, I am careful to distinguish presidential preferences and actions from agency ones. Although President Obama famously declared his ability to accomplish executive action by stating, "I've got a pen and I've got a phone," presidents do not write or promulgate rules. Instead, they rely on agencies to accomplish this task. Presidents sometimes work in concert with agencies, but at other times they work toward opposing ends. It is precisely this variation in presidential support and opposition that I intend to highlight in conceptualizing the political environment.

her own parking space on Capitol Hill. True to this pledge, in the first year
after Republicans took control of the House, Administrator Jackson testified
before the House a total of twelve times.[14]

In this kind of environment—where a principal is hostile to the agency's
actions—rules are at high risk of failing. Anticipating this threat, an agency
can maneuver to help its rules succeed in the face of adversity. That is, while
most theories of agency policy making suggest that the EPA should have
abandoned its rulemaking projects in this environment, the agency nonetheless persevered. In spite of Congress's increased scrutiny of the EPA, under
Jackson's leadership the agency issued a number of critically important environmental rules during the 112th Congress. These included a rule to curb
greenhouse gas emissions from new coal-fired power plants, a rule that addressed air pollution associated with hydraulic fracturing (or "fracking"), and
a rule that required power plants in twenty-seven states to cut their emissions
by between 54 percent and 73 percent. These were not trivial policy changes.
For instance, most observers considered the fracking rule to be the first federal foray into regulating this then-emergent drilling technique. The rule was
ambitious, too; the agency used its extant authority under the Clean Air Act
to issue the rule despite the opposition of industry and many in Congress.[15]
Meanwhile, the agency did not slow the rate of its regulatory activity, issuing
more than 150 "significant" rules during this time period.[16] In other words,
the agency was doing something to shore up its regulatory agenda despite
strong congressional opposition. I argue that strategic policy and procedural
choices allowed the agency to proceed in the face of this adversity.

POLICY CHOICES

The rulemaking process begins once an agency has decided to issue a rule—
either because some other actor (e.g., Congress, the courts) has prompted it
to do so or because it has independently recognized a need.[17] The question
then becomes, what policy should the agency propose?

14. See the *Economist* (2011). By contrast, Jackson's predecessor, Stephen Johnson, testified
before Congress only four times in his two-and-a-half year tenure.

15. Pub. L. No. 91-604.

16. This figure is based on the number of "significant" rules that the Office of Management
and Budget selected for review during the 112th Congress. It is on par with EPA's regulatory
volume in previous Congresses.

17. See chapter 2. Although there is a principled distinction between rules that are mandated (i.e., directly required by statute or judicial order) and those that are discretionary (i.e.,
initiated by the agency), that distinction becomes blurred in practice. Even when a policy is

A policy choice is an agency decision about the direction in which the agency should take a regulatory program. Sometimes, the question of precisely which policy to propose is a relatively trivial one, such as whether the agency should require regulated parties to submit a form on a monthly or a quarterly basis. However, policy questions lie at the very heart of rulemaking, and agencies often have considerable discretion over them when preparing a draft rule. For instance, the agency may decide to include or exclude entire industries from the scope of a rulemaking that imposes new regulatory burdens. One such policy choice occurred in 2010, when the Federal Aviation Administration issued a proposed rule to extend its commercial service pilot fatigue and rest regulations to cover charter and cargo flight operations.[18] This policy choice created winners (e.g., safety advocates) and losers (e.g., charter and cargo carriers who subsequently faced stricter pilot service times).

In the face of opposition, an agency cannot usually just propose its preferred, or ideal, policy when making a rule. Rather, as numerous theoretical models of agency policy making demonstrate, agencies are constrained and therefore strategic in which policies they can offer in a system of separation-of-powers oversight.[19] These models are typically based on a spatial logic and show how tools of political oversight—like the regulatory veto—ensure that agencies take the preferences of political overseers that possess this power into account when proposing policy. For example, if an agency proposes a policy that is too extreme compared to the preferences of, say, the president, that rule is likely to get overturned through the course of OIRA review. The veto results not only in wasted agency effort but also, presumably, in a worse policy outcome from the agency's perspective because either policy will revert to the status quo or some other actor will set policy. As a result, agencies propose policies that are as close as possible to their own ideal policy while

---

mandatory, the agency can have considerable discretion over how the policy is implemented, or it may attach additional provisions to the rule that Congress or the courts in no way intended. In a recent study Haeder, Yackee, and Yackee (2016) examine congressional regulatory mandates to the Department of Interior over a forty-year period. They find that the DOI has routinely failed to issue rules that are required by statute. Upon further scrutiny, then, mandatory rules may be much more discretionary in nature than they initially appear. Thus, rather than being a dichotomous concept, is it more appropriate to consider this as a continuum with fully mandatory and fully discretionary rules at each end.

18. "Flightcrew Member Duty and Rest Requirements," 75 FR 55852, Sept. 14, 2010.

19. This general result follows from a series of well-known models of delegation in which overseers set some sort of constraints and agencies maximize within these bounds. See, e.g., Bawn (1995); Epstein and O'Halloran (1999); Ferejohn and Shipan (1990); Shipan (2004); and Volden (2002). See also McCubbins, Noll, and Weingast (1989).

still being tolerable for the president. The same logic applies to congressional and judicial oversight.

Put more precisely, agencies propose policies that are a constrained optimum, or the best policy they can achieve in a world where they are subject to political checks. However, even with a policy that is constrained, agencies are still at an advantage when they propose a policy compared to having some other entity such as Congress make the policy instead (e.g., by passing a law). This is because, were Congress to set the policy, Congress would not have to take the agency's preferences into account at all and would simply offer its own ideal policy. Because the agency proposal factors in the agency's preferences, while the congressional proposal does not, there is real value—from the agency's vantage point—in being the agenda setter and being able to propose policies through the rulemaking process.[20]

Understanding agency choices about where to set policy has been a central theme of previous scholarship. My argument is that procedures also play an important role in influencing the outcome of the administrative process. Importantly, the use of procedures may alleviate some of the constraint on the policies that agencies select. That is, by employing procedures strategically, agencies may not need to make as many policy concessions and may even gain policy benefits in the process. This is not to say that agencies do not make constrained policy choices, but rather that procedural tactics may free agencies up more than in a policy-making scenario that does not take procedures into account.

PROCEDURAL CHOICES

Procedures are an established way that an agency does something, usually in a certain order. While procedures imply routine and predictability, they do not mean that rulemakings will be carried out in the same way every time, but rather that there is an infrastructure in place that sets an expectation about how things should generally follow from rulemaking to rulemaking. Procedural questions permeate every stage of the rulemaking process. They include considerations such as the following: How should the initial proposed rule be drafted and who should do it? Should the process begin with a proposed rule, or is the policy action urgent enough to warrant the agency invoking "good cause," which skips the proposed rule and begins the process with an emer-

20. The value of agenda setting is another established result from the formal modeling literature. As Ferejohn and Shipan (1990, 7) succinctly state, "By being empowered to make the first move, the agency has an important strategic advantage."

gency interim final rule (thereby bypassing the public comment period)? Who should be consulted, when, and how often?

Procedures are not optional; some choice has to be made at each step of the process or a rulemaking cannot proceed. Procedures are not neutral, either. For example, in writing a rule an agency can choose to make it accessible, thereby engaging a broader audience, or obscure, thereby limiting outsider participation. Each procedural decision factors into the final outcome of the rulemaking process. Procedural politicking is rooted in the idea that bureaucrats have expert insight into the consequences of these procedural choices and, accordingly, can capitalize on them for political advantage. Doing so bolsters the prospects of a rule surviving and eventually becoming a binding final rule in an inhospitable political environment.

If bureaucrats build a rulemaking process around procedures that are not carefully selected and managed, opposition can foment, introducing opportunities for intervention from principals. In contrast, a process that is skillfully orchestrated can help to suppress potential opposition and open a path to success where none previously existed. Some procedural tools raise monitoring costs for principals, whereas others build support or minimize opposition.

Procedural politicking is often intended to manage external audiences. However, it does not affect all audiences equally. For the mass public, some tactics make it less likely that individuals will engage with a rulemaking— they will be less likely to read and digest the rule, less likely to submit a comment on the rule, less likely to contact a political principal about a rule, and so on. However, given the low level of public engagement in rulemaking overall, the impact may be minimal. Organized interests—affected industries and interest groups—are much more likely, ex ante, to participate in the process; procedures also affect these stakeholders, albeit in a different way. Not only does procedural politicking "up the ante"—requiring groups to devote more resources to the rulemaking process—it also makes it harder for these groups to expand the scope of the conflict beyond their particular interests (i.e., get outside audiences to engage with the rule). This may result in procedural tactics reinforcing already-existing participatory disparities in the rulemaking process.

As I explain in the remainder of this chapter, there is no one way to maximize procedures; the exact manner in which procedures are strategically employed depends on both the political environment and the stage of the process at which it comes into play. There are, nonetheless, systematic trends worth uncovering. As a strategic tool, procedures are particularly advantageous for agencies, because on their face they appear to be a "neutral" part of an administrative process; the agency had to make a choice, so choosing, say, a relatively long comment period rather than a shorter one is part of a choice set that can be considered (or at least argued to be) routine and pro forma.

The Role of Bureaucrats

The theory advanced in this book holds that agencies strategically respond to the political environment, but agencies are not monolithic entities. Rather, as I noted in chapter 1, agencies are collections of individual bureaucrats, and those individuals may differ in important ways. It can be useful to aggregate these actors for the sake of analysis, but doing so runs the risk of missing insights that arise from understanding variation in motivations among the individuals within an agency. As it turns out, irrespective of individual motivations, all types of bureaucrats are likely to benefit from a successful rule-making project and suffer setbacks from a failed one.[21] As a consequence, it naturally follows that, at an aggregate level, agencies pursue policy success, because all of the agency's constituent parts share this preference for success. In other words, the theory is still sound when reconstituted on an individual-level foundation.

To understand why, it is illustrative to examine the effects of a rulemaking failure at one agency—the Department of Transportation (DOT)—on four types of bureaucrats: zealots, or those who are policy motivated; climbers, or those who are career motivated; professionals, or those who closely adhere to professional norms and practices; and slackers, those who are motivated to minimize their own workload or to attend to other internal agency dynamics that are not policy related.[22]

---

21. The extent of the impact may vary by type. In this section, I consider differences in bureaucratic types according to their motivation, but another distinction that scholars frequently draw is between political appointees, who are "in and out" of the agency, and careerists, civil servants who spend major portions of their careers at the agency. However, the four types of bureaucrats considered here neatly address this divide. Political appointees are much more likely to draw from the ranks of zealots and climbers. As Kerwin and Furlong (2011, 274) explain, "Involvement in rulemaking provides political appointees one of the best ways to leave a mark on an agency that they will probably be with only for a short time." For some leaving their mark means affecting policy (i.e., zealots), whereas others hope to leave a mark in order to achieve career gains (i.e., climbers). Careerists draw from all four types, although Downs (1967, 96) characterized slackers as typically populating the lower tiers of the agency hierarchy.

22. This section draws on and expands the discussion in Potter and Shipan (2018). However, while they focus on the importance of policy production, the argument here centers on the importance of the procedural components of rulemaking. The categories in this paragraph should be considered loosely stylized groupings of bureaucrats rather than mutually exclusive

In 1995, Congress directed the DOT to amend its regulations on truckers' work hours to incorporate the latest science about human fatigue and alertness.[23] A revision was sorely needed, since the existing rules had not been updated since 1939 and there had been numerous societal advances, as well as technological advances in the trucking industry, in the intervening years.[24] Five years later, in 2000, the Federal Motor Carrier Safety Administration (FMCSA) issued the so-called hours of service (HOS) proposed rule, which was the culmination of years of research and stakeholder consultation. What followed for the agency was an epic saga that involved the courts, Congress, and multiple proposed and final rules on HOS. After FMCSA finalized the rules in 2003, it was sued and lost three separate times over the course of six years. Each lawsuit forced the agency to revisit some part of the 2003 final rule and reissue a new final rule. By October 2009, the weary agency abandoned the rulemaking and agreed to start the entire HOS rulemaking process anew.[25]

The enterprise had failed. Despite nearly ten years of effort to craft and revise its rule in a way that would make it stick, the agency had not succeeding in creating a new HOS policy.[26] This failure was costly. FMCSA was created by

---

classifications. These are my own categorizations of bureaucratic types, but they align well with those of previous scholars. Policy-motivated zealots have been described in numerous studies (see, e.g., Dilulio 1994; Feldman 1989; Golden 2000; Meier and O'Toole 2006). Meanwhile, the term "climbers" is borrowed from Downs (1967), although the archetype has been described by others (Fiorina 1989; Kerwin and Furlong 2011; Niskanen 1971), and professionals are aptly characterized by Dilulio (1994) and others who focus on norms and organizational culture (Golden 2000; Brehm and Gates 1993; Wilson 1989). Last, while there are many negative stereotypes about bureaucrats who are on a "9 to 3" schedule, some scholars have developed a more nuanced definition of the slacker category (Brehm and Gates 1993; Gailmard and Patty 2007). Of course, as Golden (2000) argues, most people are likely motivated by a host of incentives; it follows, then, that these typologies serve as useful illustrations rather than as strict categories.

23. See § 408 of the Interstate Commerce Commission Termination Act (Pub. L. No. 104-88).

24. DOT had made minor amendments to the policy in 1962, but 1939 was the last substantive revisiting of the standard.

25. There was also a new presidential administration overseeing the agency at that point in time, which may partially explain the agency's willingness to start over. There was some speculation in the press that that the Obama administration offered up the old HOS rulemaking in exchange for a smooth Senate confirmation for the new FMCSA administrator, as the timing of the two events was suspiciously close.

26. At that point, the agency started anew, issuing another HOS proposed rule in December 2010 and a subsequent final rule in December 2011. The new regulations took effect in July 2013, eighteen years after the original congressional mandate to DOT.

Congress in 2000,[27] and its struggles with HOS occurred during the agency's infancy, as it was trying to establish a reputation as a competent and effective regulator. Indeed, the HOS rule was the new agency's first major rulemaking, and the ensuing debacle certainly did not help the agency to burnish its credentials. Two of the court rulings had taken the agency to task for a failure to be thorough—once for neglecting to address an issue that the statute had required the agency to address and a second time for not being transparent about its methodological assumptions.[28]

This unsuccessful rulemaking negatively affected each type of bureaucrat at the agency. To begin, policy-driven zealots concerned themselves with writing a rule that maximized road safety, which is key to the organizational mission of FMCSA. This ethos was echoed in my interviews with FMCSA agency staff and an industry official involved with FMCSA's regulations, as well as in the agency's strategic plan, which mentions the word "safety" no fewer than 196 times in its twenty-eight pages.[29] When the HOS policy was repeatedly rebuffed, zealots suffered, because it meant that policy remained at the status quo, a policy set in 1939 that fell far short of modern safety standards.[30] Zealots were also thwarted on other policy fronts. Agency resources were repeatedly tied up revising—and revising again—the HOS rule. This was problematic because resources at the agency were fairly constrained during the time that HOS revisions were taking place; in spite of its fledgling status, on average the agency had an annual staff increase of about 1 percent during this time period. In addition, the agency's dinged reputation further limited the autonomy that zealots required to pursue ambitious new policies.

Reputational concerns also affected the prospects of so-called climbers. Climbers are motivated by advancing their career within the agency or outside of it; as Kerwin and Furlong (2011, 35) note, those bureaucrats who work on prominent rules get "considerable visibility in an agency and may become

27. The early efforts on HOS (from 1995 to 2000) were managed by the FMCSA's predecessor agency, the Federal Highway Administration.

28. See *Public Citizen v. FMCSA* (374 F.3d 1209, 1216 (D.C. Cir. 2004)), and *Owner-Operator Independent Drivers Association, Inc. v. FMCSA* (494 F.3d 188, 206 (D.C. Cir. 2007)). In both cases the DC Circuit court ruled against the agency on the grounds that the agency had been "arbitrary and capricious."

29. Federal Motor Carrier Safety Administration (2012).

30. At least this was the status quo until 2004. After the DC Circuit vacated the HOS final rule that year, Congress passed a law (Pub. L. No. 108-310) temporarily establishing the 2003 final rule as law until FMCSA could issue a new final rule, which it did in 2005. Zealots still lost out under this new status quo, however, because it was temporary and did not set a viable, long-term safety policy for the agency.

marketable on the outside." This is, of course, contingent on the rulemaking project being successful; a botched rulemaking project is unlikely to return the same positive rewards and can even have negative reputational consequences. Further, climbers realize their career ambitions through aggrandizing their agency; as Fiorina (1989, 44) puts it: "One's status in Washington . . . is roughly proportional to the importance of the operation one oversees. And the sheer size of the operation is taken to be a measure of importance." Again, the size of FMCSA was fairly constant during this period, and the failed HOS rule did not make for a compelling argument to increase the agency's resources. Climbers' prospects were thereby limited.

Professionals seek to ensure that the agency subscribes to prevailing occupational norms and also adheres to its own internal culture. FMCSA's rulemaking staff comprises white-collar professionals, but they do not draw from any one particular field.[31] Thus, in the absence of a unifying set of occupational norms, professionals at FMCSA were most concerned about getting the HOS policy "right"—that is, selecting a policy that would ultimately be able to be successfully enforced given the agency's capacity, safety concerns, and the structure of the trucking industry.[32] Failure to evade meddling from the courts and Congress detracted from the goals of professionals. These external actors did not share the agency's outlook on safety and pushed the agency toward certain solutions and away from others. For professionals who would have preferred to make decisions based on technical and policy criteria, this was problematic. That is, political considerations may have forced professionals to de-emphasize aspects of HOS policy that may have been substantively more important. Further, the court rulings repeatedly dinged the agency for policy and procedural missteps, effectively accusing it of a lack of professionalism. Such criticisms acutely sting for those who pride themselves on knowing how to competently execute the rulemaking process.

Last (and perhaps least) come the slackers, the catchall term for bureaucrats who are motivated by factors other than policy, career, or professional considerations. Here, it is straightforward to see that slackers were worse off; whatever their individual contribution to the HOS rule, they were forced to redo it several times (likely on top of their other ongoing workload). Addi-

---

31. According to the Office of Personnel Management's *FedScope* database, in 2006 approximately 37 percent of FCMSA staff in the DC headquarters held advanced degrees. The diversity of the agency's rulemaking staff was confirmed in interviews with two DOT officials.

32. In this case, the goals of professionals and zealots aligned nicely, but this might not always be the case. For example, professionals at FMCSA could plausibly advance a policy that maximizes road safety while (deregulatory) zealots could advocate for a policy that focuses on minimizing costs on regulated parties.

tionally, the work environment for slackers likely deteriorated as a result of the HOS failure. Compared to a counterfactual world in which the proposed rule continued seamlessly to finalization and implementation after the 2000 proposed rule, agency morale was lower, since HOS was one of the agency's chief policy priorities.[33] Additionally, top DOT and FMCSA officials likely scrutinized the work products of FMCSA rulemaking staff more carefully after the rule was repeatedly rebuffed—not an ideal situation for a slacker.[34]

Although it is just one rule, the FMCSA's experience with the HOS rule in the first decade of the new millennium illustrates a larger point: each type of bureaucrat working within the agency would have preferred an outcome in which the HOS proposed rule was successful—that is, finalized quickly and subsequently implemented. Within the agency, all types were made worse off by the repeated rehashing—and eventual failure—of the rule.[35] The takeaway is that it is reasonable to assume that rulemaking success is in the shared interest of bureaucrats working within the agency, irrespective of their type.

Procedural Politicking in Practice

What does procedural politicking look like in practice? The answer, of course, is that it depends on the procedure: what does it do, and at which point in the process does it come into play? Through the course of creating a new rule, bureaucrats face a menu of procedural options. Although it is often presumed that the Administrative Procedure Act (APA) dictates the procedures that agencies must follow to create a new rule, the procedural framework established by this law is surprisingly minimal, leaving bureau-

---

33. Agency morale is often assessed via personnel surveys conducted by the Office of Personnel Management. While OPM did not disaggregate data to the bureau level, it is possible to evaluate morale at the DOT during this time frame. Between 2004 and 2008, employees at DOT were significantly more likely to respond negatively ("dissatisfied" or "very dissatisfied") when asked the question "Considering everything, how satisfied are you with your organization?" (Office of Personnel Management 2008). In 2004, 24.5 percent of DOT employees recorded negative responses, and in 2008 37.2 percent of employees responded negatively. Although this does not speak directly to the HOS issue at FMCSA, it is consistent with the notion that morale was on the decline during this period.

34. This is conjecture on my part. However, it is commonsensical to assume that a supervisor would give greater attention to a subordinate's work following a series of organizational missteps.

35. FMCSA's HOS rule is an example of a rulemaking failure. Consideration of a rulemaking success would entail the same type of counterfactual exercise, in which each type's utility would need to be considered in light of what would have happened had the rule failed. However, the result of such an exercise would yield the same result: that success is a rising tide that lifts all boats.

crats with plenty of room to maneuver. Former Supreme Court Justice Antonin Scalia (1978, 348) explained, "Insofar as the text of the APA is concerned, the choice within this available spectrum of possible procedures was left to each agency." Wiseman and Wright (2015) further note that only two-thirds of one page of the original nine pages of the enacted law actually addressed the subject of rulemaking. As I have noted, what the APA does include is four basic requirements: when writing a new rule, an agency must (1) provide notice of the proposed policy change, (2) solicit public input, (3) publish a final rule, and (4) allow some time between the final rule's publication and the effective date.[36] Even then, the law allows agencies to waive the first and fourth requirement in some cases and altogether exempts policies dealing with the military, foreign affairs, or internal agency management. In all other respects, the law is silent on procedural particulars.

There are, however, policy-specific procedural constraints imposed on agencies by other laws. Requirements included in statutory language often direct agencies about how additional procedures should be layered on top of the basic requirements. For example, the Higher Education Act (HEA) requires the Department of Education (ED) to take extra steps when writing rules pertaining to student financial assistance.[37] When drafting a new rule under this legal authority, ED is required to follow a "master calendar," whereby only final regulations published by November 1 can take effect by July 1 of the following calendar year.[38] For the most part, Congress tacks on the majority of agency-specific procedures; the other constitutional branches largely refrain from dictating procedures.[39]

I focus on three key procedural politicking tools: writing, or control over

---

36. See 5 U.S.C. § 553.

37. These additional steps were added as part of the 1986 (§ 482 of Pub. L. No. 99-498) and 1998 amendments (§ 490(D) of Pub. L. No. 105-244) to the Higher Education Act of 1965 (Pub. L. No. 89-329).

38. See § 482(c) of the HEA. The master calendar is intended to provide stability in financial aid programs, so that changes to the program do not occur in the middle of an academic year.

39. In earlier periods, particularly the 1970s, activist courts were heavy handed, in some cases directing agencies to take additional procedural steps or to make overtures to particular types of stakeholders. In the rulemaking regime studied here, procedural interference by the courts was unusual. The turning point on this front came in 1978, with a landmark Supreme Court decision on the appropriate role of the courts in evaluating the sufficiency and scope of agency procedures. In *Vermont Yankee Nuclear Power Corp. v. Natural Resources Defense Council, Inc.* (35 U.S. 519 (1978)), the Supreme Court overturned an earlier anti-agency decision by the DC Circuit. Their logic was that that agencies, not courts, were best situated to evaluate their own procedures; the question at hand involved whether the Atomic Energy Commission, which

the composition of the rule;[40] consultation, or how the agency manages its interactions with stakeholders outside the agency; and timing, or how the agency manages the temporal aspects of the process. While these three tools do not constitute the universe of procedural decisions, they are core to the process and shared across rulemakings; bureaucrats at every agency must decide about these procedures for each and every rule that crosses their desks.

THE POWER OF THE PEN

Bureaucratic authorship of rules can be an important persuasion tool. The way a rule is written can convince readers that the agency's proposed course of action is a sound one. For instance, a regulatory text that is packed with citations to scientific material may lend credence to a policy idea that might seem half-baked on its own. Alternatively, a rule may be drafted in a manner that dissuades readers from engaging too deeply with the underlying policy. Texts that are written densely or in jargon, for example, set up barriers by requiring more of a reader's cognitive energy and attention. In the procedural politicking context, bureaucrats can use writing tools to persuade or to make supervisory review more difficult; that is, bureaucrats can make it harder for principals to anticipate the consequences of their rules, or dissuade them from intervening at all. As laid out in table 3.1, agencies have numerous writing tools at their disposal, including framing, manipulating analytical assumptions, and making the policy more or less accessible.[41]

Framing is generally understood to mean selecting "some aspects of a perceived reality and make them more salient in communicating text, in such a way to promote a particular problem definition, causal interpretation, moral evaluation and/or treatment recommendation for the items described" (Entman 1993, 52).[42] The basic premise is that any issue can be viewed through a

---

had written a rule on nuclear power, had sufficiently "ventilated" the key issues in the rule so that affected stakeholders could evaluate the proposal. See Metzger (2005).

40. Some readers may question whether writing is truly a procedure. However, the definition of a procedure provided earlier in this chapter provides a broad understanding of a process-related undertaking. Given the way agencies manage the rule-drafting process—usually involving teams of people with multiple drafts circulated internally—writing should certainly be treated as a procedure.

41. The tools presented in table 3.1—and the two "tool kit" tables that follow in table 3.2 and table 3.3—should not be read as exhaustive lists.

42. Framing is conceptually distinct from priming, which suggests that the individual apply a particular evaluation criterion (which typically draws on an categories or constructs in that individual's memory) over other possible criteria, and agenda setting, which is the transfer of salience from elites to an audience (Chong and Druckman 2007; Scheufele and Iyengar 2017).

TABLE 3.1. The writing tool kit

Tool	Description	Stage
Policy framing	Agency frames policy in ways that avoid certain known political or policy land mines.	Proposed rule
Analytical assumptions	Agency generates cost-benefit analysis (or other analytical requirement) relying on assumptions that favor the agency's preferred policy.	Proposed rule
Text accessibility	Agency drafts proposed rule in a way that is inaccessible to nonexperts or raises the costs of engagement.	Proposed rule

Note: Although these tools are available at both the proposed and final rule stage, they are most formative early on at the proposed rule stage.

variety of lenses, and the interpretation of the issue may change depending on which lens is put into focus. Successful framing can shape how outsiders—principals and other stakeholders—perceive and react to a controversial rule.[43]

There is a not a one-size-fits-all frame that agencies should employ when a rule is at risk. Rather, because rules deal with so many different policy areas, the optimal frame (from the agency's perspective) will vary. A return to the FDA's tobacco rules in the mid-1990s illuminates the role of framing in rulemaking. In his account of the development of the agency's proposed rule, former Commissioner Kessler (2001) describes why the agency adopted a frame of nicotine addiction as a pediatric disease. Importantly, the agency chose not to focus on adult smoking—even though many of the rule's reforms would have limited adult access to tobacco products—and also refrained from appeals to moral authority. In a country where one in four adults smoked cigarettes,[44] these approaches might have hardened opposition, but appeals based on children's health were likely to engender more universal sympathy.

43. As Poletta and Ho (2006, 188) explain, "The ways in which political actors package their messages affect their ability to recruit adherents, gain favorable media coverage, demobilize antagonists, and win political victories." Framing effects have been demonstrated in a many contexts, including how firms' quarterly results are perceived and in the extent of public support for the Supreme Court (e.g., Nicholson and Howard 2003; Wade, Porac, and Pollock 1997). There is less scholarly understanding of how elites strategically select frames, although there is a general sense that there is a strategic element to it. For example, litigants are artful in choosing how to frame their briefs before the Supreme Court, but the exact frames selected depend on the context (e.g., petition or respondent, how the issue was framed in the lower courts). See Wedeking (2010).

44. Between 1995 and 1997, 24.7 percent of adult Americans were cigarette smokers (Centers for Disease Control and Prevention 2016).

Framing the issue in this way allowed the FDA to outcompete other actors and achieve its preferred outcome.[45] Framing is important because it establishes the terms on which stakeholders will encounter a rule and how they respond to it.[46]

Framing a proposal in an advantageous light can also include appeals to authority, which can burnish a rule's bona fides in high-risk scenarios. Steeping a proposal in scientific, technical, or legal citations enhances a policy's external validity and demonstrates that the agency has done its homework.[47] This can signal to overseers and interest groups that the agency would be a formidable adversary if challenged. For example, the FDA's completed proposed rule on tobacco regulation, issued in 1996, included references to 118 scientific studies and ran 221 pages.[48] Only four of those pages contained the proposed regulatory language that would make the legal changes to the *Code of Federal Regulations*. The remainder of the text included 169 pages of preamble text explaining the legal authority, impact, and implementation plan for the proposed rule, and 51 pages of analysis addressing the rule's costs and benefits, as well as its impact on the economy, families, federalism, paperwork, property rights, and the environment. This was an explicit strategy on the agency's part: as Kessler (2001, 296) explains: "We had allowed ourselves to become vulnerable to criticism by making statements without having all the supporting facts behind them. . . . I decided that everything we did must be totally data-driven."

Agencies can also select scientific or technical assumptions to bias a rule's analysis toward the agency's preferred outcome. For instance, one industry official I interviewed complained that the FMCSA adopted a "tortured logic"

45. The agency achieved its preferred outcome (i.e., a binding final rule) in the short term. In the longer term, the Supreme Court overturned the rule in *FDA v. Brown & Williamson Tobacco Corp.* (529 U.S. 120 (2000)).

46. This does not mean that stakeholders will necessarily accept the agency's frame or that the frame will be successful. Opponents often introduce competing frames that challenge the agency's frame (see Chong and Druckman 2007; Sniderman and Theriault 2004). In the case of the FDA's tobacco rulemaking, the tobacco industry responded with a frame that the agency's proposal impinged upon individual freedoms and was evidence of regulatory overreach and a nanny state. The presence of competing frames is par for the course in contested policy areas, but the agency gets the opening shot at persuading audiences of its perspective.

47. Strategic appeals to authority have been identified in other contexts as well. For example, in a study of how firms justify chief executive officer compensation, Wade, Porac, and Pollock (1997, 641) find that "when companies have more concentrated and active outside owners, they are much more likely to justify their compensation practices by citing the role of compensation consultants as advisors in the compensation-setting process."

48. See 61 FR 44396; Aug. 28, 1996.

in its technical assumptions for the Obama-era HOS rule.[49] On the benefits side of the ledger in the cost-benefit analysis, the agency assumed that, by forcing truckers to take more breaks, truckers would sleep more hours, which would then lead to greater health, which in turn would increase longevity. Thus, the costs of the rule were offset in part by estimated returns in reduced mortality for individual drivers.[50] Industry officials found this assumption to be questionable—truckers might choose to sleep more with mandated breaks, but they also might choose other activities instead.[51] While arbitrating between whether industry or the agency had a better grip on how truckers would spend an additional hour-long break is beyond the purpose here, it is indisputable that this assumption aided in justifying the agency's analysis. In the end, FMCSA's analysis yielded a positive net benefit for its preferred policy of approximately $205 million per year.[52]

Agencies may also draft rule texts in ways that obscure the intent or the impact of the policy. By writing a rule that is dense or that relies on technical jargon, agencies can discourage nonexperts from engaging with the rule. Additionally, the agency creates uncertainty among principals (who are likely nonexperts) about the precise consequences of the policy. Specifically, agencies can draft proposed (and, subsequently, final rules) in ways that make it hard to discern exactly what the rule does and how it will have an impact on

49. Interview with trucking industry official, June 2016.

50. Reduced mortality was then monetized in terms of the value of a statistical life, which, consistent with the DOT's standard practice, was set at $6 million. See chapter 5 of the agency's regulatory impact analysis for an explanation of the FMCSA's analytical methodology for the final rule (Federal Motor Carrier Safety Administration 2011).

51. See the preamble to the final rule for discussion on this point (76 FR 81134; Dec. 27, 2011).

52. Wagner (2009) raises a similar critique regarding a controversial EPA rule known as the Clean Air Interstate Rule, or CAIR. In conducting the required regulatory impact analysis, the EPA produced a report that was 240 pages long and included more than four dozen tables and a separate 180-page appendix. The agency presented a cost-benefit analysis of the proposed option and only one other policy option: the status quo. While the principles of good policy analysis generally require consideration of many policy alternatives, "by providing such a limited glimpse of the policy alternatives, EPA [reduced] the risk of being hung up in litigation about the viability of close competitor approaches" (Wagner 2009, 59). Additionally, the EPA relied on highly conservative estimates of many of the most controversial points of the rule and conducted excessive uncertainty analyses around these estimates. The intent was to make the rule unassailable on these points and to appease industry critics. In the end, Wagner concludes that the EPA's approach to the RIA in this case was a masterful manipulation; it resulted in a benefit-to-cost ratio of 25 to 1 for the agency's proposed policy and served as an advocacy mechanism to promote the agency's preferred course of action. For more on manipulation of assumptions in cost-benefit analysis, see Livermore (2014).

different constituencies. This overlaps with appeals to authority because it can emerge as a consequence of peppering the text of the rule with scientific and technical citations, but it can also exist independently of that strategy. Agencies can simply craft rules using more obfuscatory language that requires a higher level of sophistication or takes more time to comprehend; in so doing, the agency raises the costs for outsiders—whether it be staffers on Capitol Hill, OIRA desk officers, interest group officials, or individual citizens—of meaningfully engaging with the rule.[53] Similarly, rules that extensively appeal to scientific authority can still be written in an accessible and straightforward way.

Stepping back, the manner in which a proposed rule is written, then, can be used to make it more difficult (or less desirable) for outsiders to scrutinize or attack the policy. Following the procedural politicking logic, agencies will be more likely to use writing tools to obfuscate, insulate, and convince when their rules are at greater political risk. That is, if one of the agency's political principals is not aligned with it, that agency will be inclined to write the rule in a way that protects it from a potential political interference.

Of course, the stakeholder groups that are affected by the agency's rules play a particularly important role in monitoring rule documents. After all, these groups are likely to be directly affected by the rule (should it become final) and may also have insight into the details of how a particular proposal is likely to play out in the real world. It follows, then, that if the agency anticipates that affected groups will oppose a proposed rule—and that principals are likely to agree with any complaints groups raise about the rule—writing strategies will become particularly useful in fending off political incursions.

THE POWER OF THE PARTICIPATION VALVE

Public participation in rulemaking is the hallmark of notice-and-comment. Consulting with stakeholders is a way that agencies can both gather information from regulated parties about policies and legitimate the policies that they have developed. It is also, however, a way that stakeholders can find problems with the agency's proposal and throw up roadblocks that could potentially lead to political problems down the line.

The actual participatory requirements in rulemaking are minimal. The APA merely dictates that the agency "shall give interested persons an opportunity to participate in the rule making through submission of written data,

53. Owens, Wedeking, and Wohlfarth (2013) make a similar argument in the context of the Supreme Court, where they show that justices write opinions in a more obfuscatory way when their decisions are at greater risk of being overturned by Congress.

TABLE 3.2. The consultation tool kit

Tool	Description	Stage
Advance notice of proposed rulemaking	Agency chooses whether to publish an ANPRM.	Prerule
Regulatory negotiation (regneg)	Agency decides whether to develop the proposed rule in concert with a negotiation committee comprised of stakeholder entities.	Prerule
Advisory committee meetings	Agency consults with its advisory committee in the process of writing a rule.	Prerule, proposed rule
Length of comment period	Agency chooses how many days to allow the public to comment.	Proposed rule
Timing of comment period	Agency chooses when public comment period will occur.	Proposed rule
Outreach forum	Agency holds outreach forums, including public hearings, focus groups, listening sessions, etc.	Public comment period
Interim final rule	With "good cause," the agency waives the notice stage of the process and solicits comments on a final rule that takes effect immediately.	Final rule

views, or arguments with or without opportunity for oral presentation."[54] This means that while the agency must allow for some level of public participation, the extent of that participation is largely at the agency's discretion.

This is where procedural politicking comes into play; an agency can choose to expand or restrict participation opportunities depending on the nature of the feedback they anticipate receiving. If stakeholder feedback is expected to reflect positively on the rule (or to be relatively innocuous), it can bolster the rule's prospects going forward. Negative feedback can have the opposite effect. Recognizing this, agencies can adjust participation opportunities accordingly. Crucially, agencies are better positioned than their principals to forecast the tenor of participation.

Table 3.2 lists several procedural choices that affect stakeholders' participation opportunities. Some of these tools—such as publishing an Advance Notice of Proposed Rulemaking (ANPRM), holding a hearing, engaging in negotiated rulemaking, or having a longer period for public comment— increase stakeholders' access to a rulemaking.[55] To take one example, if an

54. 5 U.S.C. § 553(c).

55. These tools should not be considered equivalent to one another. For example, choosing to engage in negotiated rulemaking is a considerable resource investment on the part of

agency opts to have a hearing on a proposed rule, that hearing is held in addition to the opportunity for stakeholders to submit written comments on a proposed rule (one of the APA's few requirements). Accordingly, the choice to have a hearing is a "bonus" of sorts; it expands the ways in which a stakeholder can offer feedback on a rule in progress and encourages participation by a larger set of stakeholders.

There are other tools, however, that decrease access for stakeholders, making it more difficult—at the margins—for stakeholders to participate or diminishing the impact of their feedback if they do. These tools include having a shorter public comment period, timing the public comment period at an inconvenient time (for either stakeholders or political principals), and publishing an interim final rule. For instance, as explained previously, one procedural choice is for the agency to avail itself of the APA's "good cause" exception and to publish an interim final rule rather than a proposed rule. Although interest groups still are given the opportunity to submit written comments on an interim final rule, those comments come after the interim rule has taken effect. Stakeholder comments may still influence the agency's final decision, since the agency is still supposed to issue a subsequent final rule. However, the effect of group concerns—and especially the weight such concerns carry with principals—are muted because the policy is effectively the new status quo and, for the most part, represents a done deal.

There are meaningful potential benefits to consulting with external stakeholders through these procedures. By engaging with key groups, the agency can improve the policy and perhaps enhance its implementation prospects.[56] For example, holding a public forum (e.g., a hearing about the proposed rule) allows stakeholders from both sides of an issue to air out their grievances, which may give stakeholders a greater appreciation of other perspectives on an issue and help neutralize opposition. Creating more opportunities for public participation may also generate buy-in from stakeholders. One agency rule writer explained that his agency held lots of listening sessions for some rules, because the listening sessions "allows folks to have their piece," and those individuals were less likely to oppose the rule as a result.[57] In ad-

---

the agency (because selecting a negotiating committee is burdensome and committees typically meet numerous times to craft a proposal), much more so than, say, the one-time cost of the agency hosting a hearing on the proposed rule.

56. Coglianese and Lazer (2003) summarize this position with respect to environmental policy, stating that "firms are often better positioned than government regulators to know important details about the environmental risks created by their production processes." See also Moffitt (2014); and Woods (2013).

57. Interview with DOT official, May 2016.

dition to policy legitimacy, offering greater consultation opportunities can enhance an agency's reputation.[58]

However, unlike consultation that occurs during the proposed rule development stage (i.e., ex parte consultation), the participation procedures listed in table 3.2 are all public, on-the-record consultations.[59] This means that the feedback that the agency receives through these avenues becomes part of the rulemaking record and can be used in the event that some stakeholder chooses to take the agency to court over the rule at a later date. That is, stakeholder participation can lay the groundwork for future litigation.[60]

There are other costs to increasing participation opportunities. Facilitating participation requires agency resources, since agency personnel must be assigned to engage with stakeholders and read and respond to comments. Stakeholder management and comment processing can also slow down the rulemaking process. From an informational perspective, public feedback on an agency's proposal may not be all that valuable either. For instance, one EPA official I spoke with estimated that fewer than 10 percent of comments that agency receives contain new or noteworthy information.[61] After all, if agencies gather information from key stakeholders privately in advance of the public portions of notice-and-comment, then they may already possess the information required for implementation.

In short, stakeholder participation in rulemaking can yield both substantive costs and substantive benefits to the agency. However, there is also a political calculation that an agency must make with respect to participation opportunities. If groups are not supportive of an agency or a proposed rule and principals are also skeptical of the agency, the risk increases that the entire rulemaking enterprise is upended. In this situation increased participation opportunities can mean greater opportunities for fire alarms to be pulled and responded to in adverse ways. This puts the agency under heightened political scrutiny and enhances the likelihood of a veto. Further, if stakeholders make a case that the agency is incompetent or overstepping its author-

---

58. There is a considerable literature on the benefits of public engagement as a way of enhancing an agency's reputation and legitimacy; see Carpenter (2001, 2010); Carpenter and Krause (2012); Krause and Douglas (2005); Maor, Gilad, and Bloom (2013); and Moffitt (2010, 2014).

59. A notable exception is consultation with the agency's advisory committee; these sessions can be open or closed. Though relatively rare, closed sessions are confidential and not publicly observable.

60. Schmidt (2002).

61. Interview with EPA official, May 2013. See also Chubb (1983); Naughton et al. (2009); Yackee (2012); and West (2004).

ity, other political consequences may ensue. This means that when political principals are not aligned with the agency and the agency anticipates negative stakeholder feedback, it is in the agency's interest to reduce participation opportunities: complaints about the agency or the rule are more likely to find a sympathetic ear among the agency's adversaries. In contrast, in circumstances where groups are likely to bolster the agency's position, the agency may find itself increasing participation opportunities. That is, if groups support the agency's position and principals do not, having groups weigh in on the agency's proposal may yield the substantive benefits discussed earlier and serve to convince overseers that the agency proposal has merit—or at least that intervening in the rulemaking may raise issues with a groups of powerful interests.

Historically, scholars have focused on the benefit agencies receive from obtaining information from regulated parties through the notice-and-comment process.[62] In evaluating the level of participation that an agency allows for, I am not assuming that agencies already have complete information and that public consultation is entirely uninformative to the agency. Rather, my point is that sometimes agencies do not need information from regulated parties, as the policy itself is straightforward, or they have already acquired the requisite information. At other times, agencies do need information. In these cases, the agency can get information publicly through the public comment period or, if public consultation is too risky given the political environment, can collect it through more private means (e.g., conducting research, holding off-the-record meetings with individual stakeholders).

THE POWER OF PACING

Rules surface and come to the attention of political overseers at different points in their life cycle. For instance, a rule is more visible and receives more attention when it is published (either at the proposed or the final stage) than when the agency is quietly working on the policy behind closed doors. Although exogenous events may occasionally bring rules to light at other points, in general, agencies control when their rules enter the spotlight. Temporal control over the moments when a rule is publicly prominent is, therefore, another arrow in the bureaucrat's quiver. While some procedures are used

62. The basic idea is that expertise is costly to acquire, and agencies must make decisions about whether to acquire it internally or externally. See Gailmard and Patty (2013); Stephenson (2008, 2010).

TABLE 3.3. The timing tool kit

Tool	Description	Stage
Publication timing	Agency chooses when the rule is published.	Proposed rule, final rule
Effective date	Agency decides when the final rule should take legal effect.	Final rule
Implementation delay	Agency postpones the effective date of the final rule after publication.	Final rule

to strategically raise a given principal's monitoring costs or to persuade principals of a proposal's merits, timing tools may allow bureaucrats to choose which principals will respond to the agency's rule in the first place.

Table 3.3 lists the temporal decisions that bureaucrats make when issuing a rule. These include controlling when the rule is published and when the rule takes binding effect.[63] Sometimes, the agency can draw attention to its rules at points when principals are more sympathetic to the agency's goals. All else equal, an agency would prefer to make policy in a situation where its principals are favorably predisposed than in a situation where they are not. By slowing up or speeding down the process, bureaucrats may be able to choose whether the principals who review their policies are more or less receptive to their goals.

Control over timing is useful for the agency because what might be perceived as a rash or ill-conceived policy in one political environment may be regarded entirely differently in another. What this means in practice is that agencies may delay a rule to have it surface in a more advantageous political clime. At other times, agencies may speed up the process to take advantage of a favorable moment. Regardless of the climate, timing tools can be used to limit the amount of scrutiny a rule receives overall.

63. Timing when the public comment period occurs is another tool by which bureaucrats can control the temporal dimension. However, I consider this consultation, because it directly affects the level and impact of interest group participation during the consultation phase of rulemaking rather than changing who the principals in question are. I include implementation delays—where the agency delays the effective date of the rule after the rule has been finalized—as part of the timing tool kit, even though their use is heavily constrained by the courts. There are several ways such delays can occur—rules may be postponed at the start of a new administration or while ongoing litigation is settled (see § 705 of the APA). However, excessive or prolonged use of implementation delays is an invitation for groups to bring suit against the agency. Courts do not typically side with agencies in these cases, making it an inherently risky strategy.

Delay can have considerable upside for an agency. When the political environment is disadvantageous, waiting to issue a decision allows for more attractive possibilities to develop; exogenous events may shift political priorities in ways that make the agency's decision less salient to political overseers. More significant, the overseers themselves may change. Sitting on a rule, a tactic that is known colloquially as slow-rolling,[64] can mean that a new coalition of political overseers will be responsible for evaluating the agency's decision when the decision finally becomes public.

Consider a hypothetical draft final rule that is particularly contentious. Perhaps OIRA signaled political opposition to the proposed rule during its review. Interest groups may also have become animated during the public comment period and gotten Congress involved. The release of the final rule is an important moment when the agency fully reveals its final policy, and if a political principal remains dissatisfied, war can be waged. However, until the final rule is released, no one outside the agency knows what the final policy will be. The agency may resolve issues in a way that a principal finds satisfactory, or it may stick with its original proposal. As long as this ambiguity remains, the agency deflects interventions by claiming to be "working on it."

Central to the logic of delay is the reality that the time horizon of bureaucrats is typically longer than that of political overseers. Recall that agencies often take years to finalize a proposed rule. So, if an agency wants to finalize a rule that may face opposition, it can play the waiting game, idling until the environment improves when a new principal takes over. This is much more than an issue of term limits and transitions. Politics is unpredictable. For example, few would have predicted Senator Jim Jeffords's (R-VT) 2001 decision to caucus with the Democrats, which caused a switch in party control of the Senate. Nor would many have counted on President Richard Nixon's sudden decision to resign in the face of the Watergate scandal or Justice Antonin Scalia's untimely death in 2016 and the vacancy it introduced on the Supreme Court. While unexpected, such events do happen and often reshape the political landscape in surprising ways. Unforeseen shake-ups can make agencies worse off, but they can also make them better off. When the present situation is adverse, it can make sense to hold out for a better day to come.

Conversely, if the political environment is favorable for the agency, it can issue the rule quickly to capitalize on the situation. This is "fast-tracking," the opposite of slow-rolling. An oft-cited example of agency fast-tracking is the midnight rulemaking phenomenon, by which, at the tail end of a presidential administration, agencies rush to complete rules that are supported by the

64. See Labaton (2004).

outgoing president.[65] While midnight rulemaking is controversial, this may only be because it is more readily observed than other types of fast-tracking, as otherwise expeditious rulemaking may be perceived as routine, or even efficient. Consistent with the idea of procedural politicking, agencies should thus use their control over the pacing of the rulemaking process to try to ensure that rules come to fruition when compatible principals are in power.

Importantly, agencies may not be able to wait out interest groups in the same way that they can slow-roll a principal. No one interest group oversees an agency; constellations of interest groups are typically involved in providing oversight.[66] Therefore, should one group lose clout, other like-minded groups may step in to fill the void. In other words, macro-level changes in the power and mix of interest groups in an agency's sphere are slow to occur and may not transpire in the amount of time that individual bureaucrats have to carry a particular rule to completion—even with bureaucrats' extended time horizons. This implies that the relationship between regulatory pacing and political principals is not conditioned on the interest group environment, as it is for other procedural politicking strategies.

Politics by Other Means

Procedural politicking helps to explain a puzzle posed in chapter 2—why are regulatory vetoes so rare? Federal agencies issue thousands of proposed and final rules each year that deal with all manner of policy issues. Political principals frequently, and often publicly, find fault with the rules that agencies write. For example, in a 2013 decision on the DOT's HOS rule, the DC Circuit court opined that the agency had made "unwise policy decisions."[67] Yet, despite such critiques, overseers interfere in the rulemaking process infrequently. OIRA reviews only a fraction of the rules agencies produce, and among the rules it does review, vetoes less than 10 percent of them. Congress gets involved even less frequently, and, when rules are litigated in court, judges support agencies more often than not. To wit, even while chastising the DOT for being "unwise," the court still upheld the rule, stating that the agency "won the day not on the strengths of its rulemaking prowess, but through an artless war of attrition" (21).

---

65. For an evaluation of the merits and frequency of midnight rulemaking, see Copeland (2008); O'Connell (2011); and Stiglitz (2013).

66. Sometimes these groups even band together to lobby an agency; see Nelson and Yackee (2012).

67. *American Trucking Associations, Inc. v. FMCSA*, Case No. 12-1092 (D.C. Cir. 2013), p. 21.

In the legislative process, scholars have traditionally pointed to anticipatory policy concessions as the primary explanation for the dearth of vetoes. Charles Cameron (2000) shows that presidents do not need to actually issue a veto to influence the bills that Congress passes.[68] Rather, the mere specter of a veto can shape the bills that Congress writes, a behavior that Bachrach and Baratz (1962) refer to as the "second face of power," wherein power operates through anticipation and does not require visible compulsion. In other words, because the president has the power to veto, when drafting bills Congress makes policy concessions before sending the bill down Pennsylvania Avenue.

In the regulatory context, the natural extension of this model is that agencies make policy concessions so as to avoid regulatory vetoes. However, regulators are far from passive actors in this exchange, and in some ways they are even advantaged. While concessions undoubtedly occur, their procedural control over the process allows agencies to be less constrained than they first appear when it comes to rulemaking. Procedural power, in turn, not only can enable agencies to avoid vetoes (and other political consequences) but also can, if used strategically, introduce a way for agencies to get more of what they want in terms of policy leeway. In other words, procedures exist as a pathway outside of policy concessions for agencies to dodge the regulatory veto and extract policy benefits.

Summary

Agencies can deploy their procedural prerogatives to sidestep political oversight, either by incrementally raising oversight costs or by sapping a principal's desire to provide oversight in the first place. This chapter has unpacked the strategic logic of procedural politicking, including the role that it plays in the rulemaking process and how it interacts with the motivations of individual bureaucrats.

Focusing on three distinct aspects of the rulemaking process—writing, consultation, and timing—I explained how and when agencies deploy particular types of procedures to their advantage. This theoretical discussion has testable empirical expectations, which, for ease of reference, are summarized in table 3.4. These hypotheses are not specific to any one agency, since the

---

68. However, issuing a veto can be useful to the president in extracting concessions in successive rounds of bargaining, a process that Cameron (2000) refers to as veto bargaining. For additional work on anticipatory power, see also Ferejohn and Shipan (1990); Howell and Pevehouse (2011); and Tsebelis (2002).

TABLE 3.4. Summary of procedural politicking hypotheses

Strategic Writing Hypothesis	Agencies will use writing tactics to raise oversight costs when the political environment is adverse.
Conditional Writing Hypothesis	Agencies will use writing tactics to raise oversight costs when the political environment is adverse and when relevant interest groups are predisposed against the agency.
Expanded Consultation Hypothesis	Agencies will expand participation opportunities when political principals are not aligned with the agency and when relevant interest groups are predisposed in favor of the agency.
Limited Consultation Hypothesis	Agencies will limit participation opportunities when political principals are not aligned with the agency and when relevant interest groups are predisposed against the agency.
Strategic Timing Hypothesis	Agencies will use timing tools to release rulemaking decisions in more favorable political environments.

incentives created by the notice-and-comment process and political oversight are expected to have a comparable effect on similarly situated agencies.

The political environment is a key component of each hypothesis. When that environment is adverse, agencies have an incentive to engage in some level of procedural politicking. Critically, an adverse political environment does not require the extreme case, where all three constitutional branches are aligned against the agency. Rather, when assessing the political environment, an agency takes stock of each branch and adjusts its response accordingly. In other words, this is a question of degree, and one should expect procedural responses to be calibrated to the extent of political opposition the agency faces at that point in time. However, the opposition of just one principal is sufficient to imperil a rule and invoke procedural politicking.

Over the course of the next four chapters, I explain individual procedures in greater depth and empirically evaluate the expectations. The hypotheses are not tied to one specific branch or form of oversight. Instead, I allow the empirical tests to distinguish how an agency chooses from the menu of procedural tools available. To foreshadow, the results are nuanced, suggesting that agencies may view particular procedures as more influential at fending off oversight from one overseer rather than another. Additionally, I do not provide an empirical test for each and every procedural tool discussed in this chapter. Rather, I assess a representative set of tools that are systematically observable across agencies and rules. The goal is to substantiate the empirical reality of procedural politicking rather than unpack its every nuance.

I begin in the next chapter with an investigation of writing as a tool of procedural politicking. I also introduce the *Regulatory Proposals Dataset*, a trove of approximately eleven thousand agency proposed rules that informs the analyses throughout the remainder of the book. I rely on the texts from agency proposed rules to explore the Strategic Writing Hypothesis and the Conditional Writing Hypothesis. Using text analysis tools, I show that agencies do indeed use composition to insulate rules from political risk by strategically manipulating the accessibility of their rules. In chapter 5, I continue this investigation with a careful look at the ways that agencies engage with the public when escorting a rule through notice-and-comment. Focusing in on the public comment period, I consider whether the evidence supports both the Limited Consultation Hypothesis and the Expanded Consultation Hypothesis.

In chapter 6, I give close consideration to one timing tactic: the release of an agency's final rule. I show that agencies strategically slow-roll and fast-track rules as a way of evading political oversight. This analysis provides strong evidence in support of the Strategic Timing Hypothesis. And in chapter 7, I study one rulemaking at the FDA as a way of gauging how these procedural tools work in the context of a real-world case. Strictly speaking, chapter 7 does not test the hypotheses developed here, but it does allow for a nuanced consideration of many strategies in the case of one important rule. It also allows me to draw a connection between procedural politicking strategies and policy choices.

All told, these empirical explorations provide a rich and nuanced understanding of how agencies strategically manage the procedural aspects of rulemaking. Importantly, the argument does not suggest that agencies never make policy concessions to avoid having rules overturned. Rather, taken together, the preponderance of evidence suggests that concessions are not the only avenue to success in the rulemaking process. Procedural means offer a way for entrepreneurial bureaucrats to get what they want.

4

Writing as a Tool

President George W. Bush's signature domestic policy achievement was, arguably, primary education reform.[1] With the passage of the No Child Left Behind (NCLB) law in 2001,[2] Bush ushered in an enhanced federal role in K–12 education, including more stringent standardized testing for students, more rigorous qualification standards for teachers, and increased accountability and transparency for schools and state and local education authorities. After the fanfare around the law's passage subsided, much of the actual implementation of the law fell to the Department of Education (ED). The department, and the Office of Elementary and Secondary Education (OESE) in particular, then used rulemaking to fill in many of the important policy gaps.

One such regulation was a 2005 proposed rule that allowed students with disabilities to take different standardized tests (i.e., modified assessments) from those for the rest of the school population. The rule was referred to colloquially as the 2 percent rule, because it allowed school districts to give these alternate tests to up to 2 percent of their students. The proposal addressed demands from school districts for additional flexibility in the law. The department's announcement of the precise number of special education students who could be excluded from the regular tests and how flexibility would be monitored had been eagerly awaited by relatively small but con-

---

1. In his 2010 memoir, *Decision Points*, Bush states that he wanted his legacy to be that of the "education president" (275).
2. Pub. L. No. 107-110.

centrated groups of stakeholders in the education and disability advocacy communities.[3]

However, when the proposal was published in the *Federal Register*, its purpose and the means by which it accomplished that goal were largely obscured. The proposed rule's executive summary was dense and hard to read.[4] Although the summary is just 130 words, in that short space it mentions three separate statutory authorities and includes jargon such as "local education agency," "instructional interventions," and "Title I." Further, it provides little to no substantive policy information, conspicuously making no mention of the key 2 percent threshold, even though this was the centerpiece of the proposal. It also does not use the word "test" even once. The rule's title— "Title I, Improving the Academic Achievement of the Disadvantaged; Individuals with Disabilities Education Act (IDEA), Assistance to States for the Education of Children with Disabilities"—is equally uninformative.

ED's abstruse language could be construed as sloppiness on the agency's part, except that this stylistic choice had implications for monitoring and oversight—implications that point to savvy strategy rather than incompetence. News coverage of the rule referenced its colloquial name (the 2 percent rule), so a congressional staffer or interest group official who read an article about the proposal and wanted to read the entire text would have little luck finding it by entering the informal name into an internet search engine.

---

3. The response from the disability advocacy community, particularly special education advocates who had lobbied for a more nuanced approach, was far from enthusiastic. For example, in a letter to Secretary of Education Margaret Spellings, the Consortium of Citizens with Disabilities (2005), a group representing more than twenty-five disability advocate organizations, excoriated the proposed rule, noting that it "should have focused on increased and improved access to the general curriculum, an investment in training highly qualified special education teachers, the development of valid and reliable universally designed assessments, and a rededication to scientifically-based instruction."

4. The executive summary read as follows:

The Secretary proposes to amend the regulations governing programs administered under Title I of the Elementary and Secondary Education Act of 1965 (ESEA), as amended by the No Child Left Behind Act of 2001 (NCLB) (referred to in these proposed regulations as the Title I program) and the regulations governing programs under Part B of the Individuals with Disabilities Education Act (IDEA) (referred to in these proposed regulations as the IDEA program). The proposed regulations would provide States with additional flexibility regarding State, local educational agency (LEA), and school accountability for the achievement of a group of students with disabilities who can make significant progress, but may not reach grade-level achievement standards within the same time frame as other students, even after receiving the best-designed instructional interventions from highly trained teachers. (70 FR 74624; Dec. 15, 2005)

Further, even the most scrupulous policy analysts would struggle to critique the proposal from the executive summary, because it neither mentioned the 2 percent threshold nor offered any insight into how the policy would be implemented or monitored. In fact, it says nothing about what the rule would actually do, promising only the anodyne-sounding "additional flexibility."

The rule needed all the cover such writing could provide. While the 2 percent rule was associated with one of the president's core policy priorities, it was proposed nearly four years after the NCLB law was passed. In the intervening years, political support for the policy had waned, particularly among those most engaged in implementing the policy. When polled about their opinions on NCLB in 2005 (the same year the proposed rule was published), 38 percent of Americans viewed the policy unfavorably, while 75 percent of high school teachers expressed unfavorable feelings toward the policy.[5] Meanwhile, the extent of opposition to NCLB from the states, specifically states that were considered Republican strongholds, was "unprecedented in its scope and depth" (Sunderman and Kim 2007, 1066). This, in turn, put pressure on Republican majorities in Congress—a partisan alignment that tends to be skeptical of ED and federal intervention in education more generally—to do something to combat NCLB and its ambitious policy reach.[6] In other words, key stakeholders were opposed to the tenets of the rulemaking and in a position to mobilize and take action with a receptive Congress.

This account exemplifies two ways—using obfuscatory language and omitting key pieces of information—in which an agency can strategically use writing tools to shield a proposed rule from potentially hostile oversight. Writing is the phase that sets the course for the remainder of the process. While chapter 3 laid out a theory of how agencies employ procedures to influence the course—and ultimately the outcome—of the rulemaking process, this chapter is where the rubber meets the road. That is, I move from a

---

5. The Educational Testing Service conducted a poll about public sentiment regarding NCLB and disaggregated the results by subgroup. Among all Americans surveyed about NCLB, 45 percent expressed favorable opinions, 38 percent expressed unfavorable opinions, and 17 percent indicated that they either were neutral or did not have enough information to form an opinion. Among K–12 parents, the results were fairly similar, with 46 percent favorable, 39 percent unfavorable, and 15 percent no opinion or not enough information. Among high school administrators, opposition was slightly greater, with 48 percent favorably disposed to the policy, 43 percent unfavorably disposed, and 9 percent with no opinion or not enough information. High school teachers were strongly opposed, however, with 19 percent expressing favorable opinions, 75 percent expressing unfavorable opinions, and 5 percent with no opinion or not enough information. See Hart and Winston (2005).

6. By 2005, some GOP conservatives in Congress were already hostile to the law, resenting what they regarded as NCLB's federal intrusion into education, typically a state prerogative.

theoretical exercise to an empirical one to uncover the reality of procedural politicking. I begin by drawing a concrete connection between the theoretical tenets in the previous chapter and the empirical expectations in this one. I then introduce the *Regulatory Proposals Dataset,* a new dataset that underpins the empirical analyses throughout the remainder of this book. The chapter culminates with an examination of the language used in proposed rules at eight agencies.

Connecting to Theory

The departure point for the theory of procedural politicking is that agencies make calculations about the political environment, specifically how each of the three constitutional branches—the president, Congress, and the courts—is predisposed to their interests, as well as the willingness of interest groups to closely monitor them. When political overseers are inclined to agree with what the agency is trying to accomplish in their rulemakings, there is no need for the agency to use procedures to strategically maneuver. However, in the face of more hostile political oversight, procedural politicking takes on a new urgency, as agencies strive to protect the investments they have made in their rulemaking projects and guard their organizational reputations. The Strategic Writing Hypothesis reflects this, holding that when political overseers are not aligned with the agency, agencies will use writing tactics to raise oversight costs or neutralize opposition.

Interest groups also figure into an agency's writing strategy; agencies must forecast and manage the role that relevant interest groups play in mediating the agency's relationship with its political principals. The Conditional Writing Hypothesis takes this calculation into consideration, stipulating that strategic writing is conditioned on the willingness of interest groups to bring complaints to the attention of unfavorably disposed principals. When these groups are aligned with the agency's goals, agencies do not have a need to use procedural maneuvers to protect their rules. However, when groups are ideologically opposed to the agency and principals are sympathetic, agencies can use writing procedures to insulate their rulemakings.

There are several ways that an agency can write strategically. The example of the 2 percent rule suggests two with respect to the accessibility of a text: making the prose harder to digest with dense language and altogether omitting key pieces of information. These are, however, not the only writing tools at an agency's disposal. An agency may also adjust the framing of the proposed rule or manipulate the assumptions used in the regulatory analysis. While each of these tactics serves to insulate a rule, the tactics offer delivery by different routes. A less accessible text raises the costs to readers of engaging with the text, whereas a change in the frame or the assumptions may diffuse opposition, either through persuasion or co-option.

I do not test of all these writing tactics in this chapter. The reason for this is simple. My focus in this chapter—and the two that follow—is on detecting systematic patterns that emerge across a large sample of rules at many agencies. Using frames or analytical assumptions strategically is highly context specific. For example, a frame that is controversial in one instance or at one agency may have a completely different connotation in another.[7] For this reason, the study of frames (and other writing tools like analytical assumptions) is best suited to a qualitative case study approach, which I take on in chapter 7.[8]

Here, I leverage differences in text accessibility—a feature of strategic writing that is consistent to measure across rules and within agencies. My expectation is that when faced with a hostile political environment, agencies should write less accessible proposed rules. Texts that are written in an inaccessible manner can deter oversight (or at least make it more costly) by making it difficult for laypeople to ascertain the true consequences of a policy proposal. Put differently, forcing readers to digest a lengthy proposal that is written in technical jargon or legalese raises monitoring costs; it may require a congressional staffer to find a lawyer to review the agency's proposal or a judge's law clerk or a desk officer at the Office of Information and Regulatory Affairs (OIRA) to invest hours deciphering what the agency is proposing and precisely how that differs from the status quo.[9] As one regulatory observer puts it, "Overworked journalists, OMB economists, and Hill staff are not going to slog through forty to fifty *Federal Register*-length pages of technical jargon for each major rule in an effort to tease out the agency rationale for its action" (Parker 2006, 398). To engage with prolonged and obscure agency

7. Importantly, with respect to framing, my argument is not that bureaucrats ignore framing considerations when the political environment is relatively favorable; all documents have some frame, so framing is always a consideration. (Indeed, one would hope that identifying a target group, connecting the problem to the proposed solution, and justifying policy action would be routine, since it is part of writing good and detailed policy.) My point is that in a contentious political environment framing takes on increased importance and becomes a *strategic* consideration rather than a normal part of the workflow.

8. Following this logic, I also do not study the omission of key words here, as doing so would require a case-by-case consideration of a rule, which words were important, and whether those terms were included or excluded.

9. Similarly, as in the case of the 2 percent rule, the omission of important information (e.g., the key threshold) from the executive summary makes readers have to search for that threshold later in the text.

rulemaking documents, overseers must expend already-scarce resources; as a text becomes lengthier or more opaque, the resource expenditure required also increases.[10] Of course, the effect of this strategy may differ depending on the audience; while the general public or a busy staffer may be dissuaded from engaging in the first place, an organized interest group with a concrete stake in the proposal may be forced to devote more upfront resources toward the rule. Nonetheless, if the strategy is effective, it should serve as a deterrent at the margins.

Text inaccessibility offers a short-term benefit for the agency—increasing the probability of survival of the proposed rule—but it may be a double-edged sword. Ultimately, the purpose of writing a regulation is to change policy, and if agencies make it harder for parties to engage with, or even understand, a rule, they may be setting the stage for compliance problems down the road.[11] This, in part, explains why agencies do not simply write all their rules as obscurely as possible. In the end, however, compliance is a second-order consideration. It can be handled through other means at later points in the process: through a road show or supplementary guidance after the final rule is issued, or even in some cases as part of the enforcement process (e.g., inspections). The primary consideration from the agency's perspective is to create a policy that is desirable to enforce in the first place.

The Regulatory Proposals Dataset

The Strategic Writing Hypothesis and the Conditional Writing Hypothesis suggest that the kind of strategies that OESE employed in the 2 percent rule occur systematically in response to adverse political environments. To evaluate these theoretical expectations in a broader setting, I created a catalog of regulatory actions. To begin, I consulted the *Unified Agenda of Regulatory and Deregulatory Actions*, an accounting of agency rulemaking activity that is published semiannually in the *Federal Register*. The *Unified Agenda* offers a brief description of prospective rules, rules in progress, and completed rules, including dates and basic characteristics such as whether the rule was economically significant, its legal basis, any associated deadlines, and so on. Agencies are expected to report a rule to the *Unified Agenda* through each

10. Owens, Wedeking, and Wohlfarth (2013) explain this logic with respect to how the Supreme Court writes its decisions so as to avoid congressional review. They argue that, "by writing a less readable opinion, justices might craft a desired judicial policy while simultaneously deterring a legislative response by making it more difficult for Congress to address it" (39).

11. This boils down to an empirical question, and as I show in the tests that follow, compliance issues appear to be secondary to political oversight ones.

stage of the process until it is completed (i.e., prerule stage, proposed rule, final rule, and completed action).

The *Unified Agenda* is the most comprehensive and systematic accounting of agency rulemaking available to scholars. There are, however, some drawbacks to it as a data source. Foremost, though mandatory, it is self-reported by agencies, meaning that agencies could plausibly make systematic errors or omit certain types of actions.[12] Additionally, the data do not include the texts of the rules themselves, which required that I take additional steps to link the data to the actual language agencies use in their proposed rules (as I do later in this chapter).

In the data appendix at the end of this book, I detail the method I use to remove duplicate observations and to clean the data, but the result of this exercise is a dataset of approximately eleven thousand proposed rules over the study period (1995–2014). While not all of these proposals went on to become binding final regulations, the vast majority (84 percent) did. In other words, the successful completion of a rule is the most common outcome.

In evaluating the rules in the *Regulatory Proposals Dataset*, I take into account the lowest-level unit responsible for creating the rule. So, for example, if a rule was sponsored by the Animal and Plant Health Inspection Service (APHIS) within the Department of Agriculture (USDA), I consider the characteristics of APHIS, as it is the unit most responsible for the rule. This aligns with recent scholarship that focuses on the bureau—rather than the department—as the appropriate unit to study bureaucratic behavior.[13] However, to the extent possible, I also account for the fact that APHIS is a subdivision of USDA. The dataset covers 150 agencies, including 135 bureaus housed within 15 executive branch departments and 15 independent agencies.[14]

Figure 4.1 shows the total number of proposed rules issued by the top thirty agencies (by proposed rule volume) in the *Regulatory Proposals Data-*

---

12. Agencies sometimes omit rules that they find to be inconsequential and not worthy of reporting. Additionally, Nou and Stiglitz (2016) find that agencies fail to report some proposed rules during periods of divided government. They argue that agencies do this to limit the advance notice given to Congress about rules in periods when congressional actors may not agree with them. However, agencies eventually do report these proposed rules to the *Unified Agenda* (i.e., they appear in a later version of the *Unified Agenda*). For my purposes, then, this strategic element of self-reporting is not a serious issue, because I rely on retrospective reports of a rule. Put differently, even if a rule does not appear in the *Unified Agenda* as a prospective action, it should eventually show up and be counted in the *Regulatory Proposals Dataset*.

13. See, for example, Selin (2015); and Wilson (1989).

14. The names of the bureaus and departments are listed in table A.1 in the data appendix. By focusing on executive branch agencies, I consider only rules over which the president has oversight through OIRA.

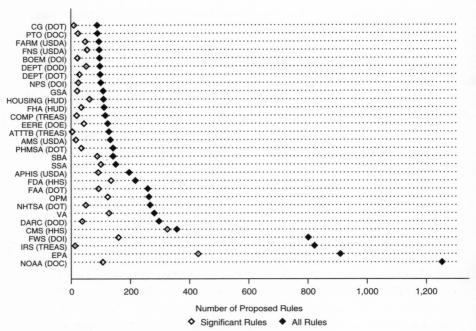

FIGURE 4.1. Total number of proposed rules issued by select agencies

Note: Solid diamonds indicate the total number of rules for each agency in the *Regulatory Proposals Dataset*. Open diamonds indicate the number of proposed rules for which the agency granted a priority status of either significant or economically significant in the *Unified Agenda*. For clarity, data are shown for the top 30 agencies (by volume of proposed rules issued) only. When appropriate, bureaus are listed with their respective department name in parentheses. See table A.1 in the data appendix for a complete listing of agency names and acronyms.

set. While some agencies like the National Oceanic and Atmospheric Administration (NOAA) and the Environmental Protection Agency (EPA) issued several hundred proposed rules during the study's time period (1,253 and 909 rules, respectively), other agencies like the Forest Service and the National Institutes of Health (not shown) issued many fewer (53 and 20, respectively).[15]

The *Regulatory Proposals Dataset* includes rules that range from those that made important public policy changes to those that dealt with mundane administrative details. In other words, the rules vary in their substantive importance and the level of underlying policy complexity. For instance, returning to an example from the introductory chapter of this book, the Office

15. NOAA stands out as a clear outlier in terms of rules produced. This is because the agency houses the National Marine Fisheries Service, which issues a considerable number of rules that are specific to species of fish in a particular region (e.g., Snapper-Grouper Fishery of the South Atlantic Region, Eastern Pacific stock of northern fur seals). Many of these rules are of low salience except to those in the fishing industry. In the statistical analyses that follow, I address variation in a rule's salience by including controls for each rule's impact and complexity.

of Personnel Management (OPM) issued a proposed rule in June 2006 that adjusted the amount that federal agencies reimbursed civilian employees for uniform purchases from $400 to $800 per year. This is clearly a trivial change when compared with the ED's proposed rule to set benchmark standards for college and university participation in federal student aid programs (the gainful-employment rule) or the Occupational Safety and Health Administration's (OSHA) 1999 proposal to enact nationwide workplace ergonomics standards. Many studies address this variation with a litany of control variables to roughly approximate a rule's impact or complexity. However, that approach essentially assumes that the observed variables effectively capture the nuance of a rule's impact and complexity.

I take a different approach to unpacking these dimensions of a proposed rule. I assume that a rule's impact and complexity are latent characteristics instead of things that can be directly observed. I then gather an array of variables that are related to these two characteristics of a proposed rule. These data include measures that draw directly from the *Regulatory Proposals Dataset*—such as whether a proposed rule was economically significant or whether it affected small businesses, as well as whether the *New York Times* covered the proposed rule's release.

I rely on a statistical technique known as principal components analysis (PCA) to reduce these variables into two uncorrelated measures: *Impact* and *Complexity*.[16] The PCA approach has an important advantage: it allows me to more precisely identify the actual dimensions of interest—*Impact* and *Complexity*—rather than variables that are merely related to them.

The first component, *Impact*, loads from measures that reflect the extent to which the rule is expected to have an effect on different societal groups. A proposed rule with a high *Impact* score has a broad societal reach, whereas one with a low *Impact* score has a more limited reach. Specifically, *Impact* builds from variables that capture whether the rule had a large economic impact, whether it affected small businesses, whether it affected other governmental units, and whether the *New York Times* covered the proposed rule's publication. The *Complexity* dimension addresses whether the rule tackled a difficult policy problem. A complex proposed rule does not address a simple fix to the regulatory code, but rather has many dimensions to what it aims to accomplish. *Complexity* loads from measures that assess the number of statutory authorities cited in the rule and whether the number of words included

16. An examination of the eigenvalues suggests that there are indeed two dimensions to the data. For a discussion of the PCA method and the measures that feed into the analysis, see section B of the data appendix.

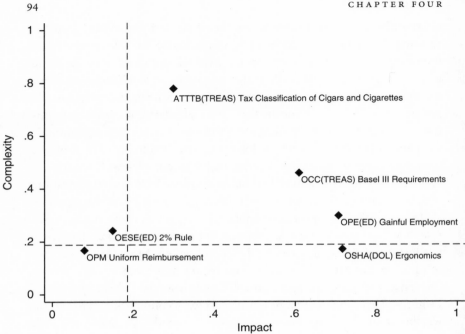

FIGURE 4.2. Illustration of proposed rule *Impact* and *Complexity* scores
Note: Solid diamonds represent the respective *Impact* and *Complexity* scores for a select set of proposed rules. Dashed lines indicate the mean value of each measure.

in the rule's abstract is greater than or less than the mean for that bureau.[17] Both *Impact* and *Complexity* are scaled between 0 and 1 to ease interpretability, with higher values indicating that the rule had a greater impact or was more complex.

Because of the central role that these scores play in the analysis, it is worth establishing their validity. Figure 4.2 shows the *Impact* and *Complexity* scores for the three proposed rules discussed earlier. As expected, the gainful-employment rule and OSHA's ergonomics rule net high *Impact* scores (*Impact* = 0.707 and 0.716, respectively), both of which fall in the 99th percentile of *Impact* scores. In contrast, OPM's uniform rule scores much lower (*Impact* = 0.080, 10th percentile). Meanwhile, OESE's 2 percent rule (discussed in the introduction to this chapter) scores slightly below average for *Impact* and

17. Previous research suggests that longer abstracts may be associated with more complex rules (Yackee and Yackee 2010) and that rules that cite to more policy topics (e.g., laws) have greater breadth (Boushey and McGrath 2015). Both of these measures are captured in comparison to the bureau's typical use, as bureaus may approach citations and abstract writing differently.

slightly above average for *Complexity*. The figure also provides the scores for two proposed rules from the Treasury Department, one about banking requirements emerging from the financial crisis (the Office of the Comptroller of the Currency's, or OCC, Basel III requirements) and another from the Alcohol and Tobacco Tax and Trade Bureau (ATTTB) relating to how excise taxes for cigarettes and cigars should be categorized. These two proposed rules both score high on the *Complexity* dimension. Banking regulations and tax policies are notoriously complex, so it is to be expected that these two proposed rules load positively on this dimension. In contrast, OPM's uniform rule, which was relatively straightforward, scores low in terms of *Complexity*. All told, these scores appear to do a good job of capturing these two dimensions of a proposed rule.

Writing as Procedural Politicking

In principle, the text of a proposed rule should be accessible to a wide audience. For decades, policy makers have pushed agencies to be more transparent in their rulemakings and to use "plain language" to make rules comprehensible to nonspecialists.[18] For example, Executive Order 12,866, which President Clinton issued to govern rulemaking in executive branch agencies (and that remains in effect today), directs each agency to "draft its regulations to be simple and easy to understand" and to use "plain, understandable language" in "all information provided to the public."[19] Clinton followed this order with a subsequent memorandum on the necessity of plain language in government documents, including rulemakings.[20] Subsequent presidential orders and even laws passed by Congress have reaffirmed the importance of making regulatory texts easy to comprehend. In 2010, Congress passed the Plain Writing Act,[21] which required agencies to "designate one or more senior officials to oversee plain writing initiatives, create a plain writing section of their websites, establish training and compliance processes, and publish annual reports."[22] It applied to certain government documents, including the preambles to proposed and final rules. Executive Order 13,563, issued by President Obama in 2011, followed up on this action, stating that agencies

18. Farina, Newhart, and Blake (2015) discuss top-down attempts, particularly from the president, to improve the readability of rulemakings dating back to the 1960s.
19. Exec. Order No. 12,866, Oct. 4, 1993; 58 FR 51735.
20. Clinton (1998).
21. Pub. L. No. 111-274.
22. Farina, Newhart, and Blake (2015).

should produce regulations that "are accessible, consistent, written in plain language, and easy to understand."[23]

Yet despite these political pronouncements, for the most part, proposed rules remain highly inaccessible documents. For example, in a study of rule-making abstracts for proposed and final rules, Farina, Newhart, and Blake (2015) find that, on average, rules are written at about a fifteenth-grade level, even though 80 percent of US adults read below the tenth-grade level.[24] And a casual glance at the *Federal Register* indicates that rules frequently run dozens—or even hundreds—of pages long, which makes reading them a time-consuming task.

To evaluate whether textual obfuscation is a tactic agencies use intentionally to evade oversight, I use the *Regulatory Proposals Dataset* to identify eight of the largest rulemaking bureaus (by volume of proposed rules produced); these are the Animal and Plant Health Inspection Service (APHIS), the Centers for Medicare and Medicaid Services (CMS), the Environmental Protection Agency (EPA), the Food and Drug Administration (FDA), the National Highway Traffic Safety Administration (NHTSA), the National Oceanic and Atmospheric Administration (NOAA), the Office of Personnel Management (OPM), and the Department of Veterans Affairs (VA). These agencies were selected on the basis of three criteria: the total number of proposed rules the agency produced, the substantive interest of the rules the agency produced, and my ability to consistently identify and locate the relevant rule texts. I also sought to include a mix of agencies that serve liberal- and conservative-oriented missions.[25]

Because the *Regulatory Proposals Dataset* includes only descriptive information about rules and not the texts of the rules themselves, I identified proposed rules using that dataset and then searched the *Federal Register*—the daily digest where proposed rules are published—for the body of each rule. This resulted in a dataset of 2,870 proposed rule texts, accounting for slightly more than a quarter (26.3 percent) of rules.[26]

For each proposed rule, I develop two measures of the text's accessibility. The first measure, *Preamble length*, draws on the text of the preamble, the

23. 76 FR 3821; Jan. 21, 2011.

24. In comparison, journalists generally aim to write news articles at about an eighth-grade reading level.

25. As I discuss in the next section, I use Clinton and Lewis (2008) measures of agency ideology to characterize an agency as liberal or conservative.

26. For an explanation of how I compiled and analyzed the proposed rule texts, see section C of the data appendix. Because of how the *Federal Register* formats texts, the analysis does not include proposed rules issued prior to 2000.

part of the rule that is intended to explain in detail—and in plain English—the purpose, logic, and consequences of the policy proposal. Specifically, I count the logged number words in the preamble text.[27]

When an agency writes a long and detailed preamble, it accomplishes two goals simultaneously. First, by thoroughly expounding the logic of its approach, it plays defense, attempting to persuade readers that it has a taken a sound course of action. Recall the example of the FDA's tobacco rule in chapter 3, where the agency head admitted that the agency wrote an exceptionally long preamble to the rule to prevent the agency from being "vulnerable to criticism."[28] This "drown them in detail" approach is not limited to the FDA. Parker (2006, 395–98) observes that in writing a controversial 2001 regulation on arsenic standards in drinking water, the EPA spent considerable effort explicating the rationale for its course of action. While the regulatory text associated with the rule ran only six pages in the *Federal Register*, the agency devoted twenty-nine pages to explaining its reasoning, fifteen pages to summarizing the policy and providing procedural background, and another eight pages to addressing administrative requirements. A longer preamble is an effective way for the agency to demonstrate to external audiences that it has done its homework and thought through all the implications of its proposed policy action.[29]

Parallel strategies can be found in the private sector. One study finds that firms tend to write longer (and less readable) annual reports when they have poor earnings. The author of that study explains: "Because the information-processing cost of longer documents is presumed to be higher, assuming everything else to be equal, longer documents seem to be more deterring and more difficult to read. Therefore, the length of an annual report could be used strategically by managers in order to make an annual report less transparent and to hide adverse information from investors" (Li 2008, 225).

Returning to the rulemaking context, a longer preamble does not mean that the agency necessarily provides more or better information to the regulated community. As Parker (2006, 396) concludes in his account of the EPA: "One will search that notice in vain for anything resembling a concise, readable explanation of why EPA chose the particular maximum concentration limit (MCL) for arsenic (10 micrograms/liter) that it adopted." The EPA is

27. Logging this variable is necessary given the skewed nature of preamble text length.

28. Kessler (2001, 296).

29. Parker (2006) attributes this behavior to agencies taking preventive measures in anticipation of judicial review in particular. The argument I make here extends that logic beyond the judiciary to the other political branches. While his example of the EPA centers on the final rule, the same logic applies to proposed rule preambles.

not alone in this approach. Parker (2006, 397) notes that "the implicit assumption behind current practice seems to be that if the APA requires 'a concise general statement' of a rule's basis, then an extremely detailed, lengthy, and arcane explanation is so much the better." The implication is that a longer preamble may serve a secondary goal: discouraging more casual readers from engaging too deeply (or at all) with the text. After all, the average preamble in the sample is more than 6,300 words, or about twenty-five double-spaced pages in a standard typed document. Assuming that most educated adults read at a rate of about two hundred words per minute, this means that the typical preamble takes more than thirty minutes to read—and this is surely an underestimate given the difficulty level of these texts.

The second measure examines the clarity of the abstract, the part of the proposed rule that is intended to briefly convey what the regulation aims to accomplish and why. As the 2 percent rule illustrated, abstracts can be dense and loaded with jargon, making them harder to understand and discouraging readers from wanting to engage with the remainder of the text. Given the attention that prior presidents and Congress have devoted to getting agencies to write in a more intelligible manner (via, for example, executive orders and laws), it is reasonable to expect that, in terms of procedural politicking, this tool may be more constrained than manipulating the length of a text.

Nonetheless, to evaluate the accessibility of each abstract, I consider its readability. Readability metrics are designed to evaluate how difficult it is for an individual to understand a text. They have become increasingly common in studies of political institutions.[30] As Farina and colleagues' (2015) study illustrates, readability is often conveyed in terms of the grade level at which an individual would need to read in order to comprehend a text. Perhaps because it can be easily calculated in Microsoft Word, the Flesch-Kincaid grade-level metric is the most widely employed readability measure. However, it is but one of dozens of readability measures that experts use to evaluate texts. While different measures focus on different aspects of a text, such as word length (based on characters, number of syllables, or both) or sentence length (again based on either number of characters, syllables, or both), no one mea-

---

30. For example, Owens, Wedeking, and Wohlfarth (2013) show that Supreme Court decisions are written in a more obfuscatory fashion when Congress is more likely to overturn the court's actions, and Curry (2015) argues that legislative bills are written in a harder-to-read fashion when party leaders want to keep rank-and-file members from meaningfully engaging with a bill that is under consideration. See also Black et al. (2016).

sure has emerged as the generally accepted best practice, and all measures have their detractors.[31]

In light of this, I follow the approach of Black and colleagues (2016) and use twenty-eight distinct and widely used measures of text readability to assess proposed rule abstracts. I then employ the same latent variable approach used to obtain the *Impact* and *Complexity* measures—principal components analysis—to reduce these metrics into one measure that draws on the commonalities among the many metrics.[32] As Black and colleagues (2016, 50) note, this approach "captures what is common among [the readability metrics] without being skewed by various idiosyncrasies of each individual formula."

The resulting measure, *Abstract readability*, ranges from −21.1 to 27.7, with negative values indicating a harder-to-read text, and positive values indicating a relatively easier-to-access text. The scores are commonsensical. Applying this method to OESE's 2 percent rule yields a score of −13.1, which puts it in the lowest 1 percent of abstracts and makes it one of the least readable in the dataset. At the other end of the spectrum, consider the abstract for a proposed rule from the VA titled "Hospital and Outpatient Care for Veterans Released from Incarceration to Transitional Housing"; it reads:

> The Department of Veterans Affairs (VA) proposes to amend its regulations to authorize VA to provide hospital and outpatient care to a veteran in a program that provides transitional housing upon release from incarceration in a prison or jail. The proposed rule would permit VA to work with these veterans while they are in these programs with the goal of continuing to work with them after their release. This would assist in preventing homelessness in this population of veterans.[33]

31. Critics take issue with the formulae associated with individual measures or point to the fact that, across the board, readability measures are only weakly correlated with one another (e.g., Stokes 1978; Schriver 2000). The most biting criticisms, however, hinge on the fact that readability measures are necessarily divorced from the text's broader context. As Bruce, Rubin, and Starr (1981) explain, "Because most of the formulas include only sentence length and word difficulty as factors, they can account only indirectly for other factors that make a particular text difficult, such as degree of discourse cohesion, number of inferences required, number of items to remember, complexity of ideas, rhetorical structure, dialect, and background knowledge required."

32. To score the twenty-eight measures I rely on the koRpus package in R. I then use PCA to reduce the dimensionality of the measures and uncover a latent *Abstract readability* measure. See section C of the data appendix for more detail on how the measure was constructed.

33. 75 FR 26683; May 12, 2010.

While still formal in tone, this abstract is clearly more accessible than the one for OESE's 2 percent rule; it uses shorter words, relies on shorter sentence structures, and avoids jargon. Accordingly, it receives an *Abstract readability* score of 5.4, placing it among the more readable abstracts (in the 85th percentile). The scores are valid beyond the realm of abstracts. By way of contrast, applying the same readability scoring method applied here to *The Cat in the Hat*, a well-known children's book by Dr. Seuss, results in a readability score of 27.6, making it more readable than any text in the dataset. Executive Order 12,866, which is a legal document, weighs in at 1.0, making it slightly more readable than the average abstract.

Table 4.1 provides detail about the two text accessibility measures for each of the eight agencies under study. No immediate patterns emerge from an examination of this table. Both among and within agencies there is considerable variation in *Preamble length* and *Abstract readability*. For instance, in terms of readability, the EPA tends to write some of the longest preambles, but it writes relatively average abstracts. CMS follows a similar pattern. Meanwhile, the FDA drafts long preambles and writes relatively unreadable abstracts. However, even in these cases the range of accessibility values remains comparable to those of other agencies.

While this variation is interesting in its own right, the question for the present purpose is whether agencies use texts to obfuscate as a means toward strategic ends. To evaluate the expectations laid out in the Strategic Writing Hypothesis and the Conditional Writing Hypothesis, I assess whether *Preamble length* and *Abstract readability* vary according to the political environment that agencies face.

TABLE 4.1. Summary of proposed rule text accessibility measures

Agency	Preamble length Mean [range]	Abstract readability Mean [range]
Animal and Plant Health Inspection Service	8.5 [6.7, 11.0]	−0.4 [−19.0, 10.1]
Centers for Medicare and Medicaid Services	9.8 [5.3 12.9]	−0.6 [−17.8, 14.0]
Environmental Protection Agency	9.4 [4.8, 12.6]	0.1 [−16.4, 14.0]
Food and Drug Administration	9.3 [7.2, 11.9]	−1.0 [−14.5, 8.0]
National Highway Traffic Safety Administration	9.0 [6.3, 12.6]	1.8 [−11.8, 16.5]
National Oceanic and Atmospheric Administration	8.4 [6.1, 11.7]	0.2 [−21.1, 13.8]
Office of Personnel Management	6.9 [4.5, 10.0]	0.4 [−14.4, 10.5]
Department of Veterans Affairs	8.0 [6.07, 11.9]	−1.1 [−19.1, 10.4]

Note: Cell entries are agency means with the range of values in the data displayed in brackets. See section C of the data appendix for a detailed explanation of how the parts of each proposed rule were parsed and how the abstract readability measures were calculated. Lower *Abstract readability* scores indicate texts that are more difficult to read, whereas higher values suggest easier-to-read texts.

MEASURING THE POLITICAL ENVIRONMENT

To capture the level of anticipated ideological opposition from each of the constitutional branches, I employ three separate variables. For the presidency, I rely on Clinton and Lewis's (2008) estimates of agency ideology, which are based on expert surveys about the ideological orientation of a particular agency's mission.[34] I use these estimates to distinguish liberal-leaning agencies from conservative-leaning ones and then match the agency's ideological predisposition with the party of the current president. The resulting variable, *Unaligned president*, is a dichotomous variable that takes a value of 1 when the president does not share the agency's ideological predisposition, and 0 when he does.[35]

There is no widely agreed-on measure of agency expectations about the potential for congressional opposition. What is needed is a measure that takes into account the ideological positions of both the agency and key congressional actors, as well as the ability of members of Congress to overcome their collective action problems and constrain agencies for their regulatory infractions. To generate such a measure, I again separate agencies by ideological orientation using the Clinton and Lewis scores. I then create a size-unity ratio for the agency's opposition party in Congress—that is, the size-unity score of the Democratic (Republican) party for conservative (liberal) agencies.[36] For a liberal-leaning agency like the Department of Health and Human Services (HHS), for example, it is calculated by averaging the scores for the House and the Senate, as follows:

$$(1) \qquad Congressional\ opposition_{lib} = \frac{Republican\ size \times Republican\ cohesion}{Democrat\ size \times Democrat\ cohesion}$$

34. Clinton and Lewis (2008) conducted a survey of experts and asked them to rate the ideology of agencies. They aggregate these responses using a multirater item-response model to create an estimate of each agency's ideology. These scores range from -2 to 2, with negative values indicating a more liberal agency and positive values indicating a more conservative one. I consider an agency to be liberal if its Clinton-Lewis score falls below 0 and to be conservative if its score exceeds 0.

35. This way of operationalizing the ideological agreement of an agency and the president based on Clinton and Lewis's (2008) scores and the president's party has become increasingly common (see, e.g., Bolton, Potter, and Thrower 2016; and Ostrander 2016).

36. The size-unity ratio is substantively similar to Hurley, Brady, and Cooper's (1977) legislative potential for policy change but is easier to interpret. Again, I count an agency as conservative if its Clinton-Lewis score is greater than 0, and liberal otherwise.

CHAPTER FOUR

The resulting measure takes on values greater than 1 when the agency's partisan opposition is strong—both in terms of seats held and cohesiveness—and values less than 1 when the opposition is weak. Presumably, as *Congressional opposition* increases, agencies should be more concerned with the threat of hostile congressional actions. The measure has the advantage of being continuous, which allows for a nuanced consideration of changes in the relative strength of a particular party. Most important, it addresses the two key congressional attributes required: the size of the agency's opposition (party size) and how well the party holds together (party cohesion).[37]

Finally, the courts figure prominently into agency calculations about the political environment, since an unfriendly court is more likely to overturn a rule than a friendly one. To gauge the court's influence, I include *Court cases*, the volume of court cases involving the agency.[38] I focus on the DC Circuit court because it is widely considered the most important for agency cases. Federal administrators tend to be most aware of this circuit's decisions and take them most seriously.[39] There are other advantages to focusing on the appellate level. For example, focusing on the circuit court avoids selection problems that appear at the district and the Supreme Court levels. Additionally the appellate courts hear enough agency cases for each agency to develop expectations, and the cases they decide carry weight in terms of setting precedent.

To create a measure of the agency's expectations about the courts, I used LexisNexis to identify every DC Circuit court case in which an agency was a party in every month. *Court cases* is the monthly moving average of the number of appellate court cases involving the agency over the previous twelve months.[40] This measure builds on agency perceptions of the likelihood that groups will use the judiciary as a means to pursue relief.

A key element of my argument is that agencies anticipate how interest groups will react to their rules and craft their procedural choices in response to this expectation. There is no simple measure of either interest group predisposition toward specific rules or agency perceptions about anticipated group responses. Developing such a measure is problematic because agency perceptions are not observable, but one way to work around this is to look

37. Party cohesion is evaluated using party unity scores (Brookings Institution 2017).
38. I consider cases where the department (not necessarily the bureau) was involved in litigation.
39. See Hume (2009).
40. Logging this variable produces essentially the same results for the regression models in this chapter and the ones in subsequent chapters. Accordingly, I use the unlogged specification because it is easier for readers to interpret its meaning.

at the amount of money interest groups devote to political influence in an agency's policy area, or more specifically, the balance in giving to the agency's copartisans and out-partisans.[41]

Political giving is an admittedly crude measure of interest group activity, but it has several advantages. First, it allows for variation between agencies. So, for instance, an agency working on foreign aid is considered separately from an agency working on defense issues, even though both fall under the foreign policy umbrella. Second, spending may vary across time, though rarely dramatically so. This approach allows for within agency variation, although it mostly picks up large changes in relative group power across time. Finally, spending is observable by agencies themselves, which means that it plausibly factors into an agency's perceptions of group orientation.

To measure interest group political contributions, I match annual aggregate interest group spending by industry to policy topic areas developed by the Policy Agendas Project.[42] I also match agencies to their substantive policy topic area according to each agency's core function. I then use the policy topics to bridge agencies and interest group spending, adapting a method developed by Curry (2015).[43] The result is data on political spending in the agency's issue area for each year. Again building off the agency's categorization as liberal or conservative, I assess the balance of party spending in that area. For a liberal agency, for example, it is possible to examine whether political giving to Republicans in the agency's policy area exceeded donations to Democrats

41. Both the *Congressional opposition* and the *Group opposition* measures focus on parties within the congressional chambers. This focus assumes that parties, and particularly the majority party, play an important role in dictating the oversight agenda for agencies. Although there is considerable support for this assumption in the congressional literature (e.g., Cox and McCubbins 1993, 2005), it stands in contrast to a long-standing argument that congressional committees hold the key to agency oversight (e.g., Shipan 2004; Lowande, forthcoming; Weingast and Moran 1983). Importantly, my assumption should not be read to make the case that congressional oversight committees do not matter to agencies; rather, it implies that other actors in Congress, in addition to oversight committee members, also matter. This holds for two reasons. First, rules are often cross-cutting in that they affect industries or groups of people that do not neatly align with a member's committee assignments. This means that oversight can come from outside of committees, since constituents can activate their representatives to engage on a rule, irrespective of committee membership. Second, in recent years committee oversight has become increasingly overlapping, as more committees and subcommittees claim oversight over agency turf (see Clinton, Lewis, and Selin 2014). This means that, empirically speaking, it is not clear exactly which committee(s) the agency views as its oversight committee.

42. Baumgartner et al. (2016).

43. Data on political spending by industry are from the Center for Responsive Politics. See section D of the data appendix for a more complete explanation of the measure and for the mapping between industries, topics, and bureaus.

in a particular year. *Group opposition* is the resulting dichotomous measure, which takes a value of 1 when, on balance, groups from across the aisle are more politically active and engaged in an agency's policy jurisdiction and a value of 0 when groups that share the agency's ideological orientation are more politically active.[44]

Although creating this variable involves many steps, the effort yields a time-varying and agency-specific measure of the predisposition of an agency's interest group constellation. To test the argument laid out in the Conditional Writing Hypothesis, I interact *Group opposition* with each of the key theoretical variables: *Unaligned president*, *Congressional opposition*, and *Court cases*.

In addition to the core theoretical variables, I also include *Impact* and *Complexity*, as well as measures intended to address features of the rule in question that may affect the accessibility of a rule's text more broadly. *Statutory deadline* and *Judicial deadline* are dummy variables that indicate, respectively, whether Congress or the courts has issued a deadline by which the agency is required to issue the rule. Although agencies often fail to meet the deadlines set by these actors, they still may give expedited treatment to rules that have a deadline.

Finally, I include two measures of an agency's capacity on the logic that, at different points in time, agencies may be more or less capable of engaging in procedural politicking. Bureaucratic capacity is "the ability [of the agency] to accomplish intended actions" (Huber and McCarty 2004, 481). This is inherently a multidimensional concept, encompassing management, resources, and expertise. The measures I adopt focus on two prominent and observable features of capacity.[45] *Employees* is the total number of employees at the agency (in thousands), and it serves as a proxy for agency resources. This variable addresses the possibility that agencies may be less willing to engage in outreach when they have fewer staff to manage the process. The number of employees in an agency is particularly advantageous as an indicator for resources because it is comparable across agencies and because previous research finds that agencies with a greater number of employees perform

44. The empirical results that I present in this chapter and the next (chapter 5) are robust to using the ratio of opposition group spending to supportive group spending in lieu of the blunter *Group opposition* measure. However, for ease of exposition, I present the *Group opposition* measure.

45. One could conceivably focus on any number of attributes of an organization's capacity (e.g., budgetary resources, ratio of political appointees to careerists); future research identifying those dimensions of capacity that most meaningfully affect bureaucratic outcomes is certainly welcome.

better.[46] Second, I include *Expertise*, which is the proportion of the agency's workforce that has worked at the agency for at least five years. An agency with a more expert workforce may be able to navigate the pathways of the regulatory process with greater ease and speed. While these variables are correlated (ρ = .39), they represent theoretically distinct aspects of an agency's capacity; *Employees* captures the raw resources at the agency's disposal in terms of personnel, whereas *Expertise* addresses how experienced an agency's staff is in terms of knowing the ropes of rulemaking.

Assessing Text Accessibility

Although the preamble and the abstract are distinct parts of a text, they are both part of the same document, and agencies make decisions about their level of accessibility simultaneously. To jointly model the effects of the political environment on the text accessibility measures—*Preamble length* and *Abstract readability*—I use seemingly unrelated regression (SUR) models.[47] The results are displayed in table 4A.1 at the end of this chapter. The first set of models shows the results for a basic model of the direct effects of the political environment, as laid out in the Strategic Writing Hypothesis, while the second set of models shows the effects of *Group opposition* on the political environment variables, in keeping with the conditional logic outlined in the Conditional Writing Hypothesis. I include presidential administration fixed effects to account for unobserved heterogeneity within specific administrations.

Overall, the models indicate a strong and consistent court effect, and weaker but still clear evidence of agencies responding to Congress and the president. The basic model—which is designed to test the Strategic Writing

46. For example, some have argued that having more employees enables organizations to be better at problem-solving and to deal with difficult situations. See Hill (1982). As Haleblian and Finkelstein (1993, 846) explain, having a relatively larger organization can "enhance problem-solving capabilities by (1) increasing the number of items of information that can be absorbed and recalled, (2) increasing the number of critical judgments available to correct errors in inference and analysis, (3) increasing the number of potential solution strategies, and (4) increasing the range of perspectives brought to bear on a problem." For a contrary perspective, see Lee and Whitford (2012).

47. The SUR approach allows for correlation of the error terms across the two equations (Zellner 1962). Results of Breusch-Pagan tests suggest that the equations are not independent. In order to properly specify the model, I include the two capacity variables in the *Preamble length* equations only. All results remain substantively similar when I calculate separate ordinary least squares models with random effects at the agency level and robust standard errors clustered on the agency.

Hypothesis—shows that when the courts are serving as more active monitors, agencies respond by increasing the length of preambles and decreasing
the readability of abstracts. Looking at *Preamble length*, for an agency with
an average level of court scrutiny, the preamble will be 6,572 words long (approximately twenty-six double-spaced pages); however, for an agency with
an above-average caseload (one standard deviation above the mean number
of cases), the preamble is predicted to increase to 10,194 words, or roughly
forty-one pages total. This represents an increase of approximately 58 percent. The court results for *Abstract readability* are similar; increasing from
the mean number of court cases to one standard deviation above the mean
results in a reduction of 0.4 units on the readability scale. While this is small
in terms of the full range of this variable, it is in line with the idea that readability is strategically manipulated. These findings are consistent with prior
research that identifies court oversight as a key influence in how agencies approach the drafting of proposed rule texts.[48]

The effects with respect to Congress and the president are more mixed
in the basic model. For both dependent variables, *Unaligned president* is not
statistically significant, and in the case of *Abstract readability*, it is incorrectly
signed. While the coefficients for *Congressional opposition* both carry the expected sign, the variable achieves statistical significance only in the *Preamble
length* model. In that case, moving from the minimum to the maximum value
of *Congressional opposition* results in about a 1,425-word increase in preamble
length, or about five and a half pages. Overall, the results of the basic model
lend additional credence to the idea advanced by legal scholars that agency
preambles function as a way for agencies to communicate directly with the
courts.[49]

The results from the conditional model, however, bring the findings for
all the branches into focus in favor of the notion that agencies manage the
writing of rules as a political instrument. Across the board, the results with
respect to *Preamble length* conform to theoretical expectations; when interest groups in the agency's policy area are likely to be predisposed against the
agency's proposals and the complaints they raise may resonate with any of the
constitutional branches, agencies tend to write verbose preambles.

For the president, the results of the conditional model suggest that having an unaligned president and strong group opposition affects the length

48. Parker (2006).
49. The intent of this communication is to persuade judges of the agency's position in the
event of judicial review. See, e.g., McGarity (1991); Morse and Osofsky (2018); and Stack (2016).

of proposed rule preambles. Figure 4.3 shows the results of this interaction graphically, plotting the difference between having an aligned president and an unaligned one, when interest groups are supportive or in opposition. In this figure—as well as figures 4.4 and 4.5 and most of the figures in the next chapter—I show the marginal effect of changes in a principal's disposition (i.e., $\partial y/\partial x$). This means that the graphs should be read in a comparative fashion as the change in the dependent variable as the opposition from the principal in question increases.

With respect to *Preamble length*, when interest groups are supportive of the agency's goals, there is no difference predicted between having an aligned and an unaligned president (see the left half of figure 4.3). Turning to the right half of the figure, however, the level of presidential support matters when interest groups are opposed to the agency. Compared to having an ideologically aligned president, an agency with an unaligned president and opposed interests groups will write a preamble that is 1,239 words longer, or about five additional pages. The results for *Abstract readability* (not shown)

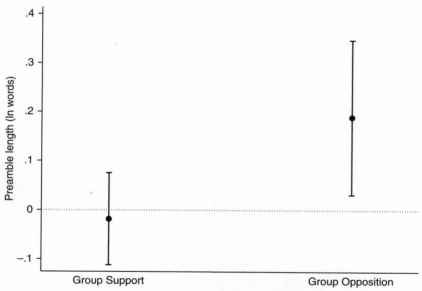

FIGURE 4.3. Effect of shifting from aligned to *Unaligned president* on *Preamble length*, contingent on *Group opposition*

Note: Circles indicate the predicted changes in *Preamble length* when moving from an aligned to an unaligned president, in cases where the agency's interest groups are supportive (left) or opposed (right). Estimated from the conditional model in table 4A.1. Bars indicate 95% confidence intervals.

do not show meaningful differences across the various configurations of interest groups and the White House.

The models suggest analogous effects for congressional oversight on text accessibility; in terms of *Preamble length*, agencies adapt their behavior when opposition groups are likely to bring it to the attention of the legislative branch. Starting with the left half of figure 4.4, when interest groups are supportive of the agency's goals, there is no change in the length of preambles as congressional opposition increases from weak to strong. However, when interest groups are opposed to the agency's goals (see the right half of the figure), as congressional opposition becomes stronger, agencies respond by increasing the length of their preambles. The effect is stark: the addition of more than 6,200 preamble words, or an additional twenty-five pages. Again, however, the results for *Abstract readability* indicate that agencies do not manipulate the readability of a text in the same way in response to hostile congressional oversight.

Again, the most robust evidence of strategic manipulation of text accessibility can be seen in response to court oversight. The top panel of figure 4.5

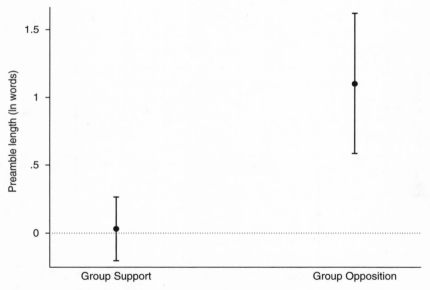

FIGURE 4.4. Effect of shifting from weak to strong *Congressional opposition* on *Preamble length*, contingent on *Group opposition*

Note: Circles indicate the predicted changes in *Preamble length* when moving from a weak to a strong congressional opposition, in cases where the agency's interest groups are supportive (left) or opposed (right). Estimated from the conditional model in table 4A.1. Bars indicate 95% confidence intervals.

depicts the results for *Preamble length*, and the bottom panel shows the results for *Abstract readability*. Increasing levels of court oversight result in a shorter average preamble when interest groups are supportive of the agency—to the tune of about eight additional pages. However, when interest groups are opposed under these same conditions, preambles increase by approximately forty-four pages in length. These results are depicted graphically in the top panel of figure 4.5. Similarly, as shown in the bottom panel of the figure, agencies write much less readable abstracts when faced with a watchful court and opposed interest groups. Specifically, abstracts decrease in readability by about -0.3 on the readability scale, a small but statistically significant effect. Taken together, these results suggest that court oversight in conjunction with interest group monitoring powerfully shapes the manner in which agencies draft proposed rules. That is, when courts are actively monitoring and groups are positioned against the agency, agencies respond with longer preambles and less readable abstracts.

It is worth noting that the findings from both the basic and the conditional models hold after controlling for the features of a rule that might naturally influence its difficulty level. That is, the models take into account both *Impact* and *Complexity*, as well as the other measures identified earlier, although no consistent patterns emerge from an evaluation of these control variables.[50]

Stepping back, the *Preamble length* results from the conditional model are strongly supportive of the theory, whereas those with respect to *Abstract readability* are less so; what should one make of these results? Interpreting null results is notoriously rocky terrain, but there are a few possible interpretations. First, the readability measures are inherently noisy. In constructing a composite measure of readability, I have attempted to reduce the noise that exists among the different measures, but it might be the case that the mea-

---

50. For instance, the models indicate that proposed rules that have a high impact score have longer preambles. While the sign for *Impact* is negative (as predicted) for the readability model, the results are not statistically significant. For *Complexity* the converse is true; it has a statistically significant effect in terms of decreasing the readability of a proposed rule, but although the coefficient for *Preamble length* carries the predicted positive sign, it is not distinguishable from 0. Essentially this suggests that *Impact* and *Complexity* both matter to rule writing but have a different effect depending on the tool in question. The results for the remaining control variables also elude consistent meaning. With respect to *Preamble length*, having either a statutory or judicial deadline is associated with a longer preamble, but this takeaway does not travel to *Abstract readability*, the other measure of text accessibility. The first agency capacity measure, *Employees*, is not statistically significant, while the second measure, *Expertise*, is associated with a shorter preamble. This indicates that having a more stable and expert workforce may lead agencies to avoid excessive detail in preamble statements.

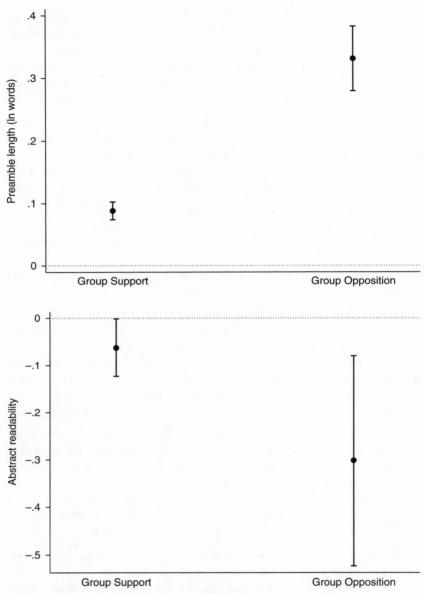

FIGURE 4.5. Effect of shifting from a low to a high number of *Court cases* on *Text accessibility*, contingent on *Group opposition*

Note: Circles indicate the predicted changes in *Preamble length* (top) and *Abstract readability* (bottom) when moving from a low to a high number of *Court cases*, in cases where the agency's interest groups are supportive (left) or opposed (right). Estimated from the conditional model in table 4A.1. Bars indicate 95% confidence intervals.

surement challenges are too great to overcome in order to detect what may be small effects. Second, compared to increasing text length, agencies may be more reluctant to employ readability tactics. The distinction relates to implementation; while agencies may be interested in discouraging certain groups of readers, they may be reluctant to repel those in the regulated community who will eventually be required to comply. While a long preamble may be tedious, it might not obscure the actual intent of the policy. In contrast, highly complex text may open the door for misinterpretation of the agency's intent by the regulated community or even the courts. Finally, agencies may simply not be able to use text accessibility as a tool to stave off certain forms of oversight where overseers have an expressed interest in text clarity. Not only does OIRA retain a heavy editorial pen, but also, as noted earlier in this chapter, rectifying the readability of text has historically been something of a presidential priority. Congress, too, has passed laws encouraging agencies to write more clearly. Given the direct attention these principals have devoted to readability, it may be an ineffective way to respond to their oversight, since they are likely sensitive to its use.

Summary

How a proposed rule is written can shape how audiences respond to it. As the opening example of the 2 percent rule demonstrated, the political environment can create an incentive for an agency to make a proposal more—or, in that case, less—accessible. Reducing text accessibility raises the costs for vested interests to meaningfully engage with the rulemaking process, and it may deter less attentive publics from participating altogether. By finessing text accessibility at the drafting stage for the proposed rule in response to the political environment, the agency enhances the prospects of a rule's political success in the longer term.

Of course, this strategy is not without its perils. Manipulating text accessibility may introduce potential compliance problems in the longer term. If regulated parties do not fully read or understand a proposed rule, down the line, they may struggle to decipher precisely what they need to do in order to comply with the regulations. Complex texts may create openings for novel, unanticipated legal challenges. As a result, agencies must exercise this strategy with caution. That is, as a tactic, text accessibility addresses a short-term need for proposed rule survival but may introduce the need for more education or guidance at the final rule and implementation stages, things that are not costless from the agency's perspective.

One interesting result that emerges from this chapter is that the political results are not consistent across the two measures of text accessibility. That is, while agencies use preamble length to respond to potentially adverse oversight from all three principals (conditional on interest group opposition), the results with respect to readability are more mixed, suggesting a consistent effect with respect to the courts but not the other two branches. Rather than interpreting the disparate results as evidence against the theory, I take it as evidence that agencies approach each step of the process in a nuanced way, fashioning the procedures to best suit the institutional constraints that they face at that particular point in the process.

In other words, the results are indicative of the inherent differences between the two strategies.[51] Compared to writing a less readable rule, an agency that writes a longer preamble may encounter fewer obstacles; as explained earlier in this chapter, numerous presidents have pressured agencies to make their rules more readable. Readability also has different implications with respect to the compliance problems discussed above. Whereas a less readable text may create confusion, a longer text may provide greater guidance to regulated parties on what they are supposed to do, which could potentially help with compliance. The takeaway, then, is that agencies "microtarget" their procedures, deploying them differentially with respect to a consideration of the tool itself, the branch in question, and how effective the tool is expected to be at that stage of the rulemaking process.

Text accessibility is just one way that agencies can use writing tools to raise monitoring costs for principals and insulate their rulemaking proposals. While the empirical test in this chapter focused on two accessibility techniques—length and readability—agencies also can apply a different frame to the rule or manipulate the assumptions used in the rule's analysis. In chapter 7, I explore both of these tools in the context of the FDA's rulemaking on menu labeling. However, now I continue on down the rulemaking path, turning in the next chapter to an exploration of procedural politicking at the consultation stage.

---

51. Alternatively, the differences in results could result from underlying problems with readability metrics, as discussed earlier in this chapter and outlined by Bruce, Rubin, and Starr (1981) among others. While I do not rule this out, the empirical results I report in later chapters in this book bolster the notion that agencies strategically tailor their procedures.

Appendix to Chapter 4

TABLE 4A.1. Seemingly unrelated regressions of proposed rule text accessibility

	Basic model		Conditional model	
	Preamble length	*Abstract readability*	*Preamble length*	*Abstract readability*
Unaligned president	0.013	0.216	−0.018	0.022
	(0.042)	(0.177)	(0.048)	(0.206)
Group opposition × Unaligned president			0.208*	0.650
			(0.094)	(0.407)
Congressional opposition	0.232*	−0.146	0.031	0.178
	(0.109)	(0.464)	(0.119)	(0.513)
Group opposition × Congressional opposition			1.069***	−1.376
			(0.291)	(1.207)
Court cases	0.104***	−0.075***	0.088***	−0.062*
	(0.007)	(0.030)	(0.007)	(0.031)
Group opposition × Court cases			0.242***	−0.239*
			(0.027)	(0.117)
Group opposition	−0.123*	−0.747*	−1.798***	0.865
	(0.055)	(0.212)	(0.308)	(1.278)
Impact	4.882***	−0.591	4.309***	0.022
	(0.211)	(0.880)	(0.215)	(0.916)
Complexity	0.217	−13.230***	0.904	−14.057***
	(0.684)	(2.908)	(0.676)	(2.925)
Statutory deadline	0.448***	0.147	0.327***	0.260
	(0.055)	(0.232)	(0.055)	(0.237)
Judicial deadline	0.851***	0.286	0.913***	0.258
	(0.079)	(0.334)	(0.078)	(0.336)
Employees	0.0002		0.0001	
	(0.0003)		(0.0003)	
Expertise	−0.928*		−1.255**	
	(0.364)		(0.360)	
Constant	7.184***	2.328***	7.513***	2.104***
	(0.155)	(0.628)	(0.161)	(0.658)
Presidential administration controls	Yes	Yes	Yes	Yes
Observations		2,870		2,870
Breusch-Pagan test		52.996***		50.763***

Note: The analysis includes proposed rules issued between 2000 and 2014 (inclusive) for the following eight agencies: APHIS, CMS, EPA, FDA, NHTSA, NOAA, OPM, and the VA. Table entries are coefficients from seemingly unrelated regression models.

*p < 0.05. **p < 0.01. ***p < 0.001. All two-tailed tests.

5

Consultation as a Tool

The writing stage is a critical juncture in the creation of a new rule, but it is just the beginning of a long process. After a rule is written, the next stage is public consultation on the proposal. As the previous chapters alluded to, there is considerable variation—both across and within agencies—in how this phase of rulemaking is handled.

Adopting a procedural politicking lens, during the consultation phase bureaucrats cautiously anticipate the type of feedback they may receive and craft their approach in response. This perspective diverges from much of the literature on agency consultation (reviewed in chapter 1), which holds that agencies either sincerely consider the feedback they receive (in a "take all comers" approach) or routinely ignore all the feedback they receive. Instead, I argue that agencies forecast the political response that may be elicited through the course of consultation and vary their approach depending on whether this feedback will help or hinder a rule's prospects.

While this logic is sound theoretically, is there empirical evidence that agencies actually concern themselves with what stakeholders are likely to say and politick accordingly? This chapter takes up that question directly by examining how agencies engage their audiences through the public comment period—the primary mechanism by which agencies gather public feedback on a proposed rule.

Connecting to Theory

Rulemaking has the potential to be open and democratic; as Michael Asimow (1994, 129) puts it, "Rulemaking procedures are *refreshingly democratic*: people who care about legislative outcomes produced by agencies have a structured opportunity to provide input into the decision-making process" (my emphasis). However, while anyone with internet access and a computer can look up an agency proposed rule in the *Federal Register* in mere seconds,[1] very few people actually do. Most citizens have a poor grasp of regulation and how far the arm of the regulatory state reaches into their lives;[2] this means the prospects for average citizens effecting change in regulations is rather dim, since an even smaller set understands how the rulemaking process works in the first place.[3]

Although the average person rarely engages with rulemaking, interest groups are much more active in monitoring agencies and their regulatory proceedings. For instance, both the Sierra Club and the Farm Bureau closely track the rules issued by the Environmental Protection Agency (EPA). These groups have a professional interest in ensuring that the EPA's regulatory policies align with their organizational goals. They also have the resources—in terms of both knowledge of how the process works and staff to carry out the task—to conduct the requisite monitoring. When agency activities are particularly salient to the broader public, these groups may mobilize their constituents and citizens more broadly to participate in the rulemaking process, which they do so by translating arcane rules into simple concepts and using their resources to rally a public response.

Many studies take the participatory gulf between citizens and interest groups as a given, part of the natural state of things given the differences in resources, attention, and incentives between the two types of stakeholders. This may well be the case, but I argue that the consultation choices that agencies make may exacerbate this disparity. The two participation hypotheses laid out in chapter 3 depart from the notion that the direction of interest group oversight varies—it can be supportive of an agency's goals or antithetical to them. Accordingly, agencies must consider what the position of relevant interest groups means if those groups get the attention of political overseers, particularly those who may be hostile. As the Expanded Consultation Hypothesis states, when agencies expect that interest group feedback may help their cause, they increase opportunities for participation by in-

1. The website https://www.regulations.gov/ has served as the central portal for rulemaking documents for most federal agencies since the mid-2000s. Rules are also published online and in hard copy in the *Federal Register*.

2. For decades political scientists have lamented that Americans' overall level of political knowledge is quite low (e.g., Delli Carpini and Keeter 1997; Lupia 2016), a finding that is exacerbated in the regulatory domain (Coglianese 2005; Farina et al. 2011).

3. One study notes that "even lawyers and people who work for the federal government tend not to understand the rulemaking process unless they have been personally involved in some way" (Farina et al. 2011, 9).

terest groups. The feedback that agencies receive from supportive interest groups can then be used to demonstrate to skeptical principals that there is external support for the agency's rule. Expanding consultation can also enable groups to broaden the reach of the rulemaking—perhaps by rallying the group's sympathizers. In other words, facing an unfavorable political environment, supportive public feedback may help shore up a rule's prospects.

The Limited Consultation Hypothesis, in contrast, anticipates that the mechanism may work in the reverse. When political principals are not aligned with an agency and when relevant interest groups are predisposed against an agency, that agency will work to limit consultation. Negative feedback arising from public consultation is the fodder of "fire alarms," whereby disaffected groups bring their complaints to principals. If principals are sympathetic to group concerns, agencies face the potential of a regulatory veto or other sanction. Further, formal consultation that occurs during the rulemaking process is public and part of the rulemaking record, and it may serve to lay the groundwork for future litigation.

In this chapter, I look for empirical evidence to evaluate these hypotheses. Before doing so, however, it is worth noting that manipulating the level of consultation on a rulemaking can have negative repercussions for an agency, irrespective of which way the participation valve is turned. For example, allowing for expanded consultation when the agency expects positive feedback may enable supportive elements to chime in favorably toward the rule, but it also slows the process down and may allow a hostile minority to foment opposition to the rule. In a similar fashion, pushing through a proposed rule that is thousands of pages long and limiting the amount of public feedback on that proposal can blow back on an agency if affected groups lobby political principals to force the agency to give them more time. The agency may, in turn, be compelled to offer up additional consultation while also suffering from a reputation hit for appearing unresponsive to the "public interest." While these are real risks that agencies face with respect to consultation choices, they are subordinate to the prevailing desire to shepherd the preferred version of the proposed rule through to become binding law. Procedural politicking through the manipulation of consultation can make that happen.

The EPA and the WOTUS Rule

The politicking behind consultation is nuanced, but the basic intuition is most easily relayed with an example. In the spring of 2014 the EPA issued a controversial proposed rule on clean water.[4] The Waters of the US, or WOTUS, rule defined which rivers, streams, lakes, and marshes fell under the agency's jurisdiction under the Clean Water Act.[5] Although that law had been enacted more than four decades prior, the agency was seeking to clarify the scope of its reach. While the goal of the rulemaking was to protect a wider range of wetlands and waterways, the costs of the rule, when finalized, were likely to be concentrated among farmers, the oil and gas industry, and the construction industry. When the proposed WOTUS rule went out for public comment, however, there was overwhelming public support for it. More than one million public comments were received, of which 90 percent supported the agency's action, a statistic that Administrator Gina McCarthy of the EPA eagerly referenced when the Republican-controlled Congress called her to testify about the WOTUS rule several months after the proposed rule's publication.[6]

The widespread support for the agency's proposal was not coincidental; in this case the EPA was actually accused of drumming up support for its own proposed rule. According to one journalistic account, "The agency orchestrated a drive to counter political opposition from Republicans and enlist public support in concert with liberal environmental groups and a grassroots organization aligned with President Obama."[7] The agency's efforts included social media outreach encouraging allies to share the message: "Clean water is important to me. I support EPA's efforts to protect it for my health, my family and my community." Additionally, an EPA staffer wrote a blog post indicating that he did not "want to get sick from pollution." The post included a link to an advocacy group's website, which then entreated readers to "tell Congress to stop interfering with your right to clean water."[8]

The EPA's behavior in this case was clearly an outlier—so much so that the story netted two front-page headlines in the *New York Times*, a subsequent investigation by the Government Accountability Office (GAO), and a determination that the agency had violated federal anti-propaganda laws.[9] However, what sets this case apart is the lack of subtlety rather than the tactics themselves. The case offers two important lessons regarding the role of feedback from the public during the rulemaking process. First, agencies are often quite

---

4. The proposal was issued jointly with the Army Corps of Engineers. However, I focus on the EPA here, since it was the lead agency in the rulemaking.

5. Pub. L. No. 92-500.

6. Lipton and Davenport (2015).

7. Lipton and Davenport (2015).

8. Lipton and Shear (2015).

9. In a legal opinion, the GAO (2015) decreed that the "EPA's use of [social media] constitutes covert propaganda, in violation of the [federal] publicity or propaganda prohibition."

adept at anticipating the response from different affected publics to a particular proposal. In this case, the EPA foresaw that farmers and other industry groups were likely to oppose the rule and might get Republican support if they attempted to block the rule; the agency then targeted its efforts at countering that opposition.[10] Second, the EPA actively used support from stakeholders as a way to bolster the prospects of the proposed rule's survival. The very fact that the agency tried to engineer supportive responses from the public—and then later referenced these responses in congressional testimony—suggests that public support can strengthen a proposed rule that is under close political scrutiny.

Of course, stakeholders do not always weigh in favorably on an agency's proposed rule. Often the public comment period is an opportunity for stakeholders to identify problems with the agency's proposal and to air grievances, a concern taken up directly in the Limited Consultation Hypothesis. Just as favorable comments can enhance a rule's prospects, criticisms can prove detrimental to a proposed rule's prospects. Particularly when political principals are inclined against the agency, these critiques can have repercussions, ranging from mere annoyances (e.g., requests for more information from principals) to the catastrophic (e.g., the issuance of a regulatory veto). Taken together, the two strategic consultation hypotheses suggest that depending on the tenor of the responses received and the disposition of political overseers, public feedback on a proposed rule can alternatively help or hinder a proposed rule. I now turn to empirical tests of the effects of these relationships on the participation opportunities that an agency offers, specifically with regard to the public comment period.

The Comment Period as Procedural Politicking

There are very few ironclad requirements—legally speaking—with regard to consultation on rulemaking. Although some amount of consultation with stakeholders outside of the agency is generally required, what that consultation looks like in practice varies across the spectrum of rules issued by an agency. Sometimes agencies go out of their way to engage stakeholders, by publishing an Advance Notice of Proposed Rulemaking (ANPRM) to solicit feedback from stakeholders early in the development of a rule, or seeking advice from the agency's advisory committee in a public session, or holding

---

10. While the WOTUS rule was finalized under the Obama administration, the agency's premonitions later proved to be accurate. In February 2017, President Trump, a Republican, signed an executive order directing the EPA and the Army Corps of Engineers to review the WOTUS rule and consider revising or rescinding it (Exec. Order No. 13,778, Feb. 28, 2017; 82 FR 12497).

hearings during the public comment period at which members of the public can give testimony about the rule. At other times, however, the agency may do only the bare minimum in terms of consultation; for example, the agency could offer a very short comment period (e.g., less than thirty days) and do nothing else. In other words, agencies have wide latitude and can decide to limit or expand the amount of consultation they solicit on a particular rule.

With respect to the public comment period, what the Administrative Procedure Act (APA) does stipulate is that agencies should allow the public a meaningful opportunity to comment on proposed rules. But the law does not state how long the public comment period need be. As Lubbers (2012, 251) notes, "A common misconception is that the APA prescribes a thirty-day minimum comment period, a belief that may derive from the APA's requirement that final rules be published 30 days prior to their effective date."[11] In 1993, the Clinton administration clarified that agencies should provide "a meaningful opportunity to comment on any proposed regulation, which in most cases should include a comment period of not less than 60 days."[12] More recently, President Obama reaffirmed this policy in an executive order that indicated comment periods should be "at least 60 days."[13]

In practice, however, the sixty-day standard is not closely followed. Figure 5.1 shows that while sixty days is the modal number of comment days for proposed rules in the *Regulatory Proposals Dataset*, there is considerable variation. To better understand this variation, it is instructive to compare two bureaus within the same department—the US Department of Agriculture (USDA). One bureau, the Animal and Plant Health Inspection Service (APHIS), tends to allot a relatively long amount of time for its comment period, with a low level of variation (median = 61 days, s.d. = 13.0 days). In contrast, the Agricultural Marketing Service (AMS), typically sets a lower number of days, with greater variation (median = 32.0 days, s.d. = 20.9 days). This type of intradepartment and even intrabureau variation suggests that decisions about the length of time allotted for comment are not only bureau specific; they are also rule specific. I argue that they are also strategic.

The amount of time that the public has to comment on a proposed rule matters to interest groups; Kerwin and Furlong (2011, 67) explain that "it takes time to assemble the essential information needed to evaluate and then respond to what can be highly technical and complex rules. In the contemporary political environment, time allows people to get organized, to build

11. See Balla (2015) for a thoughtful account of the duration of comment periods.
12. Exec. Order No. 12,866, Oct. 4, 1993; 58 FR 51735.
13. Exec. Order No. 13,563, Jan. 21, 2011; 76 FR 3821.

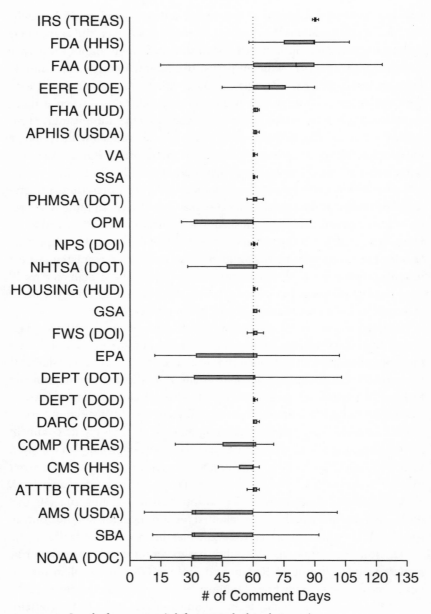

FIGURE 5.1. Length of comment periods for proposed rules, select agencies

Note: Boxes show the upper and lower quartiles of the observed data. Bars represent the agency median. The vertical dotted line indicates the 60-day mark. For ease of interpretation, the figure focuses on the top 25 agencies (by volume of proposed rules issued) from the *Regulatory Proposals Dataset*. Where appropriate, bureaus are listed with their respective department name in parentheses. See table A.1 in the data appendix for a complete listing of agency names and acronyms.

coalitions, and to orchestrate a response to the agency's proposals." It matters particularly for individuals and less moneyed interests. For example, one blogger complained that the EPA allowed only twenty-four days for public comment on a "massive 1,572 typescript pages, or 377 printed tri-column pages, proposal [that] would adopt California emissions standards for the entire United States."[14] The blogger further lamented that this was inadequate, since "limiting the period for public comment, and the load of material that must be reviewed, adversely affects the ability of any potential litigant to recognize, understand, and preserve his or her objections for judicial review."[15]

To assess whether agencies adjust the comment period in the manner suggested by the Limited Consultation Hypothesis and the Expanded Consultation Hypothesis, I count the number of days in the public comment period for every proposed rule in the *Regulatory Proposals Dataset*. The resulting dependent variable, *Comment days*, ranges from 3 to 276 days. It includes the days the bureau initially set for the public comment period; although agencies sometimes extend or reopen the comment period later on (which adds more days to the comment period), I focus on the initial number of comment days since this is the agency's opening gambit.

Because the underlying procedural politicking mechanism remains the same, I rely on the same covariates introduced in chapter 4. The two strategic consultation hypotheses pose a conditional relationship between agency expectations about the type of response they will receive from stakeholder groups and the extent to which they will be willing to engage these groups through consultation activities; therefore, I again interact each of the three political variables with the *Group opposition* variable.

Assessing Strategic Consultation

Unlike the models in chapter 4, which focused in depth on eight bureaus, the tests in this chapter take into account all 150 agencies in the *Regulatory Proposals Dataset*. This means that there is a built-in hierarchy to the data; proposed rules are nested within bureaus, which in turn are nested within departments. Accordingly, I estimate hierarchical linear models (HLM), an approach that can accommodate this structure in the data.[16] Table 5A.1 in the appendix to this

14. Beck (2013).
15. Beck (2013).
16. Specifically, I include a random intercept for each department and each bureau, to relax the assumption of independence of errors between bureaus in a given department. See Gelman and Hill (2006) and Rabe-Hesketh and Skrondal (2008).

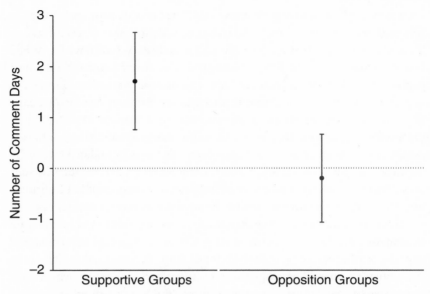

FIGURE 5.2. Effect of shifting from an aligned to an *Unaligned president* on *Comment days*, contingent on *Group opposition*
Note: Circles indicate the predicted changes in *Comment days* when moving from an aligned to an unaligned president, in cases where the agency's interest groups are supportive (left) or opposed (right). Estimated from the conditional model in table 5A.1. Bars indicate 95% confidence intervals.

chapter presents the coefficients from models of the relationship between the political environment and *Comment days*. Model 1 shows the unconditional relationship, and model 2 includes the interaction with *Group opposition*, which offers a test of the Expanded Consultation Hypothesis and the Limited Consultation Hypothesis. Again, I include presidential administration fixed effects.

The results indicate that agencies manipulate the comment period in response to both the expected response from interest groups and the political environment. Figure 5.2 shows the change in the number of comment days when interest groups are aligned with the agency, a result in keeping with the Expanded Consultation Hypothesis. Compared to a situation where the president is ideologically aligned with the agency, an agency that is not aligned with the president will increase the number of days a proposed rule is open for comment when interest groups are in the agency's corner by about two days. However, there is less clear support for the Limited Consultation Hypothesis, which suggests that when an agency faces a principal with whom they are not aligned, it will reduce opportunities for participation (i.e., shorten the length of the comment period). Although the model predicts a decrease in comment days, the effect is small (less than one day) and not statistically distinguishable from 0. Instead, the results in figure 5.2 suggest that when interest groups are opposed to them, agencies play it "safe" by choosing an average length of public comment period.

At a minimum, the findings about strategic calculations vis-à-vis the White House indicate that there is a political calculation to the length of the public comment period, a procedural step that is typically considered mundane and administrative. However, the results with respect to Congress and the courts are less stark; while the model shows a negative coefficient for both interactions (as expected), the results are not substantively meaningful. For Congress, the results are indistinguishable from 0, suggesting that agencies are not employing strategic manipulation of the comment period as a way of managing these overseers. This may be because agencies can more effectively manipulate a different aspect of the public comment period—a point I explore later in this chapter.

The results for the court mirror those of the presidency, although on a much-smaller scale. There is an effect when interest groups are supportive of the agency; specifically, the model predicts an increase of 0.24 days as the level of court monitoring changes from low to high. There is no statistically discernible effect when interest group opposition is strong. Together this suggests weak support for the Expanded Consultation Hypothesis and, as before, no support for the Limited Consultation Hypothesis. However, unlike the presidency, this effect is substantively negligible, as it does not amount to much movement in the overall length of the public comment period. This may be attributed to the courts' concern with due process, a concern that may lead agencies to pause before using this tactic to counter the judiciary. Historically, the courts have treated the public comment period as sacrosanct. Although this was less of an issue during the study's time period (since courts have tended to be less interventionist on the procedural side in recent decades), the historical precedent may make agencies wary of manipulating the comment period to gain advantage with the courts. Put differently, as there are for Congress, there may be other options on the procedural menu that more effectively build barriers to court intervention.

The models in table 5A.1 include several controls for the importance of the rule in question. The *Impact* measure suggests that when moving from the least impactful to the most impactful rule, agencies increase the public comment period by about eleven and a half days, although this effect only hovers at a statistically significant level. This is reassuring in that rules that are the most important are the ones that stakeholders might want to engage with the most. The models also suggest that the *Judicial deadline* measure is associated with nearly five additional days of public comment. Finally, each additional increase of one thousand employees in the agency is associated with only a very small increase in the average length of the public comment period. While this indicates a relationship between capacity and comment days, no comparable effect is observed with respect to *Expertise*.

Recess Commenting: An Alternate Tack

One surprising result that emerged from the prior analyses is that agencies do not systematically manipulate comment periods in response to congressional opposition. This is puzzling for two reasons. First, in the previous chapter, I showed that congressional oversight is clearly an important consideration for agencies when it comes to determining the length of a proposed rule's preamble. This establishes that, at a minimum, agencies take congressional concerns into account at the earlier drafting stage. Second, the comment period is often thought of as a point in time when interest groups can "sound the fire alarm"—an alarm that, according to most accounts, sounds most loudly in the halls of Congress.

With respect to Congress, however, there is another—perhaps better—strategy that agencies may pursue with respect to the public comment period, driving home the point that agency politicking strategies are highly tailored to the political overseers and opposition that they face. And bureaucrats are well positioned to do this careful tailoring—politicking is possible only because of the expertise and deep experience with the rulemaking process that bureaucrats derive through many repeated interactions.

If agencies are leery of the consequences of a pulled fire alarm, the most direct response maybe to enfeeble the congressional response to that alarm rather than silence interest groups, some of which may be sufficiently moneyed and organized that they are able to adapt to even the shortest comment periods. Publishing the proposed rule so that the comment period overlaps with a congressional recess may provide just such an opportunity. During recesses, members of Congress focus on activities in their home districts and are less attuned to issues in Washington.[17] From the perspective of a member of Congress, Washington business (including responding to agency rules) has essentially been "put on hold" until the session resumes.

Moreover, while some congressional staffers remain available to attend to group complaints, many schedule their vacations around recess periods.[18] Thus, while publishing during a recess period does not mean that the fire alarm will not be heard at all, it may decrease the likelihood that it engenders a substantial response. Gersen and O'Connell (2009, 1183) summarize this

17. Fenno (1978).
18. Beam (2009).

strategy in the following way: "If Congress is out of session, all else equal, the costs of mobilizing a political response to an unpopular policy should rise." This means that it may be more difficult for members of Congress to learn about a rule or to respond to the rule when they do. From the agency's perspective, this approach to handling Congress may be preferable because it prevents groups from complaining to members about arbitrarily short comment periods while also being relatively easy to implement.

To assess whether this strategy is actually employed, I consider the extent to which the comment period coincides with a congressional recess for each proposed rule in the *Regulatory Proposals Dataset.*[19] The dependent variable, *Recess overlap*, is simply the proportion of the public comment period that overlaps with a congressional recess. I include the same covariates as in the previous analyses, with one change: I add a control for the number of days in the public comment period, because proposed rules with longer public comment periods have a greater opportunity to overlap with a congressional recess. I employ the same HLM approach to account for hierarchy in the data.[20] Table 5A.2 in the appendix to this chapter presents the model results.

The takeaway is that as the strength of congressional opposition increases, agencies time public comment periods to overlap with congressional recesses. However, unlike in the previous models, there is evidence of a direct effect of congressional oversight; in model 1 the coefficient on *Congressional opposition* is positive and statistically significant. The substantive effect is considerable as well; moving from a weak congressional opposition to a strong one results in about a 7 percent increase in a proposed rule's overlap with a congressional recess. That said, these effects appear to be largely concentrated among cases where the agency's interest groups are opposed to the agency's efforts, which shows up in the conditional model (model 2). As shown in figure 5.3, the predicted increase in comment period overlap is large (11 percent) and positive when interest groups are not aligned with the agency. In contrast, the effect is indistinguishable from 0 when they are aligned (see the left half of the figure).

19. I again focus on the initial comment period and ignore instances where the agency extended or reopened the public comment period, because these decisions are not part of the original strategic calculus. Additionally, I focus on periods when the House was in recess.

20. The dependent variable, *Recess overlap*, is bounded between 0 and 1, meaning that least squares models can yield results that lie outside of this interval. However, employing a fractional logit model (Papke and Wooldridge 1996)—an approach that accounts for the proportional nature of the data—results in substantively similar findings. Additionally, jointly estimating this model with the earlier models on *Comment days* using the seemingly unrelated regression approach introduced in the previous chapter yields similar results. I present the hierarchical linear models here because they best account for the structure of the data.

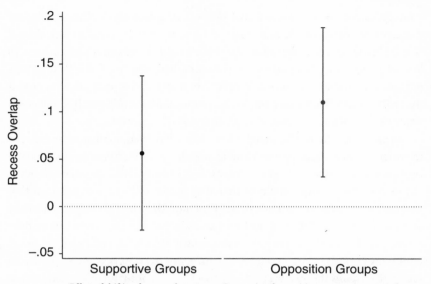

Effect of shifting from weak to strong *Congressional opposition* on comment period overlap with congressional recesses, contingent on *Group opposition*
Note: Circles indicate the predicted changes in *Recess overlap* when moving from weak to strong *Congressional opposition*, in cases where the agency's interest groups are supportive (left) or opposed (right). Estimated from the conditional model in table 5A.2. Bars indicate 95% confidence intervals.

The implication is that while agencies do not manipulate the length of the comment period, they do leverage congressional recesses as an alternate path to managing congressional oversight. This approach avoids complaints about short comment periods from reaching congressional ears and is straightforward for agencies to implement.

Summary

The analyses in this chapter suggest that agencies are keenly attuned to their stakeholder audiences and craft consultation policies according to what they expect these groups to say. The empirical focus was on two tools in particular: the duration and timing of the public comment period. The analyses of these tools did not show that agencies manipulate them consistently with each branch in mind. Instead, the results suggest a finer-grained approach in which some tools are considered more effective at targeting specific principals. In other words, the fact that I do not find statistically significant results for all three branches with respect to both tools should not be taken as evidence against procedural politicking but rather as an indication that highly strategic bureaucrats choose from a menu of procedural options and tailor their procedural strategy for each branch.

Indeed, procedural decisions do not occur in isolation; rather, they are part of a broader procedural strategy. That is, agencies may pair a lengthened comment period, for example, with other ways of enhancing participation opportunities from supportive constituents, such as publishing an ANPRM or reopening the public comment period. But when faced with hostile groups, they may employ a different procedural tool altogether. The successful use of any one of these tactics, including the strategic manipulation of the public comment period, must be nuanced; agencies that are too heavy handed call attention to themselves and lose their procedural advantage. For example, an agency that shortened the public comment period by fifteen days whenever public comments presented a potential threat would invite broad criticism from groups that were shut out of the process, introducing a new set of problems. However, by quietly accumulating small advantages across many procedures, agencies can tip the overall balance in favor of a particular outcome.

The evidence I find for the strategic manipulation of public comment periods has broad implications for the role of consultation in rulemaking. The public comment period is a point at which the agency can potentially gather information from affected stakeholders about a wide range of issues related to their rulemakings. Learning that occurs during this time is what Moffitt (2014) calls "learning in public," meaning that it is observable by others outside of the agency. The comments that the agency receives become part of the public record; they can help make the agency's case with political overseers, but they can also be used against the agency. This analysis shows that agencies are sometimes reluctant to learn in public when they can suffer political consequences. This is particularly true because agencies have plenty of opportunities to "learn in private," including meetings with stakeholders during the proposed rule's drafting stage and through informal networks that bureaucrats may share with those in their respective fields. For instance, many bureaucrats belong to the same professional associations (and attend the same networking events and conferences) as those to whom their regulations apply. This introduces opportunities for "offline" conversations about issues in industry and various regulatory approaches.

What this means is that under conditions that might lead an agency to shorten the public comment period or to publish during a recess period, agencies may have a greater incentive to learn in more private spheres, such as earlier in the process when ex parte restrictions do not apply. This is a perverse consequence of political scrutiny; since private learning is limited to parties of the agency's choosing, less meaningful deliberation between agencies and the parties they regulate may occur.

However, the public comment period is but one way that agencies manage participation when creating a new rule. As explained in chapter 3, agencies choose from a menu of options to engage stakeholders in their rulemakings. And anecdotal evidence suggests that the issues identified here with respect to strategic management of consultation mechanisms may also be at work in these other venues. For example, an agency can choose to bypass the notice provision altogether by issuing an interim final rule (IFR). IFRs, which are sometimes called emergency rules, are substantive rules that are issued without prior public notice and take effect shortly after publication. Because providing notice of a rule "makes it likely that interested parties will find out about a proposed rule and will submit comments designed to influence the decisionmakers" (Asimow 1994, 128), the substantive effect of issuing an IFR instead of a proposed rule is that the agency effectively reduces the ability of stakeholders to participate in a rulemaking.

While IFRs are supposed to be issued only if the agency has "good cause,"[21] that interpretation is left to agencies. Strategic bureaucrats can take a lax interpretation of what this phrase means and use this procedure to their advantage, much in the same way as the other tools identified here. While the good cause exemption is intended to be invoked when advance notice is "impracticable, unnecessary, or contrary to the public interest," in a 1998 report the General Accounting Office found numerous instances of agencies abusing this procedural power. For example, in one case, an agency used an IFR "'because this rule will facilitate tourist and business travel to and from Slovenia,' and therefore delaying the rule to allow for public comments before the interim rule was published 'would be contrary to the public interest'" (22). Given that an estimated twenty thousand Americans travel to Slovenia each year—less than 0.01 percent of the US population—this is a case where the public interest would likely not have been substantially harmed by going through the notice stage of the rulemaking process.

This discussion of IFRs further underlines the extent to which the consultation tactics parsed in detail here are just a snapshot of a broader landscape of consultation. Scholars would do well to consider the effects of procedural politicking across this landscape. In doing so, they must remain attuned to the reality that agencies do not employ procedural strategies to stave off each of the branches in the same way; bureaucrats tailor their strategies. In the next chapter, I turn to the final set of tools in the procedural politicking tool kit— timing—and consider how those tools are artfully employed by strategically minded bureaucrats.

21. See 5 U.S.C. § 553(b).

Appendix to Chapter 5

TABLE 5A.1. Influence of the political environment on *Comment days*

	(1) Basic model	(2) Conditional model
Unaligned president	1.074***	1.712***
	(0.314)	(0.486)
Group opposition × Unaligned president		−1.910**
		(0.715)
Congressional opposition	1.224	1.214
	(1.515)	(1.892)
Group opposition × Congressional opposition		−0.488
		(2.417)
Court cases	0.200*	0.237
	(0.102)	(0.125)
Group opposition × Court cases		−0.169
		(0.158)
Group opposition	0.796	2.425
	(0.899)	(2.371)
Impact	11.534	11.566
	(6.222)	(6.190)
Complexity	−1.143	−1.176
	(4.267)	(4.240)
Statutory deadline	−0.145	−0.151
	(1.451)	(1.449)
Judicial deadline	4.745**	4.634**
	(1.634)	(1.606)
Employees	0.003*	0.003*
	(0.002)	(0.002)
Expertise	−7.818	−7.472
	(4.423)	(4.337)
Constant	55.684***	55.188***
	(3.182)	(3.415)
Presidential administration controls	Yes	Yes
Bureau-level random effects	Yes	Yes
Department-level random effects	Yes	Yes
Observations (rules)	10,928	10,928

Note: Table entries are coefficients obtained from multilevel linear regression models with random effects at the department and bureau level and presidential administration fixed effects. The dependent variable is the number of days in the public comment period for each proposed rule. Robust standard errors clustered on the department are in parentheses.

*$p < 0.05$. **$p < 0.01$. ***$p < 0.001$. All two-tailed tests.

TABLE 5A.2. Influence of the political environment on *Recess overlap*

	(1) Basic model	(2) Conditional model
Unaligned president	0.006	0.006
	(0.004)	(0.004)
Congressional opposition	0.072*	0.056
	(0.031)	(0.041)
Group opposition $\times$ Congressional opposition		0.053
		(0.057)
Court cases	0.002	0.003
	(0.003)	(0.003)
Group opposition	0.017	−0.038
	(0.021)	(0.062)
Impact	0.013	0.013
	(0.020)	(0.020)
Complexity	0.005	0.005
	(0.050)	(0.049)
Statutory deadline	−0.003	−0.003
	(0.008)	(0.008)
Judicial deadline	0.003	0.003
	(0.009)	(0.009)
Employees	−0.000	−0.000
	(0.000)	(0.000)
Expertise	−0.087	−0.086
	(0.050)	(0.049)
Comment days	−0.00003	−0.00003
	(0.00002)	(0.00002)
Constant	0.377***	0.391***
	(0.032)	(0.043)
Presidential administration controls	Yes	Yes
Bureau-level random effects	Yes	Yes
Department-level random effects	Yes	Yes
Observations (rules)	10,928	10,928

Note: Table entries are coefficients obtained from multilevel linear regression models with random effects at the department and bureau level and presidential administration fixed effects. The dependent variable is the proportion of days in the public comment period for each proposed rule that overlapped with a congressional recess. Robust standard errors clustered on the department are in parentheses.

*$p < 0.05$. **$p < 0.01$. ***$p < 0.001$. All two-tailed tests.

6

Timing as a Tool

But a bureaucracy, above all, endures. If defeated today, it lies in wait to win tomorrow.
FORMER SECRETARY OF DEFENSE DONALD
RUMSFELD (2013, 183)

In modern construction, cranes and derricks do, quite literally, much of the heavy lifting. The Occupational Safety and Health Administration (OSHA), the federal agency responsible for regulating these machines, set new regulatory standards for their operation in 2010, but prior to that, the last set of standards was issued in 1971. In the intervening thirty-nine years between the two standards, technologies changed dramatically, making the old standards obsolete long before OSHA got around to updating them.[1] There was considerable human cost to OSHA's inaction, as crane and derrick accidents piled up at construction sites across the country at alarming rates.[2] According to one interest group's estimate, "Every year that goes by without the new rule in place another 53 people die and 155 are injured in accidents that could and should have been prevented."[3]

There are two stories of why OSHA took nigh four decades to update its regulations.[4] The first story is that regulating cranes and derricks is a

1. For example, the 1971 rules were developed around crawler cranes; much of contemporary crane usage involves hydraulic cranes and uses computers, technologies that were nascent or nonexistent in 1971. For instance, the 2010 regulations banned the use of cell phones (which did not exist in 1971) by on-duty crane operators.
2. Levine (2008).
3. O'Neill et al. (2009, 15); see also Levine (2008).
4. OSHA was not working on the cranes and derricks regulations during this entire period. In 1998, the agency met with its expert advisory committee and established a working group to recommend changes to the regulatory standards for cranes and derricks (see Advisory Committee on Construction Safety and Health 1998). Four years later, in 2002, the agency convened a regulatory negotiation committee to develop a proposed rule. The proposed rule was published in 2008, and the final rule was published in 2010.

highly complex and technical business. Figuring out the details of a policy that would apply to approximately 267,000 construction, crane rental, and crane certification establishments and affect about 4.8 million workers simply took the agency a long time.

The second story is a more political tale. OSHA began seriously working on the cranes and derricks rule in 1998, late in the Clinton administration. The agency initiated the new rulemaking in response to pressure from public safety advocates and from the construction industry itself, the latter wanting more stringent standards that would shelter it from litigation and would apply equally to all competitors. According to one public interest group, "If ever there were a rule that seemingly should have breezed to adoption, this was it" (Lincoln and Mouzoon 2011, 3).[5] Yet there was little political support within the George W. Bush administration to continue this type of reform at OSHA.[6] In fact, OSHA did not finalize the rule until 2010, when a new and more sympathetic Democratic administration led by President Barack Obama had taken office. Obama-era OSHA Administrator David Michaels admitted that there was a political component to the agency's foot-dragging: "Frankly, there were a number of years when standard setting was not given a high priority by the other administration. . . . When [Obama's Labor Secretary Hilda] Solis came in with new leadership team, we were able to then move quickly" (Walter 2010). In other words, OSHA waited until a more supportive presidential administration was in place before proceeding with the final rule.

In this chapter, I build on this second, political explanation and investigate the extent to which regulatory timing is a strategic response to the political environment. It is not uncommon for rules to take a long time—from many years to even decades—to complete. While some rules linger indefinitely, others are urgently rushed through the process. Indeed, while the cranes and derricks rule was languishing at OSHA during the Bush years, OSHA finalized dozens of rules, including a rule that would change the method for evaluating workers' risk from on-the-job chemical exposure. That proposal was perceived to make it more difficult to issue future rules regulating worker exposure and was supported by the Bush administration.[7] In the pages that follow, I argue that the considerations about the pace of rulemaking cor-

---

5. Another participant noted that both union and industry groups, "agreed that the current regulations [were] archaic and [failed] to address the daily hazards faced by construction workers" (Podziba 2012).

6. See Goldstein and Cohen (2004); and Labaton (2007).

7. *Claims Journal* (2008); Leonnig (2008).

respond to an agency's strategic calculations about what political principals are willing to tolerate and what the response might be to issuing rules that a principal does not favor. That is, I consider how strategic timing is used as a procedural politicking tool.

Connecting to Theory

As the opening quote from Washington insider and former Secretary of Defense Donald Rumsfeld suggests, agencies preside over the temporal aspects of policy making—and timing can therefore be leveraged to ensure the ultimate success of a rulemaking project. Speeding up or slowing down rules to capitalize on the political climate are strategies that are so well known inside the Washington Beltway that they have names—respectively, "fast-tracking" and "slow-rolling." Fast-tracking is the idea that an agency expedites a rule to have it come to fruition in a favorable political environment, whereas slow-rolling is the idea that an agency might draw out the rulemaking process to avoid a particularly unfavorable political environment.

As the rule on cranes and derricks demonstrates, rules can take a long time to complete. Delays like this are frustrating for the regulated community, as they create uncertainty about the future and hinder effective long-term planning. Additionally, since regulations are intended to benefit society,[8] there are presumably welfare losses associated with putting them off.

While rules that are fast-tracked often fly through without notice, rules that stagnate tend to attract the attention of regulatory observers. Many scholars attribute such delays to the onerousness of the rulemaking process. In addition to the basic requirement for notice-and-comment, agencies often have to conduct cost-benefit analysis and sundry impact analyses (e.g., effects on small business, tribes, paperwork, the environment, civil justice, children). The number of such requirements has increased over time, as political principals layer new requirements on top of old in an attempt to continue to exert influence over agencies. As a result of the growth of these requirements and an increase in the number of procedural steps, some scholars argue that the process has become "ossified."[9] In this view, agencies are so laden with all these requirements that they cannot regulate quickly—or perhaps at all.

---

8. Under Executive Order 12,866, agencies should only "propose or adopt a regulation only upon a reasoned determination that the benefits of the intended regulation justify its costs." Although there is flexibility in how this is implemented, the idea that regulation should result in net benefits is a core governing principle of the US regulatory system.

9. See, e.g., Jordan (1999); McGarity (1991); Seidenfeld (1997); and Verkuil (1995).

Judicial review also contributes to ossification; because courts strike down agency rules with some regularity, the expected return on completing a new regulation is lower ex ante.[10] This creates an incentive for agencies to move deliberately with an eye toward crossing all the *t*'s and dotting all the *i*'s, or to avoid rulemaking altogether. For instance, Mashaw and Harfst (1986) argue that legal culture and an activist court led the National Highway Transportation Safety Administration (NHTSA) to abandon rulemaking in favor of case adjudication in the early 1970s. These concerns have intensified over the years;[11] writing in 1991, McGarity noted that "it is much harder for an agency to promulgate a rule now than it was twenty years ago."[12]

Without a doubt, these factors slow the pace of rulemaking, but the object of interest here is the more political part of the story. "Midnight rulemaking" at the end of a presidential administration clearly demonstrates that agencies are capable of moving quickly when political circumstances warrant it. Moreover, there is substantial variation in timing both within and between bureaus, but the ossification thesis only explains the deceleration of the process. The reality is much more dynamic. The choice to fast-track certain rules and to slow-roll others can affect a rule's, and ultimately an agency's, fortunes. It is a political choice.

This is the logic underlying the Strategic Timing Hypothesis, which posits that agencies will use their procedural control over timing to make sure that their rules are announced in a favorable political environment. By either rushing to make a policy public when the current political configuration is supportive of the agency or slowing down and waiting in hopes that the political situation will improve, the agency can bolster the prospects of a controversial rule. Of course, agency bureaucrats cannot choose who sits in the Oval Office, on Capitol Hill, or on the bench,[13] but they can benefit from the natural transitions that occur in the political system, namely electoral turnover and changes in the courts. Critically, the Strategic Timing Hypothesis does not hinge on the disposition of interest groups, as the mechanisms

10. Jordan (1999); Livermore (2007); Pierce (1995).

11. See Pierce (2011).

12. The ossification theory has its detractors, however. In a series of articles Yackee and Yackee (2010, 2011) find little empirical evidence that the volume or the pace of rules has meaningfully slowed with the imposition of more procedural requirements; ultimately, they conclude that the ossification argument is over-egged. See also Raso (2010). And while Livermore (2007) contends that ossification exists, he suggests that it stems from a broader status quo bias rather than from procedural impediments.

13. However, bureaucrats can and do vote in electoral blocs that influence the selection of political principals; see Chen and Johnson (2014); and Moe (2006).

described in the previous chapters did. Agencies cannot "wait out" interest groups in the same way that they can slow-roll a principal. Interest group oversight is provided by networks of groups with long time horizons, meaning that oversight is not contingent on one actor and that shifts in interest group power are slow to occur.[14]

Although agencies make many timing decisions—such as when to publish the proposed rule, when the final rule should take effect, and whether to delay the implementation of the effective date—in this chapter I focus on when an agency finishes working on a final rule and the agency's ultimate policy choice is shared publicly. Until a rule reaches this point, no one outside the agency knows how an agency will address the issues, if any, raised during the public comment period. That is, by sitting on a final rule, an agency is able to effectively able to evade criticisms. From the outside the agency appears to be working out the kinks of a policy proposal, meaning that things are still prospective and potential critics must wait and see how any outstanding issues are resolved. When the final rule is actually published, only then are its contents known and can critics begin to pick it apart. If some parties are particularly opposed to the rule and the agency chooses not to accommodate them in the final rule, this is the point at which full-on war can be waged.

Strategically Timing Final Rules

To strategically time rules, agencies must have information about the predispositions of political principals. While they cannot perfectly predict, agencies can anticipate when a political principal might be more or less likely to overturn a rule, or punish the agency in some other way. At the very least, they are able to discern when the present moment is so adverse as to make delaying for an uncertain future preferable. However, given that the forms of oversight are exercised differently among the branches, the types of information available to agencies about principals' preferences also varies.

With respect to the president, rulemaking oversight is direct and explicit. By the time the agency is gearing up to issue a final rule, the agency has a good sense about where OIRA stands on it. At the proposed rule stage, OIRA gave the agency feedback on the rule: either by declining to review the rule altogether or by choosing to review it and then waving it through or pushing back on the agency. This information provides the agency with

---

14. As Harris and Milkis (1989) explain, both agencies and their attendant interest groups often arise as the result of social movements. The implication for interest groups is that their influence is tied not to any one actor but rather to a network of actors.

insight into OIRA's position on the rule, and if that stance is less than favorable, then there should be no rush to send the rule back to the same hostile reviewers.

With respect to Congress, agencies have less specific information about key actors' positions on individual rules, because legislative oversight is driven by fire alarms rather than consistent, institutionalized interaction. However, while less precise than presidential oversight, partisan cues are a useful heuristic for how rules are likely to be received. While agencies themselves are not partisan, scholars agree that some agencies have a more liberal mission and others have a more conservative one. Accordingly, agencies with more liberal missions might proceed with greater caution when Republicans are relatively strong, and vice versa.

A similar logic regarding strategic timing applies to the courts. In some periods, based in part on the extent to which monitoring interest groups are litigious, the courts closely scrutinize agency behavior. At other times the courts are sleeping watchdogs. Being sued is a setback for an agency; agencies are rarely commended for their good behavior, but they can be heavily penalized.[15] Even if the agency has a strong case, litigation is costly and watchful courts may incentivize delay. As Jones and Taylor (1995, 333) note, "The mere threat of [lawsuits], due to their concomitant delays and increased workload and costs, may influence the [agency]'s decisionmaking before decisions are even made."

When the agency is repeatedly being hauled into the courtroom, it may move slower until the court's attentiveness diminishes or until groups bring suits less frequently. With a reduced pace, the agency can digest what is happening in the courts and pay greater attention to specific issues or new doctrines that may be emerging. If the courts are quiet, though, the agency can speed up the rulemaking process to capitalize on the current repose.

These expectations about each of the branches follow from the Strategic Timing Hypothesis; as the agency's rapport with a given principal diminishes, the agency is more likely to move slower on the rule. I now look for empirical evidence to evaluate this expectation.

Measuring Timing Effects

Using the data from the *Regulatory Proposals Dataset*, it is possible to evaluate how long it takes agencies to finalize rules—from the moment that the proposed rule is published to when the draft final rule leaves the agency. The

---

15. While agencies have a high affirmance rate in the courts, they by no means win every case (e.g., Mashaw and Harfst 1986).

analyses that follow explore the political determinants of the time it takes an agency in months to finalize a proposed rule. A key prediction of the ossification thesis is that the average time to issue a rule should be quite lengthy, a conjecture that—in aggregate—is borne out empirically.[16] As shown in figure 6.1, the median time for issuing a final rule is about one year (median = 11.0 months, s.d. = 15.5 months).

There is, however, considerable variation around the average time to finalization both within and across agencies, and this is where the political story comes in. For instance, even though they are both bureaus within the USDA, the Agricultural Marketing Service finalizes rules on average in about nine months, whereas the Forest Service typically takes slightly under two years. Some rules take just over a month to move from the proposed to the final stage. Others take much longer to finalize. In the period under study, the longest time to finalization came from a Food and Drug Administration rule that set good manufacturing practices for infant formula. It was proposed in 1996 and finalized in 2014 (205 months, or approximately seventeen years later). While this is an outlier, nearly 10 percent of the rules in the *Regulatory Proposals Dataset* took longer than three years to move from the proposed to the final stage. In other words, it is not out of the ordinary for an agency to have a rule in the queue for a long period of time—long enough to outlive congressional sessions and presidential administrations.

Existing theory, be it the ossification thesis or arguments based on agency design features, do not speak to this variation. Certainly, the possibility that pace may result from internal factors—and perhaps intentional foot-dragging or acceleration by the agency—is widely overlooked. Put differently, much of the literature has concentrated on the lengthy average time it takes to finalize a rule, but few have considered the variation around that mean, and specifically the idea that the variation might be strategic.[17]

16. This should not, however, be taken as "proof" that ossification exists, as a long completion time could arise from a variety of processes.

17. The idea that bureaucrats may consider the temporal dimension is not new, however; scholars have established the judicious use of timing by agencies in other contexts. For instance, Muehlenbachs, Sinha, and Sinha (2011) show how the Environmental Protection Agency is strategic when making announcements to the press. They find that the agency tends to announce environmental awards earlier in the week, whereas enforcement actions and regulatory changes tend to be announced on Fridays and before holidays. They argue that this is an explicit strategy on the part of the agency to bury adverse news in the weekend and holiday news cycles, when the items are less likely to receive public attention and scrutiny. In a similar vein, Gersen and O'Connell (2009) consider the timing of the publication of agency final rules. They find significant effects for the publication of significant final rules during congressional recesses, but less so for Friday publication of rules. And, of course, strategic timing undoubtedly affects

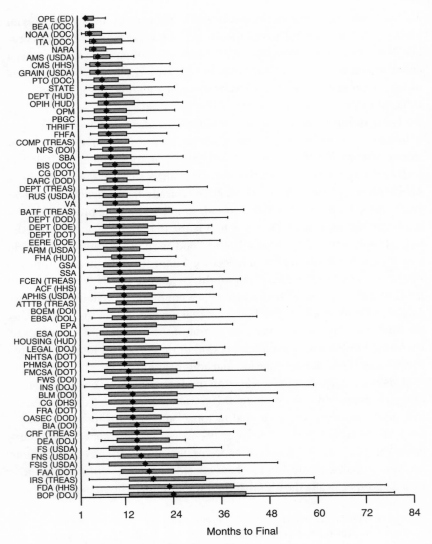

FIGURE 6.1. Time to rule finalization for select agencies, 1995–2014

Note: Solid diamonds indicate the median time to finalization for each bureau. Boxes indicate the 25%–75% range of the data and bars indicate the minimum and maximum values (excluding outliers). To aid visualization, only bureaus that produced at least 30 proposed rules during the time period under study are shown. Where appropriate, bureaus are listed with their respective department name in parentheses. See table A.1 in the data appendix for a complete listing of agency names and acronyms. Data from the *Regulatory Proposals Dataset*. Originally published in Potter (2017).

In assembling a regression model to test the Strategic Timing Hypothesis, I rely on the same covariates introduced in the previous chapter with one exception: a new measure of the level of presidential opposition to a particular rule that takes into account the rule's history at the proposal stage. As noted in previous chapters, the president enjoys a privileged position with respect to agency rulemaking; through OIRA the president's agents have the opportunity to review agency draft rules before they enter the public domain. I leverage this prior review and measure whether OIRA chose to review the proposed rule, and if so, how long that review lasted. Recent work suggests that OIRA reviews tend to last longer when OIRA and the agency disagree about the substance of the rule.[18] The result is a finer-grained measure of presidential opposition that is available for analyses only at the final rule stage.[19]

Technically, OIRA has ninety days to review an agency rule, but this standard is often not followed in practice. I rely on this variation to proxy for OIRA support or opposition to a particular rule. The variable *OIRA review time* counts every day that the proposed rule was under review at OIRA—this ranges from zero days (when OIRA declined to review the proposed rule altogether) to more than seven hundred days. Because of the skewed nature of the review length, I add one day and take the natural log of the number of days. Importantly, this review occurs before the clock starts, so it is not included in the "clock time" for the analysis.

Evaluating Strategic Timing

Because the object of interest in the analysis is the time to finalization for agency proposed rules, I rely on event history models. This approach is frequently used in medical studies to model how long a patient survives given some set of factors. The model estimates the hazard rate—usually the likeli-

---

policy makers' decisions in several other venues, including position-taking in Congress (Box-Steffensmeier, Arnold, and Zorn 1997), judges' decisions about when to retire (Spriggs and Wahlbeck 1995), and when local bureaucrats schedule elections (Meredith 2009).

18. See Bolton, Potter, and Thrower (2016); and Heinzerling (2014).

19. In chapters 4 and 5, I relied on a more blunt measure of ideological agreement between the president and the agency: *Unaligned president.* Although *OIRA review time* is a more refined measure of the level of disagreement between the agency and the president (since it is focused on the rule level), it would not have been appropriate to employ in the tests in those chapters, because OIRA review may directly affect an agency's choices about procedures relating to the proposed rule (i.e., writing and consultation). In particular, OIRA review may be correlated in systematic ways with rule readability in particular that are not related to the political argument I make. Nevertheless, the results I present in this chapter are robust to using *Unaligned president* in lieu of *OIRA review time.*

TABLE 6.1. Description of variables in the event history models

Variable	Expected effect on hazard rate	Time-varying?
OIRA review time (ln)	Negative	
Congressional opposition	Negative	Yes
Court cases	Negative	Yes
Group opposition		Yes
Impact		
Complexity		
Statutory deadline		
Judicial deadline		
Employees		Yes
Expertise		Yes

Note: "Negative" indicates that a negative coefficient is expected, which implies that the hazard rate is decreasing and the rule's expected duration is increasing. I provide sign expectations only for those variables for which there are clear theoretical predictions about the expected direction of the effect.

hood that the patient will die—at a particular point in time given a set of covariates about the patient that may be fixed across time (e.g., race) or time varying (e.g., weight). While "failure" in the prototypical medical event history model is the patient's death, in the present case failure is the finalization of the proposed rule. Specifically, the hazard rate in this case indicates the likelihood that the agency will finalize a proposed rule at time t. The unit of analysis is a rule-month, where each month that a rule remains unfinalized is an observation.

Event history models are particularly useful for this analysis because they can incorporate time-varying indicators.[20] Many models include one observation per case, typically measured at the initiation of a case and held constant for the duration of that case. Here the question of substantive interest is how agencies respond to changes in the political environment, meaning that I rely on several of the covariates to change during the course of each case. Table 6.1 lists the model variables, their expected effect on the hazard of finalization, and whether they are time varying or time invariant.

An important consideration when conducting an event history analysis of agency rule production is determining when the clock should start and when it should stop (i.e., when a rule should be considered proposed and when it should be considered finalized). While initially it may seem that the clock should start when the agency publishes a proposed rule in the *Federal Register* and stop when the final rule is published in the *Federal Register*, this approach

20. Additionally, the event history model takes into account proposed rules that were censored, meaning that they were started during the study's timeframe but remained unfinalized at the end of the period of observation.

ignores the role of OIRA review at the final rule stage. OIRA reviews a subset of what it deems to be the most important rules at the final rule stage and declines review for the remaining rules. The duration of this second OIRA review varies from just a few days to several months or longer.[21] Since the duration of this review is outside of the agency's control, I consider submission to OIRA to be the end of the agency's strategic timing efforts (for rules that OIRA reviews). In other words, I start the clock with the publication of the proposed rule and stop it when the final rule leaves the agency's control, either because OIRA selected it for review or, for rules that OIRA declined to review, because it was sent to the *Federal Register* for publication.[22]

Table 6A.1 in the appendix to this chapter presents the results of the event history analyses.[23] Table entries are Cox proportional hazard coefficients, where a positive coefficient means that the hazard rate is increasing and the rule's expected duration is decreasing (i.e., the rule will be published more quickly). A negative coefficient implies the converse: a decreasing hazard rate and an increase in expected duration (i.e., it will take longer for agency to finalize the rule). The models are stratified on the bureau, which allows the baseline hazard to vary for each bureau.[24]

The models consistently support the expectation that agencies avoid issuing rules when the political climate is less favorable. To understand the substantive magnitude of these effects, I plot the hazard ratio in figure 6.2. The dots in this figure indicate whether the key explanatory variables increase or decrease the probability of a rule being finalized in a given month.[25] The baseline for comparison is 1; a hazard ratio of 2 indicates that a one-unit in-

21. Bolton, Potter, and Thrower (2016).

22. Ideally, I would start the clock when the agency first put pen to paper to start working on a rule. Unfortunately, as I explained in chapter 2, this is not systematically recorded across agencies and rules. To the extent that the current setup misses these early stages of development, it biases against my findings, because agencies may delay at the early stages of the process rather than the later stages, when there is more public scrutiny.

23. Readers may note a slightly smaller sample size reported in table 6A.1 than in the models from chapter 5. This discrepancy owes to rules that were transferred to or merged with another RIN after the proposed rule stage. I drop these from the analysis here because it is not clear whether the "same" rule is being finalized in these cases.

24. In essence, stratification allows the researcher to control for unobserved bureau-specific factors. This is akin to including bureau fixed effects, although it does not produce bureau-level coefficients. For all models, robust standard errors clustered on the rule are included in parentheses. I also report the results of global chi-square tests of the proportional hazards assumption for each Cox model and am able to reject the null hypothesis of no violation.

25. More specifically, the points represent the estimated hazard ratio for each coefficient, and the horizontal lines denote 95 percent confidence intervals.

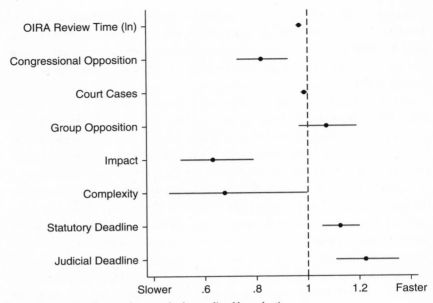

FIGURE 6.2. Finalization of proposed rules, predicted hazard ratios
Note: Hazard ratios from the basic model in table 6A.1 in the appendix to this chapter. Estimates with confidence intervals crossing the reference line at 1 are not statistically significant at the 95% level. Originally published in Potter (2017).

crease in the independent variable will make the rule two times more likely to be finalized in a month. A ratio of .5 suggests that a rule is half as likely to be finalized. As the probability of being finalized increases (decreases), rules are expected to proceed through the process more quickly (slowly).

The expectation with respect to the president is that if there was conflict between the agency and the president during OIRA's review of the proposed rule, progress toward finalizing the rule will be slower. The negative and statistically significant coefficient on the *OIRA review time* variable supports this proposition. While the magnitude of the hazard ratio seems small, this is an artifact of the logged variable. An unlogged specification (not shown) suggests this effect is substantively large: for every additional day of OIRA review, the risk of rule finalization in a given month falls by about 0.3 percent, meaning that an additional ten days of OIRA review is associated with a 3 percent reduction in the hazard of finalization in a particular month.

Agencies are also much slower to finalize rules when congressional opposition is relatively strong. Anticipation of a negative response from Congress slows the regulatory process; in a given month having strong congressional opposition (as compared to weak opposition) decreases the risk of finalization by 19 percent. The expectation regarding the courts is also borne out.

The coefficient for the *Court cases* variable is negative, as expected; although the hazard ratio appears small (HR = 0.98), this again should be considered in light of the unit. For every additional case that the agency has in the appellate court that month, the predicted incidence of rule finalization decreases by 1.2 percent.

As expected, the model indicates that there is no statistically significant relationship between *Group opposition* and the timing of rule finalization. *Impact* and *Complexity* are both associated with slower completion times. In a given month, the difference between the rule with the highest impact is associated with more than a one-third reduction in the risk of finalization; the most complex rule is also associated with a roughly one-third lower risk compared to the least complex rule.[26] These effects make sense since rules with a greater impact may require more consideration to complete, and rules that are more complex may require greater technical scrutiny, both of which require additional time.

The analysis also indicates that rulemaking deadlines are effective at prompting agencies to move more quickly. Compared to rules with no deadlines, a judicial deadline for issuing a final rule increases the hazard of issuing a final rule 22 percent, while a statutory deadline has about half that effect. These findings bolster previous work showing that deadlines influence which projects agencies consider priorities.[27] I reserve discussion of the effects of the capacity variables for a more in-depth exploration later in this chapter.

An agency's pacing strategy is, therefore, largely premised upon its relationship with each of its political overseers. As explained in chapter 3, I do not expect this relationship to be predicated on the agency's relationship with its interest group constituents (as it is with writing and consultation tools). Agencies cannot cool their heels with interest groups in the same way that they can with a principal. Interest group oversight is provided by networks of interest groups, meaning that shifts in interest group oversight are slow to occur. For instance, many groups such as the Sierra Club, the Natural Resources Defense Council, Earthjustice, and the National Wildlife Federation provide oversight of the Environmental Protection Agency (EPA). Should one group be unable to provide oversight, other groups could step up and carry the mantle. This logic applies to other context such as pharmaceutical companies and the Food and Drug Administration (FDA) and both employee and employer representatives and OSHA. Nevertheless, figure 6.3

26. Because these variables are scaled between 0 and 1, the hazard ratios can be interpreted as the difference in the effect moving from the minimum to the maximum value.

27. For example, see Gersen and O'Connell (2008); and MacDonald and McGrath (2016).

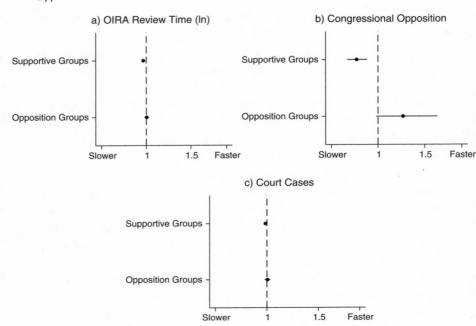

FIGURE 6.3. Conditional effects of *Group opposition*, predicted hazard ratios

Note: Hazard ratios from the conditional model in table 6A.1 in the appendix to this chapter. Estimates with confidence intervals crossing the reference line at 1 are not statistically significant at the 95% level.

explores the conditional relationship between *Group opposition* and the relative standing of each political principal. It shows the difference in pacing strategy between having an opposed principal and a supportive or opposed interest group constituency (see the conditional model in table 6A.1 for the associated model coefficients).

What emerges from the figure is that, when compared to having a supportive interest group constituency, having an opposed network of interest groups may compel agencies to speed up the rulemaking process. This relationship is apparent with respect to all three branches, although only substantively meaningful for the congressional variable. This congressional opposition effect suggests that agencies may be particularly concerned about groups activating congressional fire alarms. In particular, agencies may not want to cede additional time to opposed interest groups when that time that could be used to build a campaign against the agency's rule. Overall, the results shown in these two models indicate that the disposition of principals vis-à-vis the agency critically influences the agency's decision about how quickly or slowly to release the final rule.

Investigating the Mechanism behind Delay

Evidence of strategic behavior is notoriously elusive; what appears to be a smoking gun upon first inspection may turn out to be nothing more than smoke upon more careful consideration. With respect to regulatory pacing, it is not always easy to tell whether an agency is taking a long time because it is slow-rolling the current political regime or whether other more innocuous factors such as an authentic desire for information or consensus are producing delay. (The converse applies to rules that advance quickly through the process.)

Of course, this same ambiguity that frustrates researchers is also what allows procedural politicking to persist in the face of a naturally skeptical overseer. While my argument is that an agency's strategic calculations affect rule pacing, other pathways could plausibly lead to the same observed outcome. If I can safely "rule out" these alternate explanations, then confidence in the strategic calculations argument should increase accordingly. In this section, I do just this, looking for ways to both confirm the proposed mechanism and dispense with competing explanations.

One way to confirm that delay is strategic is to look at what happens when there are changes in OIRA leadership. The politically appointed OIRA administrator is replaced with some frequency within presidential administrations; Presidents Clinton, Bush, and Obama each had at least two OIRA administrators, with turnover occurring at irregular intervals. Each new administrator brings a fresh perspective to regulatory review. This holds even within the same presidential administration.[28] For instance, the two OIRA administrators who served under President Obama emphasized different issues and exercised distinct leadership styles. Cass Sunstein, who held the post first, was a renowned law professor who had taught alongside Obama at the University of Chicago. According to his own account of his time as OIRA administrator, Sunstein focused on behavioral economics and "nudges" (Sunstein 2013b). Sunstein was followed by Howard Shelanski, a lawyer and PhD economist, who came to the post after serving as the director of the Federal Trade Commission's Bureau of Economics. Shelanski emphasized timely re-

---

28. Another way to think about this is to note that no OIRA administrator perfectly matches the president's own preferences for regulatory review. The administrator position is highly specialized, and very few individuals are qualified, willing, and Senate confirmable. This means that presidents do not have an unlimited pool of individuals from which to select, and there is inevitably some amount of preference mismatch.

view of regulations and regulatory lookbacks, which involves removing out-dated or ineffective regulations from the books.[29]

This pattern of different emphases by the OIRA administrator, is not con-fined to the Obama administration. An examination of OIRA review times from the Reagan administration to Obama administration also supports the notion that each OIRA administrator brings his or her own "style" to review. Review of both proposed and final rules was quickest under the leadership of Chris DeMuth (Reagan appointee, 1981–1984) and slowest under James Miller (also a Reagan appointee, 1981). Following the changes to review in-stituted by Executive Order 12,866, review was quickest under Sally Katzen (Clinton appointee, 1993–1998), and slowest under John Spotila (also a Clin-ton appointee, 1999–2000). It is telling that the bookends of the variation in review time occurred within presidential administrations.

If agencies are indeed strategically timing rules, they should respond to these changes in OIRA leadership, since a new administrator may prioritize different issues in review or prioritize different agencies. This, in turn, can enhance or detract from a rule's prospects for successful finalization. Return-ing to the Obama appointees, a rule that was disfavored by Sunstein's OIRA at the proposed rule stage might have received different treatment at the fi-nal rule stage if Shelanski was at the helm, given his different leadership pri-orities. It follows, then, that having a new OIRA administrator may wipe the slate clean. Put differently, for rules that were the source of tension between the agency and OIRA at the proposed rule stage, agencies should speed up the process when there is a new (proverbial) sheriff in town. However, the agency should slow down if it faces the same leadership (again, presuming an adversarial review at the proposed rule stage), since there should be no rush to return for another hostile round of review.

To test this supposition, I create a time-varying indicator variable, *Same administrator*, which takes a value of 1 during months when the same OIRA administrator that reviewed the proposed rule is in charge, and 0 after a new administrator takes office. I then interact *Same administrator* with *OIRA review time*. The expectation is that a new administrator will lead to a break from whatever the prior reviewing regime offered (either a positive or negative review in expectation), whereas no change in the OIRA leadership suggests that the agency should anticipate the same treatment it received at the proposed rule stage to occur again.

---

29. Media accounts often highlighted the differences in the two leaders' background and how these differences presumably translated into divergent regulatory preferences. See NYU Law (2013); Weatherford (2013); and Yehle and Bravender (2014).

I present the results of this estimation in figure 6.4,[30] which plots the survival probabilities for a rule under three scenarios of conflict with OIRA: a low (10 days), medium (78 days), and high (180 days) level of OIRA review, for the same administrator that reviewed the proposed rule and for a new OIRA administrator.

Looking at figure 6.4A, the survival probability (i.e., the risk of a rule not being finalized) is consistently higher for a rule when a new OIRA administrator takes office. An OIRA review of ten days is quite short—considerably less than the ninety days allotted in the governing order (Executive Order 12,866)—suggesting that OIRA gave the proposed rule preferable treatment with an expeditious review. Figure 6.4A shows that agencies are much more likely to try to lock in that favorable treatment when facing the same OIRA administrator. Figure 6.4B shows the mean OIRA review time (seventy-eight days). Here, there is no appreciable difference between having an administrator change. The agency is no more and no less likely to finalize a rule given a change in OIRA leadership if it received the "standard treatment" at the proposed rule stage. Figure 6.4C shows the results for a rule that received an above-average review time of 180 days at the proposed rule stage. The opposite pattern from the first panel emerges; when a new administrator is in place the agency is much more likely to finalize the rule. The probability of surviving is higher for these high-conflict rules when the same administrator who reviewed the proposed rule is still in office. Put differently, agencies use the information they have about OIRA leadership and their position toward a specific rule to inform pacing strategies.

These figures, which offer a more refined test of the theory, reinforce that strategic delay is the root driver of the findings presented earlier. More specifically, the graphs show that the preferences of OIRA at the proposed rule stage—and whether they hold for the current regime—affect when an agency chooses to finalize a rule. If agencies expect favorable treatment from the current regime, they fast-track the rule (figure 6.4A), but if they expect unfavorable treatment, they are more likely to slow-roll (figure 6.4C).

Despite this affirmation, it is important to rule out other rival mechanisms that might also explain these observations about regulatory pacing.

30. See the OIRA model in table 6A.2 in the appendix to this chapter for the model estimates from this analysis. The coefficient on the interaction term is negative and statistically significant, suggesting that having a new OIRA administrator leads to a change in regulatory pace. Some of this effect undoubtedly owes to new presidential administrations. However, the inclusion of presidential administration fixed effects in the model suggests that much of this boost is attributable to having a new OIRA administrator.

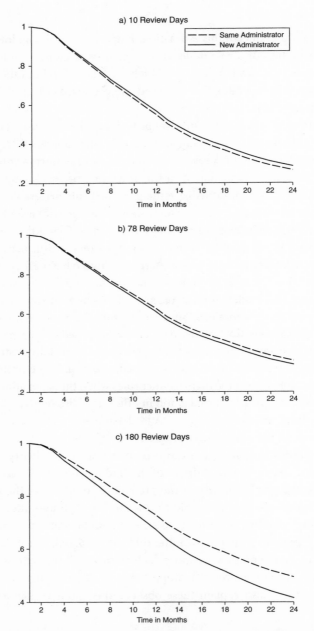

FIGURE 6.4. Probability of rules surviving to finalization under the same and different OIRA administrators

Note: Survival probabilities for a final rule for which OIRA gave a quick review of the proposed rule (10 days), average review time (78 days), and a relatively long review time (180 days) for rules that have the same OIRA administrator who reviewed the proposed rule (dashed line) or a new OIRA administrator (solid line). For model specification, see the OIRA Model in table 6A.2 in the appendix to this chapter. Probabilities were generated using an unlogged *OIRA review time* to ease interpretation. Continuous variables held at their mean and dichotomous variables held at their modal values. Originally published in Potter (2017).

One possibility is that delay in the rulemaking process could be "sincere delay," meaning that agencies work harder to get the policy right when they face an opposed principal.[31] So, rather than delay serving as an attempt to sidestep political oversight, sincere delay posits that when agencies are constrained by the political environment, they respond by working harder to please principals (e.g., by improving analyses). To distinguish between strategic and sincere delay, I interact *Complexity* with each of the three key political variables. If agencies are sincerely delaying, I anticipate that under political adversity agencies should take longer—and be less likely to finalize—the rules that are the most difficult. Complex policies require more effort, and if agencies are sincerely delaying, they should redouble efforts to "get hard policies right" when they expect serious scrutiny of their work. Put differently, if delay is primarily about improving quality, then complex rules should be the most delayed because improving their quality will take the most effort.

Although I reserve the results for the appendix to this chapter (see the second model in table 6A.2), the short version is that there is no support for the mechanism of sincere delay.[32] Of course, empirically detangling strategic delay from sincere delay is not perfectly straightforward, and while these results are not dispositive, they suggest that sincere delay is not systematically occurring across the sample of rules. This does not imply that quality improvements never occur but rather that they are not the primary driver of the observed variation in timing.

Resource shortages could also plausibly drive delays in rulemaking. Shortages can affect an agency's capacity and, in turn, its performance.[33] This is

31. A related possibility is that the observed delay could result from agencies using the additional time to learn about the preferences of political principals and adjust the rule accordingly. While empirically distinguishing between these possibilities is not clear cut, the idea that agencies are consistently changing proposed rules to suit principals is out of step with a key empirical finding in the literature. Numerous studies find that agencies make very few changes as a rule moves from the proposed to the final stage (e.g., Heinzerling 2014; Wagner, Barnes, and Peters 2011; West 2004, 2009). This literature points to the "prerule" stage as the time when agencies invest in quality and settle on policy content, and not to the publicly observable portions of the process that are the focus of the analysis here.

32. In other words, there is no statistical evidence of a significant interactive effect between any of the political variables and the complexity term.

33. This is a hard test. Given the time lags associated with decisions about budgets and personnel matters (e.g., hiring freezes) in the American system, it is an unlikely that resources can respond in real time to the political alignment of actors. Nevertheless, I consider this argument empirically and test for whether resource capacity issues underlie the results.

consistent with what is known as a "resource-based" view of organizational management.[34] The idea is that having certain resources can give a firm, or in this case an agency, a competitive edge in terms of performance. Likewise, resource deficits are understood to have a deleterious effect on performance. Since resource shortages are par for the course in bureaucratic agencies— agencies rarely have enough time, money, or personnel to accomplish all of their objectives—this could potentially explain many delays in the regulatory process.

With regard to regulatory pacing, there are two avenues by which resource shortages might lead to an outcome where agencies adjust the pace of rule-making in response to the political environment. First, political principals control an agency's resources, including authority over budget, personnel, and infrastructure decisions. Given this power, principals may reduce agency resources precisely when they are at ideological odds with an agency. In this instance, resource deficits—and not the agency's strategic calculations— might be the force behind observed delay.

Additionally, capacity deficits at OIRA, which serves a gatekeeping role for executive branch agencies, could potentially slow the pace of rulemaking. OIRA's capacity has waxed and waned across time, and when its capacity is lower, the office reviews fewer rules and takes longer to review the rules that it does bring in.[35] Limits on OIRA's capacity may disproportionately affect agencies the office is at odds with, since OIRA may deprioritize its rules. Even though OIRA review of the final rule is not included in the clock time in the prior analyses, agencies may anticipate how OIRA's diminished capacity would affect their rules and slow production accordingly. This could lead to delay occurring when the president is not ideologically aligned with the agency, although the underlying cause would be different.

To explore any potential impacts of the first type of resource constraint, I analyze the two capacity variables—*Employment* and *Expertise*—that have been included in the empirical models throughout this book. To account for variation in OIRA's resources, I add a measure of that office's capacity; *OIRA FTE* is the number of full-time-equivalent employees (FTEs) in OIRA in a year.[36] OIRA's capacity is lower when it has fewer employees on staff, as each "desk officer" (i.e., the OIRA employee who reviews an agency's rules) is responsible for a greater number of regulatory reviews.

34. See Barney and Clark (2007); Lee and Whitford (2012); Pfeffer and Salancik (2003); and Wernerfelt (1984).

35. Bolton, Potter, and Thrower (2016).

36. This measure is from Bolton, Potter, and Thrower (2016).

As it turns out, while capacity constraints at the agency producing the rule or at OIRA are theoretically plausible explanations for delay, there is little evidence that they matter in practice. The results of this test are presented in figure 6.5; table 6A.3 in the appendix to this chapter presents the capacity model, which includes the two standard capacity measures as well as the *OIRA FTE* variable. What stands out in the figure is that *Expertise* has a large effect on the hazard of rule finalization, suggesting that when an agency's staff is more familiar with the workflow and pathways of the agency (and perhaps the department), rules can move through at a faster clip. Specifically, moving from the least to the most expert staff (measured by the proportion of the agency's staff who have been there five years or more) is associated with a predicted incidence of rule finalization of 37 percent. While this is a large effect, it is worth noting that it is not statistically significant at conventional levels ($p = 0.11$), so some caution is warranted. Neither of the other two capacity variables, *OIRA FTE* or *Employment*, has a statistically distinguishable effect on the hazard of rule finalization. Overall, these results suggest that resource capacity issues—whether they be at the agency itself or at OIRA—do not systematically dictate how quickly agencies finalize rules. Importantly, the inclusion (or exclusion) of these capacity variables does not change the core

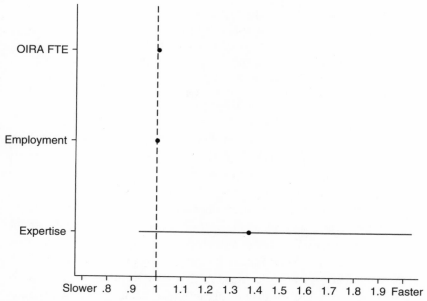

FIGURE 6.5. Predicted hazard ratios including resource capacity

Note: Hazard ratios from the capacity model in table 6A.3 in the appendix to this chapter. Estimates with confidence intervals crossing the reference line at 1 are not statistically significant at the 95% level.

results about the political environment—agencies still respond to opposition by principals by slow-rolling. This suggests that there is little evidence that agencies move slowly in response to capacity deficits, and certainly nothing that would displace the political explanation for variations in timing.

Overall, then, there is little systematic evidence to suggest that the observed delays are sincere rather than strategic or that they are driven by capacity factors (either at the agency or at OIRA). These are the primary alternatives to procedural politicking and ruling them out should increase confidence that strategic delay—or more specifically, slow-rolling and fast-tracking—is doing the work when it comes to regulatory pacing. Finally, observing the changes in timing behavior with the addition of a new OIRA leader further reinforces the argument for a strategic mechanism.

Summary

Ossification and its attendant procedural hurdles have long been held up as the root cause for regulatory delay. Returning to the OSHA cranes and derricks rule that introduced this chapter, observers were quick to blame a slow and creaky bureaucracy. For instance, in explaining why the rule took so long, one public interest group highlighted OSHA's procedural rigmarole:

> OSHA was required by a hodgepodge of federal laws, regulations and executive orders to produce several comprehensive reports, and revisions to such reports, on matters such as the makeup of industries affected by the rule, the number of businesses affected, and the costs and benefits of the rule. OSHA also was repeatedly required to prove that the rule was needed, that no alternative could work, and that it had done everything it could to minimize the effects on small businesses.[37]

Ossification is a convenient scapegoat; few would disagree with the statement that rulemaking procedures are onerous. Yet not all rules or all agencies are slowed by procedures, and if left uninterrogated, ossification actually camouflages strategic political behavior.

In this chapter, I considered whether strategic political calculations by agency bureaucrats play a role in the pace of rulemaking. Consistent with the theoretical expectations developed in chapter 3, I found that agencies have considerable mastery over timing in the rulemaking process. With respect to all three branches, the evidence suggests that agencies do fast-track or slow-roll rules. An event history analysis of more than ten thousand agency rules

---

37. Lincoln and Mouzoon (2011, 4).

from the *Regulatory Proposals Dataset* showed that rules take longer to finalize when OIRA and the agency do not agree on the proposed rule, when the
agency faces strong opposition from Congress, and when the agency is more
frequently before the courts. In other words, timing is a tool that is attractive
for agencies with respect to all three branches.

While these results indicate systematic timing effects, I found further evidence of procedural politicking when the agency faces a new OIRA administrator. Here, timing speeds up or slows down depending on whether the
new leadership is likely to help or hurt a rule's prospects. Finally, I considered
two interpretations for delay that might point in different directions. First, I
considered whether agencies simply work harder when faced with political
opposition. Second, I looked for evidence of whether resource shortages, at
either the agency or OIRA, might lead agencies to move slower in the presence of ideological discord. In both cases, the evidence supports a mechanism of strategic rather than sincere delay.

The analysis in this chapter uncovered strategic timing patterns that persist across a broad set of agencies and rules. While this evidence is consistent
with the procedural politicking theory, it necessarily glosses over the nuances
of how decisions about procedural strategies are made within agencies or
how these decisions play out with respect to individual rules. In the next
chapter, I investigate these nuances in a deeper account of how the Food and
Drug Administration employed numerous procedural tactics in the case of
one controversial rulemaking.

Appendix to Chapter 6

TABLE 6A.1. Cox proportional hazard models of time to rule finalization

	Expected sign	Basic model	Conditional model
OIRA review time (ln)	−	−0.033***	−0.035***
		(0.006)	(0.008)
Group opposition × *OIRA review time* (ln)			0.004
			(0.013)
Congressional opposition	−	−0.200**	−0.263***
		(0.062)	(0.072)
Group opposition × *Congressional opposition*			0.238
			(0.131)
Court cases	−	−0.014*	−0.014*
		(0.006)	(0.007)
Group opposition × *Court cases*			0.006
			(0.014)
Group opposition		0.070	−0.210
		(0.053)	(0.159)
Impact		−0.461***	−0.455***
		(0.114)	(0.114)
Complexity		−0.391*	−0.385
		(0.198)	(0.198)
Statutory deadline		0.118***	0.118***
		(0.033)	(0.033)
Judicial deadline		0.202***	0.201***
		(0.051)	(0.051)
Employment		0.002	0.002
		(0.001)	(0.001)
Expertise		0.363	0.382
		(0.198)	(0.199)
Presidential administration controls		Yes	Yes
Bureau-level stratification		Yes	Yes
Number of rules		10,908	10,908
Number of observations		202,068	202,068
Proportional hazards test		0.59	0.71

Note: Table entries are coefficients obtained from proportional Cox models stratified at the bureau level. Robust standard errors clustered on the rule are in parentheses.

*p < 0.05. **p < 0.01. ***p < 0.001.

TABLE 6A.2. Cox proportional hazard models of alternate pacing mechanisms

	OIRA model	Complexity model
OIRA review time (ln)	−0.019*	−0.049**
	(0.009)	(0.018)
Same administrator × OIRA review time (ln)	−0.025*	
	(0.011)	
OIRA review time (ln) × Complexity		0.084
		(0.092)
Congressional opposition	−0.178**	−0.382*
	(0.063)	(0.190)
Congressional opposition × Complexity		0.965
		(0.950)
Court cases	−0.015*	−0.012
	(0.006)	(0.015)
Court cases × Complexity		−0.007
		(0.072)
Same administrator	0.071**	
	(0.026)	
Group opposition	0.062	0.069
	(0.053)	(0.053)
Impact	−0.444***	−0.463***
	(0.114)	(0.114)
Complexity	−0.406*	−1.465
	(0.198)	(1.045)
Statutory deadline	0.118***	0.118***
	(0.033)	(0.033)
Judicial deadline	0.202***	0.201***
	(0.051)	(0.051)
Employment	0.002	0.002
	(0.001)	(0.001)
Expertise	0.326	0.358
	(0.199)	(0.198)
Presidential administration controls	Yes	Yes
Bureau-level stratification	Yes	Yes
Number of rules	10,908	10,908
Number of observations	202,068	202,068
Proportional hazards test	0.82	0.79

Note: Table entries are coefficients obtained from proportional Cox models stratified at the bureau level. Robust standard errors clustered on the rule are in parentheses. The OIRA model shows the effects of a new OIRA administrator on regulatory pacing. The complexity model examines the conditional effect of complexity on regulatory pacing to assess an alternate mechanism based on sincere delay.

*$p < 0.05$. **$p < 0.01$. ***$p < 0.001$.

TABLE 6A.3. Cox proportional hazard models of resource capacity on regulatory pacing

	Capacity model
OIRA FTE	0.006
	(0.004)
OIRA review time (ln)	−0.033***
	(0.006)
Congressional opposition	−0.201**
	(0.062)
Court cases	−0.013*
	(0.006)
Group opposition	0.086
	(0.055)
Impact	−0.454***
	(0.114)
Complexity	−0.391*
	(0.198)
Statutory deadline	0.118***
	(0.033)
Judicial deadline	0.201***
	(0.051)
Employment	0.002
	(0.001)
Expertise	0.318
	(0.200)
Presidential administration controls	Yes
Bureau-level stratification	Yes
Number of rules	10,908
Number of observations	202,068
Proportional hazards test	0.67

Note: Table entries are coefficients obtained from proportional Cox models stratified at the bureau level. Robust standard errors clustered on the rule are in parentheses.

*p < 0.05. **p < 0.01. ***p < 0.001.

7

The Case of Menu Labeling

Up until this point in the book, I have employed an aggregate, broad-brush approach to studying procedural politicking that favors generalizability over mechanisms and processes. In chapter 3, I developed theoretical expectations about how agencies use procedural powers to insulate rules that are at political risk. And in chapters 4, 5, and 6, I showed how a host of tools are used across a wide range of agencies and a large set of rules. This approach uncovered systematic patterns baked into the notice-and-comment process that are consistent with widespread procedural politicking.

This chapter considers these tools in detail in the context of one specific rulemaking case to clarify how procedural politicking actually works in practice. I examine a rule written by the Food and Drug Administration (FDA) in response to a mandate in the Patient Protection and Affordable Care Act of 2010 (ACA).[1] The rule required chain restaurants and other food establishments to display nutrition information on their menu boards. It was controversial, demanding conscientiousness on the part of the FDA's rule drafters throughout the process. To build an evidence base for this case, I rely on both primary sources (*Federal Register* documents, FDA records, and congressional hearings) and secondary sources (news accounts and blog posts about the rule), as well interviews with current and former FDA officials, local health officials, representatives from public health organizations, and conversations with those involved in the food and restaurant industry.[2]

---

1. Pub. L. No. 111-148.

2. To encourage candid discussions, I agreed with each of my interview subjects that I would not identify them by their name or their organization. Instead, I provide a general statement of the subject's organizational affiliation (e.g., restaurant industry) and the month and year in

The story of the menu labeling rule clearly reveals how rulemaking can be managed strategically to achieve policy ends. I begin this chapter with an introduction to the concept of menu labeling and then offer an overview of how the process unfolded, from the ACA's mandate to a binding FDA final rule. Next, I analyze the agency's procedural management of the rule from a strategic perspective. Finally, I consider whether we can consider the final menu labeling policy to be representative of the agency's broader policy goals.

Connecting to Theory

Menu labeling is an example of a salient rule issued in a contentious political environment. That is, it was both high impact and high complexity, and a case in which key political actors were deeply opposed to the agency's actions.

An in-depth exploration of this case clarifies how the tools described in the previous chapters play out in a specific context. This establishes mechanisms and makes concrete procedural tactics that might otherwise remain abstract. That is, in the context of the menu labeling rule, it becomes clear how procedural decisions are made in light of political realities on the ground. Because the aggregate analyses in the last three chapters did not consider all of the procedural strategies laid out in chapter 3 (e.g., there is no test of proposal framing), this case study is also useful in that it allows for a qualitative exploration of a fuller set of procedural tools than those that were quantitatively assessed.

Additionally, a case study allows for consideration of a critically important aspect of the theory that has so far gone unaddressed: how the strategies that agencies engage in when promulgating a rule connect to policy outcomes. That is, I have empirically demonstrated that agencies employ procedural tactics when managing the rulemaking process, but the idea that these strategies translate into the agency being able to secure preferred outcomes has been assumed rather than materially established. In the context of menu labeling, I trace the evolution of the policy through the rulemaking process and connect the dots from the tactics employed during the rule's development to the final menu labeling policy outcome.

Of course, relying on a case study also has drawbacks, which are worth acknowledging in full. First, the menu labeling rule transpired exactly once;

---

which the interview was conducted. These were informal conversations, typically between thirty and sixty minutes in length, designed to understand each participant's experiences with the rule and their perceptions about what happened at critical stages of the process. Their purpose in this study is to add depth and illustration.

I cannot observe a counterfactual case where the FDA pursued a different set of strategies in light of the same political constraints or where the rule proceeded in a different political context. Nor can I consider how a different agency, like the Occupational Safety and Health Administration or the Animal and Plant Health Inspection Service, might have approached a similarly controversial rule. This means that, strictly speaking, this case study rests firmly in the realm of an illustration of the theory, as opposed to an empirical test of it. Second, as will become clear, the menu labeling rule was high profile and contentious. This confers two advantages: (1) it makes it easier to observe how the case was handled (i.e., there was abundant news coverage of the rule), and (2) theoretically, we can expect that agencies engage in more careful consideration of procedural decisions when the policy at hand carries greater weight. However, the downside of studying a high-profile rule like this one is that the lessons extracted from the analysis may not extend to less salient rules.

Menu Labeling as a Policy Solution

By the dawn of the new millennium, obesity in the United States had reached crisis proportions, to the point that more than one-third of American adults were obese.[3] To address this public health epidemic, policy makers across the country implemented a panoply of programs, ranging from bans on vending machines in schools to a requirement that packaged foods disclose the amount of trans fat they contained. At the state and local levels, numerous jurisdictions began instituting requirements that restaurants provide nutrition information on their menus on the theory that providing consumers with information about nutritional content (e.g., calories, fat grams) would encourage healthier choices.[4]

New York was the first large city to adopt a menu labeling ordinance in 2006, but other cities and states followed suit in fairly short order as the policy diffused across the country. As figure 7.1 shows, by April 2011 numerous states and localities had adopted or were considering adoption of a menu labeling policy.

Because each locale formulated its own its menu labeling policy, restau-

---

3. Centers for Disease Control and Prevention (2014).

4. This approach is based on the behavioral economics theory of "nudging" consumers to make better choices (Sunstein 2013b; Thaler and Sunstein 2008) and can be traced back to ideas about using information disclosure as a form of regulation, particularly in the environmental, health, and finance arenas (see, e.g., Kraft, Stephan, and Abel 2011; Sage 1999).

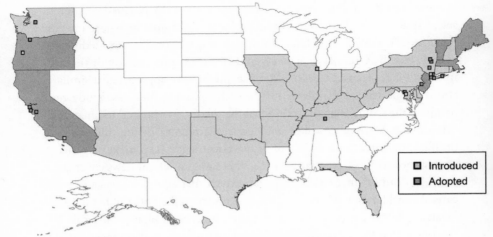

FIGURE 7.1. Map of state and local menu labeling policies as of April 2011
Note: Adapted from the Center for Science in the Public Interest. Squares indicate counties and cities that had, respectively, introduced (light shading) or adopted (dark shading) menu labeling policies as of April 2011. Counties shown: Albany County, NY; Davidson County, TN; King County, WA; Lane County, OR; Los Angeles County, CA; Montgomery County, MD; Multnomah County, OR; Nassau County, NY; Rockland County, NY; San Mateo County, CA; Santa Clara County, CA; Suffolk County, NY; Ulster County, NY; Westchester County, NY. Cities shown: New York, Philadelphia, San Francisco, and Washington, DC.

rants with a national presence rapidly began running into compliance problems. For instance, the State of California required chain restaurants with twenty or more locations to display calorie information but not other nutritional facts. The state's menu labeling law excluded alcoholic beverages and self-service buffet items. Meanwhile, Philadelphia, which had the toughest menu labeling law in the country, applied menu labeling to a lower threshold (fifteen or more establishments). The city's policy covered alcohol and buffet items, and required disclosure of nutritional information beyond calories (saturated fat, trans fat, carbohydrates, and sodium).[5] As one restaurant industry official described the problem: "We can't keep up with the patchwork of 17 different laws and have 17 different versions of calorie-labeled menu boards. This is ridiculous. We all agree that chain restaurants should be disclosing nutrition information to customers. Let's get a federal law out there that says all chain restaurants, 20 units or more, have to provide nutrition information to their customers."[6]

Because of the costs associated with complying with so many different

5. Menu labeling facts from Center for Science in the Public Interest (2011).
6. Interview with restaurant industry official, Apr. 2013.

laws, restaurants and other food groups began lobbying Congress to enact a national menu labeling standard that would preempt state and local laws. The National Restaurant Association (NRA) spearheaded the charge.[7]

Meanwhile, at the same time that menu labeling was becoming a national issue, a larger debate over how to reform America's broken health-care system was taking place on the national stage.[8] By late 2009, menu labeling discussions had been ongoing on Capitol Hill for several years.[9] When a viable health-care bill materialized—what would eventually become the Affordable Care Act—it presented a convenient legislative vehicle for menu labeling.[10] Because the White House was preoccupied with other issues related to the law's passage (and was fairly ambivalent about whether menu labeling would stay in the final bill), Senator Tom Harkin (D-IA) became the policy's champion.[11]

As a consequence of Harkin's efforts, when the ACA was signed into law in March 2010, it included a requirement that the FDA issue rules to set a national menu labeling standard to supplant the existing patchwork of state and local laws.[12] The ACA was a landmark legislative enactment—President Obama's chief domestic achievement in fact—and menu labeling was one of dozens of issues addressed in the law; only 9 of the 2,409 pages of the enrolled bill dealt with menu labeling.

The legislative language in the ACA sketched only a basic outline of the menu labeling policy. First, the rule should apply to all chain restaurants with twenty or more outlets and to "similar retail food establishments."[13] Second, it should require restaurants to disclose nutrition information on their menu boards (including drive-through menu boards). And third, restaurants should determine calorie counts according to the FDA's existing "reasonable

7. Picket (2013).

8. For a thorough discussion of the debates surrounding health-care reform in the lead-up to the passage of the ACA, see Jacobs and Skocpol (2012); and *Washington Post* (2010).

9. However, as Kessler (2001, 67–71) notes, the FDA had considered including restaurant menu labeling when it adopted package labeling in the early 1990s. At the time, menu labeling was set aside as too ambitious.

10. See Schulman (2010) and Stein (2011) for a background on menu labeling before the ACA.

11. Interview with public health advocate, July 2016.

12. See § 4205 of the ACA.

13. One interviewee noted that she thought Congress had been intentionally vague regarding which other retail food establishments should be subject to menu labeling, because members understood that this would be a sticking point. Essentially, the legislature delegated this controversy to the FDA to sort out (interview with public health advocate, July 2016).

basis" standard for determining nutrition information.[14] However, aside from these broad confines (and as is often the case with statutorily mandated rules), the law charged the FDA with determining how menu labeling would work in practice.

The FDA Tackles Menu Labeling

The FDA is considered by many to be the world's preeminent pharmaceutical regulator.[15] This reputation has been cemented through the establishment and maintenance of its scientific, multiphase drug approval process. However, beginning with then Commissioner David Kessler's efforts in the 1990s to improve nutrition labels for packaged foods and to regulate tobacco sales, the agency's role as a public health advocate has become increasingly central to its organizational reputation.

When the ACA directed the FDA to take on menu labeling, it represented a new public health foray for the agency, as it does not typically regulate restaurants. As Commissioner Margaret Hamburg would later publicly state, it was one of the thorniest issues the agency had ever encountered.[16] The law was silent on a number of issues that would prove to be major sticking points with powerful interests. For example, how would the agency handle the variability associated with different types of food establishments, such as pizza delivery restaurants, bowling alleys, carnivals, and airplanes? Would the FDA extend its current honor-system approach for package labeling to menu labeling, or would there be a more formal enforcement mechanism? How much flexibility would the agency allow restaurants with respect to the presentation of nutrition information? Would alternate forms of compliance (e.g., posting nutrition information online or on an interactive tool next to the menu board) satisfy the requirement?

From a policy perspective, developing a federal menu labeling policy should have been relatively straightforward. The "laboratories of democracy" had provided ample case evidence, as numerous states and localities had already adopted the policy and, theoretically, the agency could readily select

14. Notably, § 4205 of the ACA also directs the FDA to issue rules on labeling for vending machines. Although menu labeling and vending machine labeling were issued as separate rules, much of the FDA's work on vending machine labeling overlapped with its work on menu labeling. I focus on menu labeling here because it was a much bigger and more contentious issue than vending machine labeling.

15. See Carpenter (2010).

16. Associated Press (2013).

from among these tried-and-true options. Additionally, several officials at the FDA had worked closely with New York City officials when that city had adopted its menu labeling policy back in 2006.

Politically, however, the agency was in a tough position. The White House was decidedly lukewarm about the rule. On the one hand, menu labeling was just the sort of policy "nudge" that the Obama administration tended to favor. Additionally, menu labeling was aimed at obesity reduction, First Lady Michelle Obama's chief policy priority. On the other hand, the administration—and HHS in particular—was overwhelmed with the implementation of Obamacare, and menu labeling was not a top priority.[17] Moreover, some aides, including Nancy-Ann DeParle, Obama's health-care czar, worried that too strong a menu labeling policy could wind up being lampooned on cable news.[18] Meanwhile, Republicans had gained sixty House seats in the 2010 midterm elections and had taken aim at many ACA-related regulations, including menu labeling. This meant that some in Congress favored a weak rule—or no rule at all. In other words, key players were divided on how they FDA should proceed, and the agency's task was to navigate this political minefield.

The path that the agency followed was circuitous. It began with the publication of a *Federal Register* notice in July 2010, less than four months after the law's passage, which established an open docket where interested parties could submit comments on twenty-six open-ended questions on how the agency should implement menu labeling. As one FDA official put it, the agency did this in order to "ask basic questions about things because quite frankly we [had not] really worked with restaurants that much so this was somewhat new to us on how they do things."[19]

The following month, the FDA released a guidance document explaining how firms could comply with the menu labeling requirement before the rulemaking process was completed. After all, section 4205 took effect immediately upon passage of the ACA, and the FDA needed to clarify to which establishments the law applied and whether the agency would conduct any enforcement prior to completing the rulemaking process (it would not). The guidance was ambitious, suggesting that the policy would apply to a broad set of entities (e.g., movie theaters, grocery stores, airplanes) and types of

17. Interview with public health advocate, July 2016.

18. See Harris (2012) and Nestle (2013). This was after all, the era of Fox News and the heyday of Glenn Beck.

19. Interview with agency official, May 2013.

food (e.g., alcohol). The agency also indicated that it intended to publish final guidance four months later, in December 2010.[20] That final guidance never came, and in January 2011 the FDA withdrew the draft guidance, stating that it would instead proceed apace with the notice-and-comment rulemaking process. The agency cited "extensive comments on the draft guidance" and the need to "minimize uncertainty and confusion among all interested persons" as reasons for changing course.[21]

When the agency eventually published the proposed rule in April 2011[22]— nearly three weeks after the statutory deadline for issuing it had passed—it took strong positions on all the key issues, diverging in several areas from its earlier position in the now-withdrawn guidance. The proposed rule followed the honor-system framework associated with package labeling, meaning that the FDA would establish regulatory standards for menu labeling but would not validate the quality of the nutritional information provided.[23] Further, the proposed rule excluded establishments whose "primary purpose" was something other than food sales.[24] The proposed definition therefore excluded movie theaters, bowling alleys, carnivals, and airplanes (all of which had been covered by the guidance) but included the sale of prepared food at supermarkets. To address the issue of custom orders, the agency would allow restaurants to provide calorie ranges with lower and upper bounds for all possible variations of a particular order. Finally, the information would have to be printed on the menu board; websites, smartphone apps, and other technologies would not be acceptable substitutes.

The response to the proposed rule was mixed. Public health groups lauded the FDA's approach but felt that the agency could have gone farther by including more food venues. The National Restaurant Association, the organization that originally lobbied Congress for a unified federal standard, supported the FDA's rule and actually encouraged the agency to include a broader number of establishments in the final rule. As some commentators have noted the NRA's intent may have been to level the playing field between

20. As I explain later in this chapter, the FDA's decision to release guidance this early in the process is helpful in an analytical sense; it represents the agency's unvarnished take on what a good menu labeling policy should look like.

21. 76 FR 4360; Jan. 25, 2011.

22. 76 FR 19192; Apr. 6, 2011.

23. Neistat (2013).

24. The proposed rule defined an establishment's "primary purpose" according to whether 50 percent or more of a retailer's floor space was devoted to food sales or whether the establishment presented itself publicly (e.g., in marketing materials) as a restaurant.

its clientele (restaurants) and competitors such as convenience stores and supermarkets.[25]

Other corners of the food industry, however, were ardently opposed to the proposal. The pizza lobby took the position that the proposed rule's one-size-fits-all approach to listing nutrition information on menu boards unfairly burdened their industry.[26] The industry argued that because there are more than thirty-four million different combinations of pizza orders (including toppings, crust, pizza size, and so on),[27] the FDA's proposal to include ranges for menu items was essentially meaningless because those ranges might vary by thousands of calories. Figure 7.2 displays a mock-up of a menu board with wide calorie ranges that the American Pizza Community (APC), a formidable lobby against the menu labeling proposal, provided to the FDA during the rule's development in an attempt to illustrate the perceived absurdity of the range approach.[28] The sample menu shows an extreme case in which the calorie ranges shown for some menu options are in the tens of thousands. Not only do these ranges exceed the recommended daily intake for most adults—which is approximately two thousand calories—neither are they a useful guide for consumers in terms of helping to make selections among the options. Furthermore, the industry argued that compliance would be costly;

25. See Vinson and DeFife (2011) and Thatcher (2014). Groups lobbying for regulation to protect an industry's competitive interest is not an uncommon story. Shipan (1997) discusses a similar case where commercial broadcasters, led by the National Association of Broadcasters, lobbied the Federal Radio Commission to maintain barriers to obtaining radio licenses so as to prevent new stations from being created.

26. The pizza industry—which would prove a formidable foe in the agency's struggle to finalize the rule—opposed calorie ranges. Yet, as one interviewee noted, the intense opposition from the pizza industry over the FDA's proposed rule came as somewhat of a surprise, because pizza outfits had not been an important player in earlier fights over the adoption of state and local menu labeling policies (interview with public health advocate, July 2016).

27. ElBoghdady (2012).

28. The APC is an industry association that was launched in January 2012 with the goal of combating the FDA's approach to menu labeling. It includes more than twenty national pizza firms, representing more than twenty thousand restaurants nationwide. Since its creation, the organization has taken on new issues common to the pizza industry (e.g., agricultural policy, minimum wage policy), but menu labeling remains its core issue. The organization was extremely active in lobbying against the policy, advocating that at a minimum menu labeling should be much more flexible (i.e., include alternate compliance methods such as web-based calorie calculators and smartphone apps). In addition to submitting comments and meeting numerous times with the FDA and the Office of Information and Regulatory Affairs, the APC launched an ambitious program to lobby Congress. In 2012, 2013, and 2014, the group held "fly-ins," bringing pizza franchise owners to Capitol Hill to meet with lawmakers.

Group Specials

Pizza Only

Serves 12 – 240-400 cal/slice, 24 slices
3 Pan or Large Pizzas with up to 3-Toppings on each

$30.00
Online Promo Code:
30CATER

Serves 16 – 240-400 cal/slice, 32 slices
4 Pan or Large Pizzas with up to 3-Toppings on each

$39.00
Online Promo Code:
39CATER

Serves 20 – 240-400 cal/slice, 40 slices
5 Pan or Large Pizzas with up to 3-Toppings on each

$47.00
Online Promo Code:
47CATER

Meal Deal

Serves 10 – 7080-14350 Cal
- 3 Pan or Large Specialty or up to 3-Toppings
- 24 Papa's Wings or 30 Chicken Poppers
- 2 – 2-liters of soda

$55.00
$5.50 per person
Online Promo Code:
55CATER

Serves 20 – 12460-27890 Cal
- 5 Pan or Large Specialty or up to 3-Toppings
- 24 Papa's Wings or 30 Chicken Poppers
- 2 – 2-liters of soda

$95.00
$4.75 per person
Online Promo Code:
95CATER

Serves 40 – 26920-55780 Cal
- 10 Pan or Large Specialty or up to 3-Toppings
- Choice of 6 sides: Breadsticks,
  Garlic Parmesan Breadsticks or Cheesesticks
- 48 Papa's Wings or 60 Chicken Poppers
- 8 – 2-liters of soda

$160.00
$4.00 per person

Online Promo Code:
160CATER

FIGURE 7.2. Mock-up of pizza menu with calorie ranges
Note: This mocked-up menu board includes calorie ranges for different pizza combinations, showing that some order options could have a range of nearly 30,000 calories. The APC submitted this menu board to the FDA during the course of the rule's development; in the final rule, the FDA nonetheless required regulated restaurants to post a calorie range. From American Pizza Community (2017), produced by an independent franchisee of Papa John's.

one Domino's Pizza official stated that the proposed rule would cost the company's franchise owners $4,800 per year per store.[29]

Grocery stores were similarly opposed to the proposed rule, although their concerns stemmed not from the content of the proposal but from the fact that it applied to them in the first place. After all, the legislative text of section 4205 did not mention grocery stores, so their inclusion owed entirely to the discretion of FDA bureaucrats. The Food Marketing Institute, the chief lobbyist for grocery stores, indicated that the proposal would cost the industry $1 billion in the first year, and Kroger, the largest grocery chain in the country, stated that it would suffer $15 million in upfront costs and $4 million in annual compliance costs.[30] The grocers followed a similar strategy to the pizza industry, including submitting comments and lobbying the FDA, the White House, and Congress.

As the controversy unfolded, the FDA repeatedly pushed back the release date for the final rule, missing six self-imposed deadlines. According to the semiannual updates the agency provided to the *Unified Agenda*, the final rule was expected to be released in November 2012, April 2013, September 2013, February 2014, June 2014, and November 2014.

At long last, the final rule was published on December 1, 2014—more than four and a half years after the ACA was passed.[31] The final rule was much broader in scope than the proposed rule had been, coming much closer to resembling the original guidance. In addition to covering chain restaurants and grocery stores, the rule now included movie theaters and amusement parks, as well as alcoholic beverages. Although the final rule stated that the rule would take effect one year after its publication (December 2015), within months of the rule's publication, the agency issued a statement delaying implementation by one year—to December 2016. This delay was attributed to two factors: pressure from the regulated industries and a desire to put off the implementation date beyond the 2016 presidential election. Then, in December 2016, the agency pushed back the effective date for the rule by another six months, until May 2017, this time in response to a congressional intervention.[32] Again, in May 2017—one day before the rule was set to take

29. See Armour (2013).

30. Armour (2013).

31. 79 FR 71156; Dec. 1, 2014.

32. This delay was tied to a rider attached in the Consolidated Appropriations Act of 2016 (Pub. L. No. 114-113), in which Congress directed the agency to delay implementation of the rule until one year after it had issued final guidance to accompany the final rule. Because the agency's final guidance was issued in May 2016, this meant the rule could not take effect until May 2017, one year and five months after the agency had originally intended.

TABLE 7.1. Timeline for menu labeling rulemaking

March 23, 2010	Affordable Care Act signed into law. Section 4205 of the law directs FDA to take up menu labeling.
July 7, 2010	FDA publishes a *FR* notice establishing an open docket for interested parties to submit comments.
August 25, 2010	FDA publishes draft guidance explaining how firms can comply with menu labeling in advance of binding rules.
January 25, 2011	FDA repeals draft guidance from August.
April 6, 2011	Menu labeling proposed rule is published in the *FR*.
May 24, 2011	FDA extends public comment period for an additional 30 days (initially set to close on June 6, 2011).
July 5, 2011	FDA's extended comment period closes.
December 1, 2014	Final rule is published in the *FR*.
July 10, 2015	FDA postpones effective date of rule from December 1, 2015, to December 1, 2016.
December 1, 2016	FDA postpones effective date of rule from December 1, 2016, to May 5, 2017.
May 4, 2017	FDA postpones effective date of rule from May 5, 2017, to May 7, 2018.
May 7, 2018	Menu labeling compliance date.

effect—the FDA, now under the auspices of the new Trump administration, postponed implementation of the rule by another year, until May 2018.[33] On May 7, 2018, the rule finally became legally binding and chain restaurants were expected to comply with the new rules.[34]

All told, creating a binding final rule took the FDA more than eight years. Table 7.1 summarizes key moments in the rule's development. In the pages that follow, I trace the procedural politicking that took place behind the scenes, evaluating how the rule's path (or more specifically, the agency's tactics) accords with the theoretical claims. I conclude the analysis with the beginning of the rule's enforcement in May 2018, but as is so often the case with controversial regulatory actions, the story may not end there. Rather, the saga is likely continue for years to come as groups file lawsuits or the agency tinkers with the policy at the edges.

33. See 82 FR 20825; May 4, 2017.
34. As of this writing, interest groups are still lobbying Congress to undo the rule in one way or another. The push toward rolling back rules that occurred in the later years of this rule's development coincide with the Trump administration's broader deregulatory agenda, which, as I explain in chapter 8, may represent a new regulatory regime.

Menu Labeling in Context

Having established the basic contours and timeline of the menu labeling rule, I now consider how the FDA employed writing tools, consultation tools, and timing tools in this case.

WRITING MENU LABELING

If the pen is mightier than the sword, then the manner in which a rule is drafted can be powerful. In chapter 3, I outlined three specific aspects of how a rule is drafted that can shape its political prospects: framing, or how the agency uses language to favorably situate its policy proposal; analytical assumptions, or the assumptions that the agency uses to quantitatively justify its proposal; and accessibility, or the ease with which nonexperts can understand the policy under consideration. Each of these featured prominently in the writing of the menu labeling rule.

The preamble to the proposed rule offers a window into how the FDA framed the menu labeling rule. Preambles are an opportunity to justify the particulars of a policy proposal but also to explain the agency's rationale for choosing that proposal over others. When reading the menu labeling preamble, it is obvious that the agency heavily emphasized the proposed rule's role as a solution to the growing public health problem of obesity. What is less obvious in the preamble is how menu labeling would actually result in reduced obesity (i.e., the policy's effectiveness). Rather, the proposed rule simply states, "In recent years, there has been *growing support among public health experts* for providing calorie and other nutrition information on restaurant menus in order to help consumers make more informed food choices" (emphasis added).[35] This unattributed appeal to authority reframed the wealth of research on menu labeling's effectiveness, the overwhelming majority of which concludes that menu labeling has negligible effects on individuals' consumption behavior. As one review of the literature succinctly concludes: "The current evidence suggests that calorie labeling does not have the intended effect of decreasing calorie purchasing or consumption" (Swartz, Braxton, and Viera 2011, 135).[36] However, one would reach a very different conclusion from reading the proposed rule; the five studies the proposal cites in relation to menu labeling's effectiveness (all which are referenced in pass-

---

35. 76 FR 19193; Apr. 6, 2011.

36. For additional reviews of the literature, see also Harnack and French (2008); Hieke and Taylor (2011); Kiszko et al. (2014); and Sinclair, Cooper, and Mansfield (2014).

ing) deviate from the mainstream and report positive effects for the policy. If frames indeed "[influence] discussions, decision making, and policy outputs of other elites who must communicate used established terminology" (Wedeking 2010, 618), then the FDA's choice of an obesity reduction frame and selective use of the evidence to support it certainly put the menu labeling policy in an advantageous position vis-à-vis future policy discussions.

In making a case for menu labeling, the FDA also included numerous other appeals to authority in the preamble as a way to enhance the rule's bona fides. For instance, it would be difficult to read the rule and miss the fact that the policy was mandated by the ACA—the preamble mentions that law no less than twenty-five times. Additionally, the document included citations to fifty academic studies. The rule's analytical components were also laden with such appeals; the proposed rule's Regulatory Impact Analysis (RIA) was 88 pages and includes citations to 77 academic studies, while the final rule's RIA ballooned to 133 pages and 108 academic citations. These choices had implications for the text's accessibility, making it overall less accessible to nonexperts.

Turning to the analytical assumptions, the menu labeling rule was deemed to be an "economically significant" rule, meaning that it was expected to have an annual impact on the economy of $100 million or more. This also meant that the agency was required by executive order to consider the costs and benefits of the rule. The FDA did just this; at both the proposed and the final stage, the agency strategically selected the assumptions in the analysis so as to bias the outcome toward the agency's preferred policy.

In the RIA for the proposed rule, the agency considered the rule's costs but not its benefits. Citing a lack of "comprehensive data allowing accurate predictions of the proposed requirements," the agency instead conducted a breakeven analysis.[37] This analysis determined the proportion of the US obese adult population that would need to reduce consumption by one hundred calories per week in order to have the proposal yield positive net benefits. The result of this analysis: 0.06 percent of the obese population would have to make such an adjustment to justify the rule's costs. This analytical approach made it difficult for outsiders to evaluate the proposed policy's effectiveness, since this metric is neither relatable nor easily understood.

The proposed rule's RIA was released simultaneously with the proposed

37. Food and Drug Administration (2011, 12). Breakeven analysis still meets the spirit of the cost-benefit requirement. As Executive Order 12,866 states, "Costs and benefits shall be understood to include both quantifiable measures (to the fullest extent that these can be usefully estimated) and qualitative measures of costs and benefits that are difficult to quantify, but nevertheless essential to consider."

rule in 2011, and the FDA received several comments criticizing the agency's failure to quantify the rule's benefits. As a result in the final rule's RIA, the agency conducted a full-blown—and quite sophisticated—cost-benefit analysis. Unsurprisingly, this analysis showed that the agency's approach to menu labeling was expected to yield an annual net benefit of $511 million.

There were some surprising assumptions in the analysis, however. Most notably, the FDA assumed that, when confronted with nutrition information, some consumers would suffer a utility loss from choosing more healthy foods over less healthy ones. According to this logic, the loss in well-being occurs since healthy foods may make consumers "worse off on other dimensions such as taste, price, and convenience."[38] The FDA's inclusion of this assumption was puzzling, since it reduced the benefits side of the ledger. Although the agency had taken this approach in in at least one other high-profile RIA, it was not standard in most of the agency's cost-benefit analyses; in fact, the research underlying the agency's use of this assumption was based on one graduate student's unpublished working paper. In total, the "lost pleasure" assumption reduced the rule's benefits by between $2.2 billion to $5.27 billion, which, in turn, narrowed the margin by which the rule's benefits exceeded its costs.

Some criticized this as unnecessarily weakening the rule, suggesting that the inclusion of the calculation of lost pleasure could help companies or trade groups to challenge the menu rule in court.[39] There is, however, another interpretation of what this type of analysis added to the RIA. As law professor

---

38. Begley (2014).

39. Begley (2014). One administrative law expert that I spoke with suggested that the inclusion of the lost pleasure assumption was the work of the lead economist at the FDA at the time (interview with public advocacy official, Jan. 2017). This is plausible, as the economist in question had published work advocating for the inclusion of this assumption in evaluations of public health policies (Ashley, Nardinelli, and Lavaty 2015). The FDA was heavily criticized by the press (Begley 2014) and by academic economists (e.g., Chaloupka et al. 2014; Levy, Norton, and Smith 2016; Song, Brown, and Glantz 2014) for its application of this assumption (particularly with regard to an earlier tobacco rule). Following this backlash, HHS announced it would limit its reliance on "lost consumer surplus" in analyses of future regulations (Begley 2015). I do not view the agency's decision to avoid relying on this assumption as inconsistent with the notion of insulating it rules (i.e., bulletproofing). Because cost-benefit analysis is highly technical, it is likely that decision makers at the agency may have been aware of this assumption but may not have realized its long-term implications for future regulatory analyses. Because the benefits of menu labeling still exceeded the costs, the assumption served to bulletproof the rule. However, this is a relatively new area of jurisprudence, and the margin between benefits and costs has become a question of judicial interest in recent litigation (interview with public advocacy official, Jan. 2017). Once such concerns were publicly aired, the agency changed its approach.

Wendy Wagner (2009) argues, the use of "opponent-friendly assumptions" can make a rule less vulnerable to potential legal challenges.[40] By taking a conservative approach to the estimation of a rule's cost and benefits, agencies give opponents less fodder to work with in terms of a legal challenge to the rule's analytical merits. Given the amount of time invested in the rule, it is unlikely that FDA bureaucrats wished to see the rule weakened or overturned by the courts (who would likely adjust the rule in an ad hoc manner). It is more likely that the agency intended to "bulletproof" its analysis by cooptation (i.e., using opponent-friendly assumptions) and was able to do so while still maintaining a positive benefit-cost ratio.

Another consideration in the strategic composition of the FDA's menu labeling rule is the rule's accessibility; how easy was it for outsiders to understand exactly what the agency was proposing at each step of the process? The readability of the abstract for the proposed menu labeling rule was well below average; using the readability metrics developed in chapter 4, the abstract scores a −6.8. This is more than one standard deviation below the average preamble readability score for the sample and for the agency (sample mean = 0, FDA mean = −1.3). Additionally, the preamble was more than forty-five thousand words long (about one standard deviation above both the sample and the FDA mean), and the entire document ran forty-six tricolumn pages in the *Federal Register*. Further, the key sticking points were buried deep within these pages; grocery stores were not mentioned until the sixth page, and alcohol was not mentioned until the twelfth page. Developing an understanding of how the proposed rule differed from the earlier guidance document, then, was not a casual endeavor. Instead, it required readers to engage deeply with the rule.

All told, then, the FDA's choices on framing, analytical assumptions, and accessibility helped to present the policy in the best light and make it less assailable by critics than it might otherwise have been.

CONSULTING THE PUBLIC ON MENU LABELING

The menu labeling rule was controversial and proved to be challenging for the FDA. The rule had numerous powerful opponents—from the pizza lobby

---

40. In her analysis of RIA use at the EPA Wagner (2009, 60) argues, somewhat counterintuitively, that the agency's methods "uniformly and sometimes heavily tilt in favor of the [industry's] narrow interests." She concludes that "those who tout economic analysis as an important regulatory tool and view the rule from the perspective of hostile utilities [the opposing industry] are forced—by their own arguments and philosophies—to be mollified by EPA's conservative approach to evaluating the costs."

to grocery stores. Sympathetic to these interests, numerous congressional Republicans opposed the rule, describing it as "regulatory overreach" and "a bureaucratic solution in search of a real world problem."[41] Democrats were more supportive of the rule but also less vocal. Meanwhile, the Obama administration was tepid; while the administration supported the rule in principle, it also wanted to avoid the media battles that might ensue if the agency took too aggressive a stance on menu labeling. In total, this was an inhospitable political environment.

The interest group environment was similarly fraught. While public health and public interest groups were supportive of the rule, they were outweighed by the vociferous opposition (and resources) of the rule's industry opponents. With respect to public consultation, then, the theory laid out in chapter 3 suggests that to best insulate the proposal, we should expect to see the agency closing the participation valve to the extent possible (i.e., results consistent with the Limited Consultation Hypothesis). Yet, even though the agency was constrained from collecting information publicly from regulated parties, it still needed certain pieces of information to refine the policy it was crafting. Where possible, we should therefore expect to see the agency collecting necessary information privately (i.e., outside of the public eye).[42]

After the passage of the ACA, the FDA set to work on menu labeling right away. Within four months of the law's enactment, the agency published a notice inviting input on twenty-six different issues relating to menu labeling. The notice, which was entirely discretionary on the agency's part, established an open docket where written comments could be submitted for sixty days. At the same time, the agency began holding private meetings with affected stakeholders. These were ex parte meetings, meaning that, unlike the written comments that the agency was receiving, they were shielded from public view and did not become part of the record. There were a lot of them—one former FDA official estimated that the agency hosted fifty of these meetings.[43] The meetings engaged a diverse group of stakeholders, including chain restaurants, convenience stores, pizza delivery, grocery stores, cafeterias, coffee

41. See McMorris Rodgers and Sanchez (2013). To boot, in the 112th–114th Congresses, Republicans introduced no fewer than six bills intended to weaken the menu labeling rule. None of the bills passed.

42. This is an additional implication of the theory. The need for information collection does not recede when the agency is constrained; instead, the agency can realize this need in an alternate venue.

43. Interview with former agency official, Jan. 2017.

shops, as well as some state and local entities that had already implemented menu labeling.[44]

The proposed rule's publication opened the public comment period. The open docket and ex parte meetings clearly indicated to the agency that the interest group environment was hostile and that the learning that needed to be done was best accomplished in private. Accordingly, when setting the official comment period for the proposed rule the FDA gave stakeholders just sixty days.[45] While this met the threshold recommended in recent executive orders, it is substantially shorter than the comment period the agency typically provides (especially for such an important rule); according to the *Regulatory Proposals Dataset*, the average public comment period on an FDA rule is 83.8 days and the median is 90 days. Driving the strategic nature of this choice home, on the same day that the agency published the menu labeling proposed rule, it simultaneously published a proposed rule on calorie labeling for vending machines. While vending machine labeling was also required under the ACA, it was considerably less controversial than menu labeling. The FDA allotted stakeholders ninety days to comment on the vending machine proposed rule. While one FDA official attributed the discrepancy in the comment periods on the two proposed rules to the fact that vending machine purveyors "had never been regulated before,"[46] this explanation does not address why the more controversial of the two actions was allotted *less* time for

44. While these were ex parte meetings, one agency official indicated that it was standard practice for the agency to keep records about the meetings (interview with agency official, May 2013). Accordingly, in April 2016, I submitted a Freedom of Information Act (FOIA) request to the FDA for a list of all meetings and participants from the time the ACA was passed (Mar. 23, 2010) until the final rule's publication (Dec. 1, 2014). Six months after my request the agency responded with a memo identifying just one meeting associated with the rule. At my further prodding, the agency responded with an updated list of ten more meetings that had been held and indicated that my request had been completed in full. However, in addition to falling far short of the former agency official's estimate of fifty meetings on the proposed rule, the list excluded at least one person affiliated with a public health organization interviewed for this project, who reported meeting several times with the agency while the proposed rule was being drafted. All told, then, the FDA either does not keep accurate records regarding these meetings or was reluctant to share them in response to my FOIA request. Either possibility is in keeping with the theoretical claim that agencies prefer to keep early consultation private.

45. At the request of commenters, the agency eventually extended the public comment period an additional thirty days (to ninety days total). As in chapter 5, I focus on the initial public comment period as the unit of analysis, as this represents the agency's initial strategic choice. Agencies typically extend comment periods when commenters ask them to do so because courts are likely to be critical of agency denials of such requests.

46. Interview with agency official, May 2013.

public scrutiny. Also, as previously noted, though not unprecedented, the FDA does not routinely regulate restaurants.

After the proposed rule was published, industry leaders clamored to meet with the FDA in person so as to make their case for the final rule.[47] If such meetings were to occur, they would be part of the public record, and the agency would need to document the meeting and include it in the rulemaking docket. The FDA took the position that if it had one such meeting, it would have to meet with anyone who asked, and because the agency was hoping to the get the final rule out quickly, it therefore declined all meeting requests at this stage. Additionally, as one former agency official put it, "We felt that we had already heard from all of the relevant players."[48]

The agency's refusal to meet led to consternation within industry; as one supermarket executive lamented in a House hearing on the rule, "We meet with FDA on a regular basis on a wide variety of topics and this has been one particular topic in which they have been absolutely unwilling to meet or communicate . . . it has been a very frustrating process."[49] This sentiment was echoed by other industry representatives at the hearing and also in the interviews that I conducted. One interviewee compared his organization's experience on the menu labeling rule to another rule relating to the Food Safety Modernization Act (FSMA)[50] that his organization had also worked with the FDA on:

> When FDA started writing proposed rules on FSMA they held listening sessions and public meetings. If you couldn't make the meeting it was webcast. Everybody had a chance to talk. There were breakout groups. All of that was on the record, very transparent. They met with industry groups in the public domain. . . . Compare that to menu labeling. With this proposed rule they only talked to a certain group of folks. . . . They said they wouldn't talk with us—submit a comment and then we'll talk to you. We did. But they still wouldn't meet with us. Three and a half years later white smoke comes out and they put out a final rule.[51]

Taking stock of consultation on the menu labeling rule, the evidence suggests that the FDA managed consultation strategically. The agency tightened the participation valve by offering a relatively brief period for public com-

---

47. The agency received more than nine hundred written comments, not an unusually high volume of comments for the agency. It was actually less than some agency officials had expected (interview with FDA official, May 2013).

48. Interview with former agency official, Jan. 2017.

49. O'Quinn (2015).

50. Pub. L. No. 111-353.

51. Interview with grocery store officials, Dec. 2016.

ments, by forgoing public meetings with stakeholders after the proposed rule, and by declining to host any public hearings on the proposed rule. The agency collected what policy and political information it needed privately in numerous ex parte meetings with key stakeholders before the proposed rule's publication. However, the agency did not shut off the consultation valve completely; early on—perhaps before the agency realized the full scope of the blowback on menu labeling—the agency voluntarily established a public docket and also chose to publish draft guidance, which tipped its hand at an early stage of the process.

TIMING MENU LABELING

In chapter 6, I argued that, all else equal, agencies time the release of final rules to coincide with sympathetic political coalitions. With regard to menu labeling, despite the tough political climate, there is evidence to suggest that the agency timed the rule to achieve maximum political support. When the proposed rule was released in April 2011,[52] Republicans had won a majority in the House, a position they would hold for the duration of the rule's procedural life. Meanwhile, Democrats held control of the Senate at that point in time, suggesting support from at least one chamber.

This political configuration held—for the duration of 2012, 2013, and 2014—while the agency continued working on the final rule and while observers puzzled over what was taking the agency so long. However, the 2014 midterm elections swung the Senate into the Republicans' camp, meaning that beginning with the 114th Congress in 2015, the FDA would face a unified Republican legislature, a situation that did not bode well for the future of menu labeling. The publication of the final rule in December 2014—after the election results were in but before the new Congress was seated—minimized the chances that this unified Congress would act decisively against the rule immediately upon its release.

The timing also served to bypass potential issues with the White House. The rule came out after the midterm elections in November, meaning that it did not provide "job-killing regulation" fodder for the campaign cycle.[53] More important, from the FDA's perspective, by the time the agency sent the

52. I do not consider the agency's strategic timing with respect to the proposed rule, since Congress had placed a deadline for issuing that rule. As I showed in chapter 6, deadlines considerably increase the pace at which agencies issue rules. As a result, having a deadline constrains the agency's ability to manipulate timing vis-à-vis the political environment.

53. Some have suggested that OIRA had no small role in the postelection timing because its review of the final rule far exceeded the standard ninety-day review period.

final rule to the White House for review in 2014, Nancy-Ann DeParle, the rule's primary adversary within the White House, had left her post for the private sector. According to one former agency official, DeParle's departure freed the agency to pursue a more aggressive final rule without this opposition within the executive branch.[54]

There is also a curious bit of procedural politicking with respect to the precise timing of the publication of the final rule. While the final rule was published in the *Federal Register* on December 1, 2014, the agency actually released it to media outlets before then, on November 24. This was the Monday before Thanksgiving, and some in industry viewed this timing with suspicion. One interviewee indicated that Thanksgiving was the busiest time of year for the grocery industry—one of the industries most opposed to the rule—and suggested that the release of the rule during this week was an intentional move by the agency to bury the news story and to stifle opposition.[55]

All told, the agency did its best to make lemons out of lemonade. In an environment with many political obstacles—including hostile overseers in Congress, outspoken industry critics, and lukewarm presidential support— the agency used timing to its advantage in order to create a stronger menu labeling final rule.

There is, however, one additional procedural decision that has timing implications: implementation delays. Analyzing these delays reveals that that the agency was less strategic than it could have been. While the rule was initially set to take effect in December 2015, the rule did not actually come into effect until thirty months later (May 2018). The delay unfolded through three separate delay notices in the *Federal Register*. The first gave industry an additional twelve months to meet the menu labeling requirements. Observers at the time—even the rule's public health advocates—supported the delay as necessary to help improve compliance rates among food service providers. This was a discretionary move on the agency's part and may be evidence of trading off long-term goals (e.g., compliance) with short-term ones (policy certainty).

54. Interview with former agency official, Jan. 2017..

55. Interview with grocery store officials, Dec. 2016. One of the interviewees indicated that when the media contacted him on November 24 for a quote on the final rule, he was unable to provide meaningful comment on the rule because he had not seen it yet (the final rule was technically on a media embargo until 12:01 a.m. on November 25). However, after seeing the media stories that were published that day, he suspects that those on the winning side of the issue (e.g., public health groups) were given advance access to the rule. I was unable to verify this claim with either the FDA or any of the public health groups quoted in media stories about the final rule. Regardless of the veracity of this claim, however, this stakeholder's perception that the FDA favored one side over the other is interesting in itself.

This delay may have been shortsighted in terms of the broader political climate, however, as it ended up putting the rule's very survival into question. Industry continued to put pressure on congressional Republicans, and as the first delay period was set to expire, Congress passed a last-minute rider that forced the agency to wait six additional months. Then, by the time this second delay period was winding down, the Trump administration had taken over. The new FDA Commissioner, Scott Gottlieb, was much more sympathetic to industry concerns and willing to reconsider the basic tenets of the menu labeling policy.[56] Under his leadership, the agency delayed implementation of the rule by another year and began to consider rolling back the menu labeling regulations. Although the rule ultimately took effect in May 2018, the FDA's first decision to delay put the entire enterprise at risk.[57] Agency bureaucrats made the initial decision to delay the rule in July 2015; while it would have been impossible for these officials to foresee that additional delays would follow and a new president who had strong deregulatory preferences—and a new regulatory regime—were on the horizon, these unforeseen changes underscore the importance of locking in regulatory policy as early as possible.

Overall, the evidence accumulated in this chapter from news reports, agency documents, and interviews on menu labeling supports the theory that the FDA used writing, consultation, and timing tools in ways that promoted the rule and helped insulate the agency from potential attacks. In particular, the agency adopted a frame for the rule that highlighted the problem of obesity while conveniently avoiding research showing that menu labeling does not necessarily result in reduced caloric intake. The analytical assumptions employed in the RIA were a combination of opaque and "opponent-friendly," which helped make the analysis bulletproof while still demonstrating positive net benefits. And the consultation that the agency conducted, in terms of the public comment period and public meetings with stakeholders was minimal in comparison to other rules. At the same time, the agency held private ex parte meetings that allowed it to gather critical policy and political information privately and off the record. Finally, the timing of the final rule was shrewd in that the agency waited out a problematic White House adviser while also getting the rule out before the Senate flipped to Republican hands. On balance, then, the record supports an interpretation that the strategic use

56. Dewey (2017); Wells (2017).

57. Following the third implementation delay, the Center for Science in the Public Interest and the National Consumers' League sued the FDA, claiming the decision to delay was illegal. In September 2017, the agency signed an agreement with these parties, promising not to pursue any additional implementation delays. This legal action likely explains why the FDA chose not to delay any further under the Trump administration.

of procedures helped the FDA to create an insulated and ambitious menu labeling rule.

Connecting Strategies and Outcomes

The argument advanced in this book is that bureaucrats use their procedural control over the rulemaking process to insulate their rules and protect them from potential overturns or other repercussions from political overseers. The implication is that, by doing these things, the rules that agencies produce better reflect bureaucrats' preferred policy outcomes rather than those preferred by other actors in the political system. On the one hand, this implication logically flows from the arguments presented up until this point: why would bureaucrats bother to protect or insulate a rule that they were not partial to or did not think reflected good public policy? On the other hand, it would be more satisfying to document the effect rather than infer it. The menu labeling case can partially address this concern.

The FDA's decision in August 2010 to release draft guidance on menu labeling makes it an ideal case for this purpose. At this early stage, the path forward must have seemed like smooth sailing to agency officials. After all, industry had lobbied on behalf of a federal standard, and the policy had already been implemented in numerous locales across the country. Agency leaders therefore wanted to get the draft guidance out quickly to clarify how the agency would handle the relevant parts of the policy that were self-implementing under the ACA. As one former FDA official stated in an interview, "We were trying to push [the guidance] through fast at the time."[58] This pressure to move quickly, combined with the fact that the contested nature of the policy was yet unknown, suggests the draft guidance document revealed some of the agency's true preference—the policy it would have chosen absent any political machinations. Following this guidance document in 2010, the agency's thinking on what a menu labeling policy should look like went through two additional public iterations: the proposal that was included in the 2011 proposed rule, and the eventual policy that was laid out in the 2014 final rule. Table 7.2 includes the key components of the rule as it went through each of these stages.

The similarities between the initial draft guidance and the final binding rule are striking. Both covered a broad range of food establishments and included alcoholic beverages under their auspices. In a broad sense, the policy went from strong (guidance) to weak (proposed rule) and back to strong

---

58. Interview with former agency official, Jan. 2017.

TABLE 7.2. Policy evolution of the menu labeling rule

	Draft guidance document (2010)	Proposed rule (2011)	Final rule (2014)
Venues included?[a]	Restaurants	Restaurants	Restaurants
	Grocery stores	Grocery stores	Grocery stores
	Convenience stores	Convenience stores	Convenience stores
	Pizza establishments	Pizza establishments	Pizza establishments
	Movie theaters		Movie theaters
	Amusement parks		Amusement parks
	Airplanes		
Policy covers alcohol?	Yes	No	Yes
Calorie ranges allowed for combination items?	No	Yes	Yes
Effective date?	Following final guidance[b]	6 months from final rule	12 months from final rule

[a]Under section 4205 of the ACA, the rules could apply only to venues with 20 or more outlets (e.g., chain restaurants).

[b]The FDA's 2010 guidance was a draft guidance. Since parts of section 4205 of the ACA were self-executing, the agency initially planned to release a final guidance document in December 2010, which would take effect at that point and provide nonbinding guidance to industry. The initial plan was for the guidance to be followed up by binding regulations.

again (final rule). Politically speaking, the draft guidance document represents an unvarnished view of the FDA's thinking on menu labeling; it was published only five months after the ACA was passed and before the FDA had time to assess the prevailing political winds on menu labeling. Once those winds were assessed, the agency took a step back, retracted the guidance,[59] and, shortly thereafter, issued a weakened proposed rule.

In spite of the agency's softening of its position in the proposed rule, as previously explained, industry lobbying against the rules was intense in the months following the proposed rule's publication. As a result, the agency was under considerable pressure to issue a weak final rule. That's why the aggressive stance of the final rule came as such a surprise to observers; as professor and food politics expert Marion Nestle explains: "I was just floored. There's been so much pressure on the FDA to do nothing. And certainly not to do anything that might ruffle the feathers of industry that I couldn't believe that they went so much farther than they had even in their initial proposals."[60]

59. Industry saw the guidance document's withdrawal as a reprieve; one commenter noted that "the restaurant industry may breathe a sigh of relief" (Wiley Rein 2011).

60. Nestle (2014).

THE CASE OF MENU LABELING

Why did the FDA adopt a strong final rule? Certainly there would have been political cover for a weakened final rule, one that was perhaps even less ambitious than the proposed rule. Indeed, there was little outside support for a strong final rule—the White House's enthusiasm was tepid, and congressional Republicans were opposed to the rule, as were some very vocal industry critics. What support there was for a strong final rule came from public health advocates (and to some extent from the National Restaurant Association), but these groups were less forthcoming in their support than the rule's opponents. Additionally, as the prior discussion of the proposed rule's preamble explained, there is empirical research that would have supported the adoption of a weaker rule. In other words, the agency certainly would have been justified in choosing a weaker final policy and many observers expected as much.

The explanation is that there was support for a strong menu labeling policy from within the agency. Indeed, one former FDA official commented that, while opinion about how to proceed on the menu labeling policy was not unanimous, leadership at the top of the agency was "very supportive" from the outset and there was a general feeling that menu labeling represented good public policy.[61] A food industry executive offered a different take on this, suggesting that the agency had an "agenda" when it came to menu labeling, and that in the end, the FDA "just wanted this done and out the door."[62]

Despite the absence of sizable effects in academic studies of menu labeling, public health experts largely stand behind it as a policy tool, and alignment with the public health community is in the FDA's DNA.[63] Notably, nearly all the literature reviews of menu labeling cited earlier lament the state of the research, identify concerns with previous studies' research design or methodology, and conclude with a call for higher quality research (instead of suggesting that the public health community pursue a different policy to reduce obesity). Additionally, one public health expert who I spoke with pointed out that most of the studies have been conducted on fast food, which is only one type of eating establishment, and that most of the studies are not

61. Interview with former agency official, Jan. 2017.
62. Interview with grocery store officials, Dec. 2016.
63. Put differently, bureaucrats at the FDA are part of an epistemic community, which is "a network of professionals with recognized expertise and competence in a particular domain and an authoritative claim to policy-relevant knowledge within that domain or issue-area" (Haas 1992, 3). These communities share normative and causal beliefs, notions of validity, and a common policy enterprise, which is "a set of problems to which their professional competence is directed, presumably out of the conviction that human welfare will be enhanced as a consequence" (Haas 1992, 3). See also Savage (2005).

calibrated to pick up the small changes that consumers make when it comes to menu items (i.e., they lack sufficient statistical power).

Key FDA personnel who worked on menu labeling had backgrounds in public health, holding advanced degrees in science or public health. Using the point of contact on rule-related documents as well as meeting records and interview sources, I identified eight agency employees who formed the core team for the menu labeling rule. These eight employees collectively held nine advanced degrees, largely in fields relating to science and public health.[64] When bureaucratic agents share a common professional background, professional norms can come to guide their thinking and their policy preferences;[65] in this case bureaucrats' shared public health orientation may have encouraged the rule-writing team to pursue a more aggressive public health vision.

Overall, then, the agency's decision to have a strong menu labeling policy, a policy that accorded with its earliest unvarnished take on the policy, is consistent with the idea that the strategies the agency employed in promulgating the rule were in defense of a policy that the agency preferred over other weaker alternatives. Would such an ambitious menu labeling policy have been possible if the FDA had taken a different tack with respect to writing, consultation, or timing? It is impossible to know what would have happened if the agency had, say, allowed for more on-the-record consultation or had released the rule sooner, so I leave this for the reader to contemplate.

Summary

As the FDA was working on the menu labeling rule, it deployed its procedural tool kit strategically to enhance the prospects that a strong final rule would become binding law. The way the FDA composed the rule presented it in a favorable light. The frame the agency adopted for menu labeling highlighted the rule's orientation toward obesity reduction. The agency's argument was

64. Specifically, their degrees included master's degrees in biochemical genetics, energy and resources, microbiology, public health (two individuals); doctorates in economics, epidemiology, and nutrition; and one law degree. I also identified another fourteen agency employees who were involved in the rule but less consistently so. These fourteen employees collectively held seventeen advanced degrees in the following fields: master's degrees in food science, nutrition science, public administration, public health (two individuals) and regulatory science, doctorates in animal nutrition, nutrition, and public health, and law degrees (eight individuals). I determined employees' backgrounds via agency documents, internet searches, conversations, and the résumé site LinkedIn.

65. See Adolph (2013); Gormley (1986); Kaufman (1960); and Wilson (1989, 59–65).

based on a selective interpretation of the research, an interpretation that omitted a considerable body of work showing that menu labeling policies have negligible effects on consumer behavior. The composition was further enhanced by the way the agency conducted the empirical analysis of the rule. While still showing positive net benefits, the analysis included opponent-friendly assumptions that made it more difficult for adversaries to attack the rule on quantitative grounds.

The FDA got what information it needed early on in private, but from then on the agency limited critical participation opportunities on the rule, particularly those that were visible and on the record (i.e., the public comment period and ex parte meetings after the proposed rule), in a way that prevented opponents from being able to lodge and record their complaints. Finally, the agency timed the final rule so that the policy was less vulnerable to attacks by political opponents, by waiting out hostile elements within the White House and then finalizing the rule ahead of an incoming (and likely inimical) Republican Senate. Thus, it appears that the procedures were designed to protect the rule from political incursions.

Perhaps even more important than showing how the agency deployed its tool kit, the menu labeling case demonstrates the connection between these tools and policy outcomes. Within the agency, there was a bias toward a strong menu labeling rule, and a strong rule was the outcome that eventually materialized. While it is impossible to decisively conclude that the tools the agency deployed allowed the agency to adopt a strong final rule, the evidence suggests that the final policy accorded with the prevailing preferences of agency decision makers.

Of course, the FDA did not perfectly deploy procedures in the menu labeling case. It could not perfectly anticipate the future and, critically, the responses of other actors in the policy space. Indeed, it is easy to single out points where different choices made by the agency would potentially have led to a superior outcome. For example, perhaps if the agency had not tightened the participation valve so much after the ANPRM was issued, disaffected groups could have blown off steam during that part of the policy-making process. That outlet could, in turn, have lessened demand for recourse on Capitol Hill. Also, in hindsight, the initial choice to delay the implementation of the rule by one year, which led to implementation occurring during the anti-regulatory Trump administration, put the rule at risk. But these points amount to little more than Monday-morning quarterbacking of what would have been the optimal choice in retrospect; they do not undermine the argument that, given the information available at the time and the constraints the agency faced, bureaucratic actors deployed procedures strategically.

In sum, in a case where Congress sketched the broad confines of a menu labeling policy, the FDA used the rulemaking process to shape an ambitious rule that was both enforceable (i.e., it fit with the agency's existing honor-system approach to package labeling) and that furthered bureaucrats' public health agenda.

Procedural Politicking in Perspective

At the turn of the twentieth century, Progressive reformers envisioned a professional bureaucracy that was wholly separate from the world of politics. The idea was that the political realm should determine the tasks for bureaucrats, but then politics should not be "suffered to manipulate [administrative] offices."[1] For decades, scholars debated whether such a division between politics and administration was actually achievable. This debate has largely been exhausted, with most scholars resigned to the notion that neutrality is not possible when it comes to bureaucratic actions.[2] Yet in spite of this consensus, the mechanism by which bureaucrats shape policy is often overlooked. This book has argued for the centrality of procedures as a means by which bureaucratic actors achieve policy ends in a decidedly political world.

Conducting research on procedures is not without its challenges. By their very nature, procedures are designed to appear "neutral." Further, tracing the impact of procedural choices to policy outcomes is difficult, since it requires construction of counterfactual scenarios of what would have happened had a different procedural course been taken.[3] Nonetheless, there is clear evidence of procedural politicking through the many stages of the regulatory process and across a wide variety of agencies. Among other tools, agencies manipulate the accessibility of the texts they produce, the amount of public

---

1. Wilson (1887) as quoted in Rosenbloom (2008, 57).

2. See, e.g., Adolph (2013); Huber (2007); and Moynihan, Herd, and Harvey (2014).

3. There are other challenges to conducting research in this area, such as limitations to conducting randomized experiments—often considered the gold standard in research design—in bureaucratic settings. Additionally, while they do occur, sharp breaks in the political environment of the sort desired by scholars conducting discontinuity research are few and far between.

consultation they conduct, and the timing of the process so as to insulate their rules in the face of unsupportive political principals. The willingness of interest groups to pull fire alarms on agencies is often, though not always, an intervening factor. And, as demonstrated by the case of the FDA's menu labeling rule, the strategic use of these procedures can help an agency get more of what it wants in terms of policy outcomes, especially in an unfavorable political environment.

Procedural politicking is not confined to any one agency; its fingerprints are evident across the 150 bureaus considered in this study. Additionally, looking back on the empirical chapters in this book, it is not the case that well-resourced agencies or agencies with greater expertise were more likely to engage in this behavior. Instead, the results consistently indicate that capacity is not a driving force behind procedural politicking and that these tactics are available to bureaucrats irrespective of the resource environment in which they operate.

The politicking I have uncovered is nuanced. Not every tool is used to forestall each principal at each stage of the process; rather, agencies deploy different tools to target specific principals throughout the rulemaking process. For instance, in chapter 5 I showed that agencies do not manipulate the length of the public comment period in response to congressional oversight, but instead they manipulate the *timing* of the public comment period so that it is more likely to overlap with a congressional recess. In many cases the effect sizes associated with individual procedural tools are admittedly small. But the aggregation of procedural politicking tools amounts to "death by a thousand cuts"—the accumulation of many small procedural tweaks that result in considerable power and influence for bureaucratic actors at the margins.

The key takeaway is that procedures, which many think of as a mundane and esoteric part of the rulemaking process, are a political venue. The remaining discussion in this chapter unpacks this insight in four ways. First, I evaluate why procedural politicking has persisted as long as it has, highlighting the role of political polarization in particular. Second, I discuss the broader implications of having unelected bureaucrats influence the long-term direction of regulatory policy. Third, I consider the future of procedural politicking and evaluate the prospects of three potential reforms to the regulatory process. I conclude with directions for future research.

The Persistence of Procedural Politicking

The theory of procedural politicking holds that bureaucrats often manage the rulemaking process in ways that advantage their own interests over those of Congress and the president. It is not obvious that this equilibrium should have persisted over the twenty-year period studied in this book. After all, Congress and the president have the ability to "crack down" on agencies or to limit the scope of agency rulemaking. Why do these overseers allow agencies to continue to usurp their policy prerogatives?

There are at least two reasons why procedural politicking should be thought of as a "sticky" equilibrium. First, whether politicians like or not, delegation is a necessary part of modern governance. In 2016, the United States had a population of more than 320 million people and a gross domestic product of $18.6 trillion.[4] Given the size, scope, and complexity of the governing tasks faced by three constitutional branches, delegating to a branch of experts to devise and carry out the specifics of government's responsibilities is inevitable. Yet, as even the most basic principal-agent model predicts, having an agent carry out a task on one's behalf will nearly always result in some policy loss. So even if politicians are aware of procedural politicking and the costs it imposes on them (and they may not always be), the policy losses may be perceived as an unfortunate yet inevitable consequence of delegation. It should also not be forgotten that the administrative procedures that have become the venue of procedural politicking are themselves attempts to bind bureaucrats' hands. That is, this may be the best that political principals can do.

Second, in the contemporary political environment enacting major public policy reforms of the sort required to limit procedural politicking is not easy. It is uncontested that the two parties have polarized, and this is especially evident in the congressional setting.[5] Since about 1980, both Republicans and Democrats have been on a slow and steady march toward their respective poles, although most scholars believe that the Republicans' move to the right has been more extreme than the Democrats' move to the left.[6] Scholars have proffered numerous explanations, including a post–Civil Rights realignment of Southern politics; changes in the primary, redistricting, or campaign finance systems; and increases in economic and social inequality.[7]

The implications of increased congressional polarization are numerous, but they are rarely considered in the context of the bureaucracy. One conse-

4. Central Intelligence Agency (2017).
5. There is a wealth of literature on partisan polarization; see, inter alia, Lee (2015); and McCarty, Poole, and Rosenthal (2016).
6. See Hacker and Pierson (2006); and Mann and Ornstein (2012).
7. The influence of each these factors on polarization constitutes a literature in its own right, one in which there is often considerable disagreement. For an incisive overview of the literature, see Barber and McCarty (2013).

quence that scholars have repeatedly suggested is drift, which Lee (2015, 274) describes as "unguided policy change."[8] The basic idea is that increased political polarization has prevented Congress and the president from conducting necessary maintenance of major public policies, such as Social Security and student loan programs. As a result, changes to these program areas are made on ad hoc basis and shaped by a variety of actors outside of the legislative system.

While drift may be an unfortunate consequence of polarization, it may also be an opportunity for bureaucrats looking to leave their policy mark. That is, while policy change may appear to be unguided, strategies like procedural politicking may enable bureaucrats to steer policy in their preferred direction. Because procedures are ostensibly neutral, when bureaucrats employ them strategically, they may successfully shepherd preferred policies through the regulatory process without provoking the usual partisan, polarized opposition.

For example, Suzanne Mettler (2014) argues that the emergence and rapid growth of the for-profit college sector was precipitated by the inability of Congress and the president to address systematic problems that were evident in the structure of the federal student aid program.[9] As a result, drift led to the sector's rapid growth and also allowed for fraudulent and predatory practices to proliferate within the industry. Despite numerous red flags, a polarized Congress repeatedly failed to address these problems, and eventually it was left to the Department of Education (ED) to redress the issue through the gainful-employment rule.

As discussed in chapter 2, ED faced its own set of problems in issuing this rule, including considerable industry opposition and repeated clashes with the courts. Nonetheless, the struggle to issue a gainful-employment rule transpired in an environment where Republicans had considerable power. Had policy change been pushed through Congress in this setting, the left-leaning bureaucrats who populated ED might have been stuck with a for-profit student aid policy they preferred less than the one they finally enacted.[10] Instead, the bureaucrats at ED had the opportunity to set the policy. In

8. See also Hacker (2004). There are, of course, numerous other consequences to polarization. For instance, Binder (2008) suggests that increased polarization has enabled presidents to put more ideologically extreme judges on the federal bench.

9. See chapter 6 of Mettler's (2014) book.

10. Clinton and Lewis (2008) assign ED an ideology score of -1.22 (with a credibility interval of $[-1.78, -0.75]$), suggesting that, according to its mission, it can readily be considered a left-leaning agency.

other words, the existence of this polarized environment allowed bureaucrats to chart their own policy course.

Broadly speaking, polarization has enabled bureaucrats to play an out-sized role in the policy-making process, and because procedural politicking is not readily observed from the outside, this process has played out largely outside of public purview. From a normative perspective, having bureaucrats as the guiding force behind policy drift raises real concerns. To start, while the regulatory process is powerful, bureaucrats still face statutory limitations. They cannot provide a structural overhaul of, say, the student loan pro-gram in the same way that legislators can. This means that regulatory policy changes will necessarily be piecemeal and will not always be able to address policy problems in a holistic fashion. Moreover, bureaucrats are not elected. This suggests that we ought to be paying close attention to who works in the bureaucracy and whose values they represent.

The Influence of the Fourth Branch

The role of the bureaucracy as the fourth branch of government is one that has emerged organically. It is not a system that was optimally designed, in the sense that there are certainly more efficient and effective ways of achieving desirable policy outcomes. Nonetheless, the bureaucracy now functions as an independent force in the American constitutional system. The fact that unelected bureaucrats have political influence should not in and of itself be a cause for concern. A professionalized civil service is a hallmark of a well-functioning modern state. As bureaucrats are often experts in their respective domains, they may use their powers to steer policy toward outcomes that may make society better off.

It is important to remember that bureaucrats are not the "other." Nearly all are US citizens.[11] Demographically speaking, they are broadly, albeit not perfectly, representative of the US population. As table 8.1 shows, federal em-ployees tend to be older, whiter, more educated, and more likely to be male,

11. While there is no general constitutional or legal requirement, by convention political appointees are typically US citizens. Under Executive Order 11,935, those farther down the food chain must generally be US citizens as well; according to the Office of Personnel Management (2017), "Only United States citizens and nationals may be appointed to competitive service Fed-eral jobs. In rare cases, agencies may hire certain non-citizens when there are no qualified U.S. citizens available, unless the appointment is prohibited by statute. In addition, Congress fre-quently restricts agencies' ability to hire non-citizens into the excepted service as well, through appropriations provisions."

TABLE 8.1. Demographic representativeness of the US federal bureaucracy, 2014 (percent)

	Careerists	Agency leaders	US population
Age			
20–34	18.1	0.7	20.6
35–49	37.8	26.2	19.3
50–65	39.9	65.1	19.7
Gender			
Female	42.3	33.3	50.8
Education			
Some college, high school or less	49.2	7.8	55.5
Bachelor's	31.9	40.3	32.5
Master's	15.7	39.9	8.7
Doctorate	3.1	11.5	3.3
Race/ethnicity			
Asian	5.1	3.0	5.3
Black/African American	17.8	10.5	13.2
Hispanic or Latino	8.3	4.5	17.1
Other	3.6	2.27	2.4
White	65.2	79.7	62.6

Note: Table entries are percentages of totals and may not sum to 100 due to rounding. Agency personnel data are from the 2014 employment and diversity cubes of the *FedScope* database (Office of Personnel Management 2014). The "careerists" category includes all federal employees in cabinet agencies who are paid according to the General Schedule or an equivalently graded pay plan. The "agency leaders" category includes all federal employees in cabinet agencies who are paid according to the Executive (EX) pay schedule or the Senior Executive Service (SES) pay schedule. US population data are drawn from the US Census. Gender and race/ethnicity data are from the Census's "Quick Facts" feature for 2014. Population age data are based on the 2014 American Community Survey and, for comparability purposes, include individuals age 20–65 only. Education data are from table A4 of the Current Population Survey, Educational Attainment in the United States Report, 2014. The "other" race category includes the following groups: American Indian or Alaska Native, Native Hawaiian or Pacific Islander, and more than one race.

than the average US resident. This pattern is exacerbated among agency leaders when compared to rank-and-file bureaucrats.[12]

However, in contrast to other powerful political institutions, such as Congress, the bureaucracy ranks among the most diverse. For instance, nearly half of all members of Congress are millionaires,[13] and they come disproportionately from the upper tiers of society.[14] Members possess, on average, many more years of education than their constituents and attend elite institu-

12. The fact that the bureaucracy is broadly representative should not be read to diminish the importance of its diversity deficits. Demographic differences in leadership can have substantive policy consequences. For example, Potter and Volden (2018) point out that although women are underrepresented as bureau heads, in some agencies they are more effective than their peers in terms of both initiating and finalizing important rules.

13. Lichtblau (2011).

14. Carnes (2013).

tions of higher education at higher rates.[15] Comparatively, then, bureaucrats are a fairly representative bunch.

Of course, descriptive representation matters little if bureaucrats differ systematically in ideological orientation from those who their policy decisions affect. After all, one key implication of procedural politicking is that bureaucrats are sometimes able to advance their own agendas rather than the agendas of those who are more directly accountable for their actions, such as members of Congress and the president. However, even on the ideological count bureaucrats fare relatively well, tending not to represent extreme or highly polarized viewpoints.

In recent years, a veritable cottage industry has emerged with the goal of empirically measuring the ideology of agency leaders, as well as the careerists that constitute the rank and file.[16] While the scope, sophistication, and methodology of the approaches employed by scholars vary, they have reached surprisingly similar conclusions. First, while agencies tend to be staffed with slightly left-of-center civil servants, agency ideology estimates repeatedly show that some agencies, like the Department of Defense, attract career employees who are more conservative, whereas other agencies, like the Environmental Protection Agency, attract those with a more liberal orientation. These biases, however, are quite modest when compared to the level of polarization in Congress. Second, the preferences of appointees and careerists are distinct from one another. Third, and unsurprisingly, the preferences of political appointees tend to move leftward when the president is a Democrat and rightward under a Republican president. These findings are mirrored in surveys that ask bureaucrats both to rate their ideological orientation and to indicate their position on a host of policy issues.[17]

15. Myers and Olsen-Phillips (2017).

16. The empirical study of the ideological position of members of Congress, the president, and the judiciary is firmly entrenched in political science (e.g., Bonica 2013; Poole and Rosenthal 1997; Segal and Cover 1989). However, extending such estimates of ideology to the bureaucracy has been tricky, because bureaucrats rarely take public positions on policy issues, and when they do, it is not in a systematic and reliable manner. While early scholars relied on the president's ideology as a crude proxy for the agency (e.g., Cohen 1986; Shipan 2004) or whether the agency was created by a Democratic or Republican congress (e.g., Gilmour and Lewis 2006), in recent years scholars have begun to develop more sophisticated measures of agency ideology (e.g., Bertelli and Grose 2009; Nixon 2004; Snyder and Weingast 2000). Most recently, scores have been developed by Acs (2015); Bertelli and Grose (2011); Chen and Johnson (2014); Clinton et al. (2012); and Clinton and Lewis (2008), among others.

17. For instance, in a survey of bureaucrats working in environmental politics at the federal and the state levels, Waterman, Rouse, and Wright (2004) find that bureaucrats tend to have fairly mainstream perspectives on politics.

These points are carefully made by Clinton and colleagues (2012), who surveyed high-level careerists and political appointees and asked them to take a position on several policy issues on which Congress had recently voted. They then positioned agency-level actors in the same ideological space as the president and congressional actors. The distributions of the ideal points of various actors included in their study are displayed in figure 8.1. It is obvious that, compared to other elites, in the aggregate high-level bureaucrats tend to be more moderate and represent the middle of the ideological spectrum. Likely owing to the fact that their study was conducted under a Republican presidential administration (2007–2008), appointees skew slightly rightward (median = 0.30). Career executives, however, are slightly to the left of center (median = −0.05). Overall, then, the portrait that emerges is not one of bureaucrats as ideological extremists (despite Richard Nixon's protestations to the contrary). This stands in stark contrast to the bimodal distributions for the 109th House and the Senate (and the ideological position of President George W. Bush), also shown in figure 8.1, which clearly reflect high levels of polarization.

Ideologically speaking, it seems reasonable to conclude that the fourth branch is not particularly extreme and is, in fact, more in tune with the average American than with more polarized congressional representatives.[18] In a highly polarized environment, bureaucratic power and influence can therefore serve as a bulwark against more extreme tendencies. While politicians may be blown by the political winds, relatively centrist bureaucrats may use their procedural powers to steady the ship in uneven waters.

Overall, this examination of both the ideological and the descriptive characteristics of bureaucrats suggests that the fourth branch reflects the American public relatively well. However, just because bureaucrats may share outward traits with the average American does not mean that bureaucrats will always choose the same policies that said citizen—who is likely fairly uninformed about the particulars associated with regulatory policies—might have chosen. Miller and Whitford (2016, 80–81) explain that sometimes bureaucrats can represent underrepresented constituencies (e.g., "future" generations), serving to correct biases that exist because of majoritarian structures or the structural advantages enjoyed by powerful interests.[19] The

18. This ideological characterization, of course, relies on an understanding that the mass public is not ideologically polarized in the same way as Congress. On this point, most scholars agree that the public is largely moderate in its views (Ansolabehere, Rodden, and Snyder 2006; Bafumi and Herron 2010; Fiorina 2008), but see Abramowitz (2010).

19. It is worth noting that, to a person, each of the agency bureaucrats I interviewed for this project in one way or another expressed a desire to use rulemaking to create policy in the public interest.

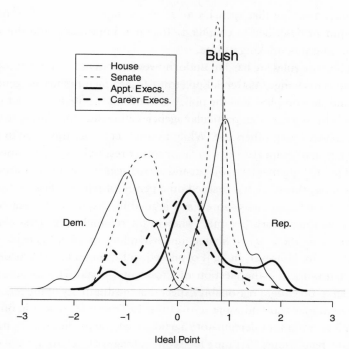

FIGURE 8.1. The ideology of appointees and careerists compared to other elites

Note: Reproduction of figure 2 from Clinton et al. (2012, 346): "The distribution of ideal points for each labeled group of political elites is plotted. All roll calls are used to estimate ideal points in the House and Senate, votes on contested conference reports are used to 'bridge' House and Senate estimates, and 14 votes are used to 'bridge' executive and congressional ideal points (seven in each chamber)."

general conclusion is, then, that procedural politicking does not necessarily steer public policy in directions that are far afield from mainstream preferences.

The Future of Procedural Politicking

Procedural politicking is about how unelected bureaucrats wield power. This power is meaningful because rules change policy in ways that are both important and lasting. Throughout this book, I have made the case that rulemaking is routinely used to move the policy needle on important issues that bureaucrats and other policy actors care about. However, rules are also relatively durable policy instruments. As former EPA Administrator Anne Gorsuch Burford (1981–1983) once put it, after "you put a regulation on the books, it is unlikely that anyone will be able to change it" (Burford and Greenya 1986, 98). Indeed, the process to undo a finalized regulation is the same as creating a new one, meaning that agencies must go through all the steps of notice-and-comment described in chapter 2. Together, importance and durability give procedural politicking its bite.

Just because rules are hard to undo, however, does not mean that they are impervious to change. As Derek Epp (2018) argues, factors such as agency capacity and the complexity of the policy at hand contribute to broader policy stability. This suggests that particular agencies and issues may be more prone to rule changes than others are. While I do not consider this issue in detail here, the insight points to a ripe area for future research exploring how procedural politicking may vary within and across agencies and policy areas.

Of course, this book has focused on a period of relative stasis in the regulatory environment (1995–2014); as I argued in chapter 1, this era constitutes its own regulatory "regime," wherein the rulemaking process changed very little and there was a shared understanding of what agencies could and should do. However, in light of subsequent changes in the broader political environment—the election of President Donald Trump in 2016 in particular—one might reasonably expect that the durability of the regulatory system itself may wax and wane across time. In Trump's first year in office he launched an ambitious deregulatory agenda, pledging to eliminate 75 percent of existing regulations.[20] Trump's focus on "rolling back" existing regulations, combined with support from a unified Republican Congress, has created a perception that rules are transitory policies. As of this writing, the jury is still out on whether Trump will succeed in accomplishing his deregulatory goals or whether the changes he has made are ephemeral. However, the shifts in norms around rulemaking for both political overseers and bureaucrats may be a harbinger that a new regulatory regime is afoot. To wit, the Congressional Review Act (CRA)[21]—successfully employed just once during the twenty-year period covered in this book—was used to repeal thirteen different agency rules in Trump's first four months in office. If it sticks, this new regime may be characterized by increasing congressional and media attention to rulemaking, and closer scrutiny (and accordingly, an increased potential for intervention) by the White House. The new zeitgeist in the Trump era is decidedly anti-agency.

Such a transition could put procedural politicking, at least as we currently know it, at risk. That is, politicians may consider serious reforms to the regulatory process aimed at reducing bureaucratic discretion and, ultimately, procedural politicking. These reforms—which would more than likely be in the form of legislative changes—would need to overcome considerable

20. Johnson and Mui (2017).
21. Pub. L. No. 104-121.

enactment hurdles. Nonetheless, there has been congressional interest in some particular reforms of the regulatory system, mostly from Republicans, but increasingly from Democrats as well. In a 2016 opinion editorial, liberal Democratic Senator Elizabeth Warren highlighted the urgent need for regulatory reform, stating that "our rulemaking process is broken from start to finish." While the emphasis of her argument—the need to reduce corporate influence in rulemaking—was distant from the concerns of her Republican colleagues, regulatory reform has been a hot-button issue in recent years. To take one recent example, during the 113th Congress no fewer than seventeen reform bills were introduced in the House and Senate. Although none of these bills received a vote in both chambers, they included many reform ideas that have been reverberating within the Beltway in one form or another for some time. The introduction of a new regulatory regime has the potential to generate new momentum for these reforms.

While pinpointing the exact nature of some future reform is necessarily speculative, three types of reforms have received appreciable attention: changes to the regulatory process, changes to the nature of judicial oversight of rulemaking, and changes to the composition of the bureaucracy. Each of these reforms would have implications for procedural politicking and for the rulemaking process, and each involves a trade-off between the between the value of the reform and the quality of the rules produced.

INCREASING PROCEDURAL REQUIREMENTS

The most commonly discussed regulatory reforms propose adding some new layer to the existing regulatory infrastructure. These procedural reforms are intended to curb bureaucrats' discretion, and they target nearly all stages of the regulatory process. Recent proposals include the addition of mandatory advance notice and a public hearing stage for any rule that would impose costs of $1 billion or more,[22] a stipulation that a rule cannot take effect unless it has been posted on the internet for at least six months,[23] and a requirement that Congress directly approve all major rules before they take effect.[24] Other reforms focus on constraining bureaucratic discretion by standardizing the rulemaking process. One recent proposal to do this would establish a

---

22. Regulatory Accountability Act, H.R. 185, 114th Congress (2016).

23. All Economic Regulations are Transparent Act (ALERT Act), H.R. 1759, 114th Congress (2015).

24. Regulations from the Executive in Need of Scrutiny Act (REINS Act), H.R. 427, 114th Congress (2015).

sixty-day floor for the length of the comment period on all agency proposed rules.[25] Another proposed by two law professors would have agencies batch release rules at prespecified points in time, to prevent agencies from strategically timing the release of their rules.[26] Finally, another class of reforms would require agencies to be more transparent about which groups they meet with and when. Proposals in this vein often include suggestions to standardize the manner by which agencies disclose this information to the public and to require regular updating by agencies.[27] It is notable that many of these reforms map directly onto the procedural tactics I outlined in the preceding chapters.

Each of these proposals holds some promise in fixing an aspect of the rulemaking process that is perceived to be broken or inefficient. To varying extents, these proposals would limit the ability of bureaucrats to engage in procedural politicking—at least as they currently do it. For instance, bureaucrats' ability to manipulate the length of the public comment period, which I uncovered in chapter 5, would certainly be diminished were Congress to mandate a floor (and possibly a ceiling). However, the nature of these reforms is necessarily piecemeal. And while this particular reform might alter one aspect of the rulemaking process, it is unlikely to reduce procedural politicking writ large.

One of the core lessons of procedural politicking is that bureaucrats respond to structural incentives and will use procedures as an avenue to realize their goals. Remedying one procedure does not change that—more likely, bureaucrats will simply shift their attention to other procedures that remain malleable. Arguably, the more complex and layered the regulatory process is, the more it favors bureaucrats. Additionally, there may be another unintended consequence of procedural reform. Agencies are already overburdened and face resource shortages. Therefore, layering on new procedural requirements may exacerbate the ossification problem. That is, agencies might be forced to move even more slowly through the rulemaking process in order to satisfy these new demands.

However, the piecemeal nature of the reforms can be considered a feature rather than a bug. Each of these reforms is premised upon achieving a specific goal—and to the extent that those goals are measurable—the reforms

25. Regulatory Accountability Act, H.R. 3010, 112th Congress (2011).

26. Gersen and O'Connell (2009).

27. The ALERT Act, for instance, would have prevented agencies from omitting rules from reporting requirements. Specifically, this would have limited an agency's ability to strategically shield upcoming rules from public scrutiny in the manner identified by Nou and Stiglitz (2016). To accomplish this the bill would have required agencies to submit monthly reports to the Office of Information and Regulatory Affairs on regulatory actions planned for the upcoming year. OIRA would then be required to publish these reports on the internet.

can be implemented in a manner that facilitates scientific evaluation of their effectiveness. For instance, working with an oversight body like the Administrative Conference of the United States (ACUS, the agency charged with overseeing the regulatory process and thinking through the big issues confronting regulators) a reform can be implemented in a way such that it is randomly assigned to certain agencies or rules. From there, it is possible to accurately identify whether or not the reform is achieving its intended goal. Approaching regulatory reform in this methodical way would serve to enhance the legitimacy of the reform process, avoid widespread unintended consequences, and possibly improve the overall quality of regulation.

CURTAILING JUDICIAL DEFERENCE

Another proposed solution to the issue of procedural discretion—and discretion in the rulemaking process more broadly—is to limit judicial deference to agencies' interpretation of statutory provisions. As explained in chapter 2, judicial deference to agencies, particularly the well-known *Chevron* deference standard, means that reviewing courts tend to grant agencies considerable latitude in their interpretation of statutes, especially when they issue regulations. Many in Congress (particularly Republicans) view judicial deference as a license for agencies to interpret laws however they see fit, regardless of the intentions of the legislative coalition that enacted the law or the current oversight coalition in Congress.

Limiting judicial deference would require courts to discard the agency's interpretation of a statutory provision and to directly review questions of law relating to statutory provisions in regulation themselves. This has been attempted. During the 114th Congress, the Republican-controlled House passed a bill—the Separation of Powers Restoration Act (SOPRA)[28]—which would have amended the Administrative Procedure Act to do just this. Although the bill died in the Senate, its intent, and the intent of other reforms like it, was to wrest power from agencies and give it instead to courts.

However, reducing judicial deference might not yield the desired effects either. First, even in the absence of formal deference standards, it is not clear that judges would necessarily arrive at different decisions. That is, given judges' considerable workload and lack of expertise in specific policy areas, they might still tend to side with agencies irrespective of whether there

---

28. Separation of Powers Restoration Act, H.R. 4768, 114th Congress (2016). This bill passed the House on a largely partisan vote (240 yea votes, 239 of which were Republican members). It was referred to the Senate Judiciary Committee but never received consideration.

is a formal norm of judicial deference. This outcome could be justified on alternate grounds, since policies like SOPRA "would not prevent the court from emphasizing agencies' competence as fact-finders and deferring in such cases."[29] Additionally, having the courts conduct statutory interpretations may actually leave Congress and the president worse off. For example, although Congress and the president were united under Republican control in 2017, the majority of appellate court judges at that time—who have lifetime appointments—were appointed by Democratic presidents.[30] This suggests that the courts might not necessarily rule in ways that favor the ideology of the current ruling coalition, and they would certainly be even less constrained than their bureaucratic counterparts.

The effects of diminished judicial deference on procedural politicking would likely be mixed. On the one hand, to the extent that I have found that agencies use procedural politics to evade court oversight, those tactics might increase. That is, agencies may find themselves with an even greater incentive to avoid judicial scrutiny. On the other hand, reduced deference might obviate the need for the type of procedural politics described herein. As Raso (2017) suggests, were such a reform to be enacted, agencies might avoid rulemaking entirely in favor of other policy-making venues: "Faced with less deference and a greater prospect of being overturned in court, agencies might invest fewer resources into interpreting statutes through resource-intensive rulemakings, instead shifting toward making policy case-by-case through a process known as 'adjudication,' which is faster and cheaper than rulemaking." In other words, judicial deference may engender a different type of procedural gaming. Given that adjudication may be less transparent and less equitable (because different policies may be applied to similarly situated individuals), this is yet another reason that policy makers should proceed cautiously with this kind of reform.

ELIMINATING MERIT PROTECTIONS

The principles of procedural politicking suggest that the makeup of the bureaucracy influences policy outcomes. When bureaucrats share an ideological orientation with political leaders, procedural politicking is less likely, simply because bureaucrats will not need to evade political oversight. Policy makers, then, ought to concern themselves with who serves in the bureaucracy. One

---

29. Raso (2017).
30. See Levin (2016, 8–10).

reform effort does just this—proposing to have politicians be able to rotate career bureaucrats out of office as they see fit.

This is less of an issue for the president, who can select political appointees (not all of whom require Senate confirmation) on the basis of their political perspectives and loyalty to the current administration. Yet even then, political appointees make up a small fraction of the federal bureaucracy, leaving lots of room for careerists to leave their mark. The principle of merit protection for civil servants means that careerists endure regardless of the current presidential administration or political environment. Established with the Pendleton Civil Service Reform Act of 1883, merit protection ensures that civil servants are structurally insulated from partisan politics.

Although merit protection is often considered a bedrock of the US bureaucracy, like any institution, it can be changed. Partisan politicians can reduce merit protections or eliminate them altogether to ferret out employees who disagree with the current leadership's policy orientation and replace them with like-minded individuals willing to toe the administration's line. These policy changes, which would reduce procedural politicking, could potentially affect not only the hiring and firing but also the promotion and compensation of bureaucrats.

This is not as far-fetched a policy reform as it may seem. Within the so-called laboratories of democracy, several states have dispensed with merit protection. For example, in 1996 the State of Georgia passed a law making all newly hired civil servants "at will" employees. Florida and Texas have also reduced merit protections, albeit to a lesser extent than Georgia. Naff, Riccucci, and Freyss (2013, 38) report that by 2005, "28 of the 50 states had expanded, or were moving toward expanding, the number of at-will positions." There have been moves toward reducing merit protections at the federal level, too. For instance, the House recently readopted an arcane procedural rule, called the Holman rule, which enables members to include amendments to appropriations bill that cut the pay of individual government employees, possibly down to $1. In theory, this tool could be used to target individual bureaucrats or groups of bureaucrats who have not performed in ways that accord with congressional wishes.[31] Similarly, bills have been introduced in Congress more recently to make all new civil servants hired on an "at will" basis, meaning that they could potentially be dismissed without cause and without a right to appeal.[32]

31. Portnoy and Rein (2017).

32. See, for example, the Promote Accountability and Government Efficiency Act, H.R. 6278, 114th Congress, which was introduced in the House in 2016.

However, while reducing or eliminating merit protections might give lawmakers and presidents more immediate control over bureaucratic actors, it also may have other, deleterious consequences that are worth considering. In the states, the results of these civil service reforms have been mixed. In Georgia, for example, the reform increased the number of new hires and the number of raises in the first two years after its implementation, but it is also believed to have created a less-trusting relationship between workers and managers.[33] While at-will employment is common in the private sector, in the public sector, where political leaders turnover with some regularity, the effect of equally high civil servant turnover could impede the overall stability of a bureaucratic organization. Reduced stability, in turn, can lead employees to adopt shorter time horizons for their work, resulting in inferior organizational performance.[34] In the extreme, were such at-will firings to be executed on a widespread basis, the result could be massive bureaucratic turnover at the beginning of each new presidential administration—perhaps even signaling the beginnings of a return to something resembling the Jacksonian patronage system, a state of affairs which Alexis de Tocqueville derided as "evil" and as leading to "a sort of a revolution" in government every four years.[35] This could potentially introduce virulent polarization into the heart of the bureaucracy. Thus, any reform to reduce merit protections should be considered in light of the trade-offs it introduces in terms of organizational stability, performance, and politicization.

Closing Thoughts

In a well-developed regulatory system like the one that exists in the United States, bureaucratic influence—particularly that exercised at the margins through procedural politics—may not be worrisome. Bureaucrats are checked by other powerful actors. Additionally, since bureaucrats are broadly representative of the populace, the agenda they pursue may mirror the preferences of the governed. As a consequence, the United States' notice-and-comment rulemaking process has repeatedly been held up as a model for

33. Kerrigan (2012).

34. Krause and Corder (2007).

35. During this period, nearly all bureaucratic positions were vacated when a new president was elected and then subsequently refilled. Tocqueville (1839, 123) noted that, with "every new election the fate of all the Federal public officers is in suspense. Mr. Quincy Adams, on his entry into office, discharged the majority of the individuals who had been appointed by his predecessor: and I am not aware that General Jackson allowed a single removable functionary employed in the Federal service to retain his place beyond the first year which succeeded his election."

bureaucratic decision making across the world. International organizations such as the Organisation for Economic Co-operation and Development and the World Bank actively proselytize the system to governments around the globe. However, in a less-developed setting—particularly one in which corruption is a potential concern—the type of bureaucratic influence described here may be much more normatively concerning.

While the focus of this book has been the notice-and-comment rulemaking process, procedural politicking is not confined to that venue. Bureaucratic agencies make myriad policy decisions—including allocating grant dollars, awarding contracts, adjudicating cases, hiring personnel, and making enforcement decisions. This study suggests that only when scrutiny is given to how the procedures associated with these technical decisions are managed is the true extent of bureaucratic power revealed.

Procedures are politics. The rules can be bent to favor particular interests or outcomes. Understanding the impact of these insights insight requires consideration of the political setting in which procedures operate and what those in charge of managing the procedures are hoping to accomplish. Rulemaking and its attendant procedures are inherently the stuff of insiders; the process is understood by relatively few, yet the regulations this process creates apply to many. This book has waded into this esoteric process, with the hope of beginning a conversation not only about what rulemaking procedures do, but also about what they should do.

Data Appendix

This appendix provides additional information about how the data used in the empirical analyses in chapters 4, 5, and 6 were collected and coded.

A. Compiling the *Regulatory Proposals Dataset*

The *Regulatory Proposals Dataset* is the primary data source for the analyses in chapters 4 through 6. It contains information on nearly eleven thousand proposed rules from 135 bureaus (housed within 15 Cabinet departments) and 15 independent agencies. To create this dataset, I relied on the *Unified Agenda of Regulatory and Deregulatory Actions* (UA), a semiannual snapshot of agency rulemaking, wherein agencies report on their prospective, ongoing, and completed regulatory activities.

To compile the UA data into a workable dataset, I follow the procedures outlined in O'Connell (2008). Specifically, I count each Regulatory Identification Number (RIN) as a unique identifier, even though in rare cases RINs are changed or reused. RINs are usually reported multiple times in the UA as a rule progresses through the through the stages of the rulemaking process; therefore, I keep the most recent UA entry for each RIN. This means that "if an earlier entry for a RIN contained certain information but a later entry for that same RIN did not, that information would not be captured in the database" (O'Connell 2008, 985). Because the UA sometimes contains incomplete or inaccurate information, where mistakes were obvious I corrected RIN entries by confirming information with the *Federal Register* or through internet searches. For instance, information about the dates associated with a proposed rule's public comment period is frequently missing or incorrectly reported in the UA. Therefore, I had teams of research assistants verify dates by examining the text of the proposed rule or consulting other agency documents that referenced the necessary information.

I exclude several classes of UA entries that are oddities from the *Regulatory Proposals Dataset*. First, I exclude rules where the proposed rule was not actually a proposed rule. This consists primarily of administrative notices incorrectly marked as proposed rules. I also exclude prospective actions, where the agency indicated in the UA that it planned to take an action but never updated that plan with a concrete action. Additionally, for the timing analyses in chapter 6, I also exclude rules that were transferred to a new RIN or merged with another RIN since it is not clear whether the "same" rule is being finalized in these cases.

Many of the analyses in the book include covariates measured at the bureau level. To identify which bureau wrote the rule I rely on the first four digits of the RIN. In most cases, this code indicates the bureau that sponsored the rule (e.g., Food and Drug Administration, Administration for Children and Families). In some cases, the four-digit code corresponds to a smaller administrative unit within a broader department (e.g., Office of the Chief Financial Officer or Office of Procurement and Policy Management, both within the US Department of Agriculture). Because many of these smaller offices issued very few rules during the study's time frame, for Cabinet-level departments that had several such offices, I group small administrative units together into a broader departmental category. In two instances (the Department of State and the Department of Veterans Affairs) the RIN indicates only the department (and not the bureau) that sponsored the rule. I was therefore unable to further disaggregate rules from these two departments and matched those rule to covariates measured at the department level. Table A.1 lists the agencies included in the dataset.

Relying on the UA has both advantages and disadvantages. On the one hand, the UA is the most comprehensive accounting of rulemaking available to scholars, including information not just on the date and progress of regulatory actions but also on other associated factors such as statutory and judicial deadlines and the legal basis for action. Additionally, many studies of rulemaking also depend on the UA, enabling comparisons between the analyses I present here and work in multiple disciplines. On the other hand, as previously noted, because UA actions are self-reported by agencies, they are subject to errors. Where possible, I have made every effort to detect and correct these errors.

TABLE A.1. Bureaus and departments included in the study

Bureau	Department	Agency name
ACF	HHS	Administration for Children and Families
AF	DOD	Department of the Air Force
AGING	HHS	Administration on Aging
AHRQ	HHS	Agency for Healthcare Research and Quality
AID[a]	—	Agency for International Development
AMS	USDA	Agricultural Marketing Service
APHIS	USDA	Animal and Plant Health Inspection Service
ARMY	DOD	Department of the Army
ARS	USDA	Agricultural Research Service
ATTTB	TREAS	Alcohol and Tobacco Tax Trade Bureau
BATF[b]	TREAS	Bureau of Alcohol, Tobacco, and Firearms
BATFE[b]	DOJ	Bureau of Alcohol, Tobacco, Firearms, and Explosives
BEA	DOC	Bureau of Economic Analysis
BIA	DOI	Bureau of Indian Affairs
BIS	DOC	Bureau of Industry and Security
BLM	DOI	Bureau of Land Management
BOEM	DOI	Bureau of Ocean Energy Management
BOP	DOJ	Bureau of Prisons
BOR	DOI	Bureau of Reclamation
BPD	TREAS	Bureau of the Public Debt
BSEE	DOI	Bureau of Safety and Environmental Enforcement
CBP	DHS	Customs and Border Protection
CCR[a]	—	Commission on Civil Rights
CDC	HHS	Centers for Disease Control and Prevention
CDIF	TREAS	Community Development Institute Finance Fund
CENSUS	DOC	Census Bureau
CG[b]	DHS	Coast Guard (DHS)
CG[b]	DOT	Coast Guard (DOT)
CIVIL	DOJ	Civil Rights Division
CMS	HHS	Centers for Medicare and Medicaid Services
CNCS[a]	—	Corporation for National and Community Service
COMP	TREAS	Comptroller of the Currency
CORPS	DOD	US Army Corps of Engineers
CRF	TREAS	Customs Revenue Function
DARC	DOD	Defense Acquisition Regulations Council
DEA	DOJ	Drug Enforcement Administration
DEPT (DHS)[c]	DHS	Departmental
DEPT (DOC)[c]	DOC	Departmental
DEPT (DOD)[c]	DOD	Departmental
DEPT (DOE)[c]	DOE	Departmental
DEPT (DOI)[c]	DOI	Departmental
DEPT (DOL)[c]	DOL	Departmental

(continued)

Bureau	Department	Agency name
DEPT (DOT)[c]	DOT	Departmental
DEPT (ED)[c]	ED	Departmental
DEPT (HHS)[c]	HHS	Departmental
DEPT (HUD)[c]	HUD	Departmental
DEPT (TREAS)[c]	TREAS	Departmental
DEPT (USDA)[c]	USDA	Departmental
DSA	DOE	Defense and Security Affairs
EBSA	DOL	Employee Benefits Security Administration
EDA	DOC	Economic Development Administration
EEOC[a]	—	Equal Employment Opportunity Commission
EERE	DOE	Energy Efficiency and Renewable Energy
EOIR	DOJ	Executive Office for Immigration Review
EPA[a]	—	Environmental Protection Agency
ESA	DOL	Employment Standards Administration
ETA	DOL	Employment and Training Administration
FAA	DOT	Federal Aviation Administration
FARM	USDA	Farm Service Agency
FAS	USDA	Foreign Agricultural Service
FBI	DOJ	Federal Bureau of Investigation
FCEN	TREAS	Financial Crimes Enforcement Network
FDA	HHS	Food and Drug Administration
FEMA[b]	DHS	Federal Emergency Management Agency (DHS)
FEMA[a,b]	—	Federal Emergency Management Agency (Ind)
FHA	DOT	Federal Highway Administration
FHFA[a]	—	Federal Housing Finance Authority
FISCAL	TREAS	Bureau of the Fiscal Service
FMCSA	DOT	Federal Motor Carrier Safety Administration
FMS	TREAS	Financial Management Service
FNS	USDA	Food and Nutrition Service
FRA	DOT	Federal Railroad Administration
FS	USDA	Forest Service
FSA	ED	Office of Federal Student Aid
FSIS	USDA	Food Safety and Inspection Service
FTA	DOT	Federal Transit Administration
FWS	DOI	US Fish and Wildlife Service
GNMA	HUD	Government National Mortgage Association
GRAIN	USDA	Grain Inspection, Packers and Stockyards Administration
GSA[a]	—	General Services Administration
HIS	HHS	Indian Health Service
HOUSING	HUD	Office of Housing
HRSA	HHS	Health Resources and Services Administration
ICE	DHS	Immigration and Customs Enforcement
IES	ED	Institute of Education Sciences

TABLE A.1. (*continued*)

Bureau	Department	Agency name
INS	DOJ	Immigration and Naturalization Service
IRS	TREAS	Internal Revenue Service
ITA	DOC	International Trade Administration
LEGAL	DOJ	Legal Activities
MARI	DOT	Maritime Administration
MSHA	DOL	Mine Safety and Health Administration
NARA[a]	—	National Archives and Records Administration
NAVY	DOD	Department of the Navy
NHTSA	DOT	National Highway Traffic Safety Administration
NIFA	USDA	National Institute of Food and Agriculture
NIH	HHS	National Institutes of Health
NIST	DOC	National Institute of Standards and Technology
NNSA	DOE	National Nuclear Security Administration
NOAA	DOC	National Oceanic and Atmospheric Administration
NPS	DOI	National Park Service
NRCS	USDA	Natural Resources Conservation Service
NSF[a]	—	National Science Foundation
NTIA	DOC	National Telecommunications and Information Administration
OASEC (DOD)	DOD	Office of Assistant Secretary for Health Affairs
OASEC (HHS)	HHS	Office of Assistant Secretary for Administration & Management
OAW	DOL	Office of the American Workplace
OCPD	HUD	Office of Community Planning and Development
OCR (ED)	ED	Office for Civil Rights
OCR (HHS)	HHS	Office for Civil Rights (HHS)
OELA	ED	Office of English Language Acquisition
OESE	ED	Office of Elementary and Secondary Education
OFCCP	DOL	Office of Federal Contract Compliance Programs
OFHEO	HUD	Office of Fair Housing and Equal Opportunity
OGE[a]	—	Office of Government Ethics
OII	ED	Office of Innovation and Improvement
OJP	DOJ	Office of Justice Programs
OLMS	DOL	Office of Labor-Management Standards
ONRR	DOI	Office of Natural Resources Revenue
OPE	ED	Office of Postsecondary Education
OPEPD	ED	Office of Planning, Evaluation and Policy Development
OPHS	HHS	Office of Public Health and Science
OPIH	HUD	Office of Public and Indian Housing
OPM[a]	—	Office of Personnel Management
OSDFS	ED	Office of Safe and Drug-Free Schools
OSERS	ED	Office of Special Education and Rehabilitative Services
OSHA	DOL	Occupational Safety and Health Administration
OSMRE	DOI	Office of Surface Mining Reclamation and Enforcement
OSPC	DOJ	Parole Commission

(*continued*)

Bureau	Department	Agency name
OST	DOI	Office of the Special Trustee for American Indians
PBGC[a]	—	Pension Benefit Guaranty Corporation
PHMSA	DOT	Pipeline and Hazardous Materials Safety Administration
PHS	HHS	Public Health Service
POLICY	HUD	Office of Policy Development and Research
PTO	DOC	Patent and Trademark Office
RBCS	USDA	Rural Business-Cooperative Service
RHS	USDA	Rural Housing Service
RITA	DOT	Research and Innovative Technology Administration
RUS	USDA	Rural Utilities Service
SAMSHA	HHS	Substance Abuse and Mental Health Services Administration
SBA[a]	—	Small Business Administration
SSA[a]	—	Social Security Administration
STATE[d]	STATE	Department of State
TA	DOC	Technology Administration
THRIFT	TREAS	Office of Thrift Supervision
TSA	DHS	Transportation Security Administration
UCIS	DHS	US Citizenship and Immigration Services
VA[d]	VA	Department of Veterans Affairs
VETS	DOL	Veterans' Employment and Training Service
WAGE	DOL	Wage and Hour Division
WCOMP	DOL	Office of Workers' Compensation Programs

Note: Departmental acronyms: DHS = Department of Homeland Security; DOC = Department of Commerce; DOD = Department of Defense; DOE = Department of Energy; DOI = Department of the Interior; DOJ = Department of Justice; DOL = Department of Labor; DOT = Department of Transportation; ED = Department of Education; HHS = Department of Health and Human Services; HUD = Department of Housing and Urban Development; STATE = Department of State; TREAS = Department of Treasury; USDA = Department of Agriculture; and VA = Department of Veterans Affairs.

[a]Indicates an independent agency within the executive branch that is not housed within a cabinet department.

[b]Indicates a bureau that was moved from one department to another during the study's time frame. The Bureau of Alcohol, Tobacco, and Firearms (BATF) was part of TREAS until January 2003, when it was transferred to DOJ and renamed the Bureau of Alcohol, Tobacco, Firearms, and Explosives (BATFE). I treat these as two distinct bureaus. The Coast Guard (CG) and the Federal Emergency Management Agency (FEMA) were incorporated into DHS when it was created in November 2002. Before then, the CG was part of the DOT and FEMA was an independent agency. Prior to DHS's creation, I consider FEMA its own agency and the CG as part of DOT; following DHS's launch, I consider both to be bureaus within that department.

[c]Indicates that I have aggregated smaller administrative units together into a broader departmental unit that issues rules.

[d]The Department of State and the Department of Veterans Affairs do not disaggregate their rulemaking activities to the bureau level. Thus, rules from those departments are counted at the department level and not the bureau level.

B. Developing Rule *Impact* and *Complexity* Scores

I use principal components analysis (PCA) to uncover an *Impact* and *Complexity* score for each proposed rule in the dataset. PCA is a widely used technique to reduce a set of variables into a smaller number of uncorrelated latent dimensions. It is typically applied to continuous data; because I include several discrete data points, I employ the polychoric PCA approach developed by Kolenikov and Angeles (2009).[1]

The information underlying this analysis is presented in table B.1, which provides a description of each of the six input variables and their associated data sources. The data are drawn from the *Unified Agenda* and from Lexis-Nexis searches. Since bureaus may have very different writing styles, I scale

TABLE B.1. PCA input data and component loadings

	Variable description	Loading
Rule impact		
Eigenvalue = 1.865		
Variance explained = 0.311		
Economically significant	1 if rule is expected to have annual impact of $100 million or more, 0 otherwise (source: *Unified Agenda*)	1.232
Small business	1 if rule affected small business or other entities, 0 otherwise (source: *Unified Agenda*)	0.361
Governmental entities	1 if rule affects state, local, or tribal governments, 0 otherwise (source: *Unified Agenda*)	0.420
Newspaper mention	1 if *New York Times* covered the proposed rule's release, 0 otherwise (source: *LexisNexis*)	1.330
Rule complexity		
Eigenvalue = 1.02		
Variance explained = 0.171		
Statutory authorities	The number of statutory cites for the rule minus the mean number of statutory cites for the bureau issuing the rule (source: *Unified Agenda*)	0.788
Rule abstract	The number of words in the rule's abstract minus the mean number of words for abstracts written by the bureau issuing the rule (source: *Unified Agenda*)	0.524

1. The polychoric PCA approach does not vary meaningfully from a standard PCA model in this case; the correlation between the two approaches is quite high ($\rho > .95$ for both dimensions).

the two variables that are based on how the rule is drafted—*Statutory authorities* and *Rule abstract*—to the mean for the issuing bureau.

In conducting PCA, the researcher must evaluate how many dimensions are present in the data. The convention is to discard any component with an eigenvalue of less than 1 (Jolliffe 2002). As shown in table B.1, both *Impact* and *Complexity* have eigenvalues greater than 1.[2] Together these two dimensions address 48.2 percent of the underlying variance in the data, which suggests that they do a good job of capturing the latent concepts.

Table B.1 also reports the component loadings for each of the data points. As expected, each of the input variables loads positively and meaningfully onto the relative dimensions.

C. Analyzing the Accessibility of Proposed Rule Texts

To create a dataset of proposed rule texts, I matched entries in the *Unified Agenda* with texts published in the *Federal Register*. This matching exercise was conducted with each rule's RIN, title, and publication date. To ensure that all texts matched precisely with data from the *Regulatory Proposals Dataset*, I first extracted all proposed rule texts from the *Federal Register*'s application programming interface (API) and then had a team of research assistants manually confirm that each proposed rule was an exact match. This latter step was necessary because many *Federal Register* texts lack the correct RIN or any RIN at all. In such cases, an internet search was performed to find the correct text. I excluded thirty-five proposed rules for which I or my team was unable to confirm an exact match with *Unified Agenda* data.

All texts were formatted in extensible markup language (XML), a programming format that structures texts according to a preset schematic of features (determined in this case by the *Federal Register*). Because I relied on automated analyses to parse the texts, I was unable to include any proposed rule from before 2000, since the *Federal Register* has not encoded documents prior to this date in XML. Additionally, I excluded an additional seven texts that were proposed after 2000 but were not available in XML format. This exercise resulted in a dataset of 2,870 proposed rule texts.

For the *Abstract readability* measure, for each XML document I extracted the abstract text, which included all text included in the summary tag <SUM>. I then use the koRpus package in R to obtain measures of text readability. Following Black and colleagues (2016), I evaluated each extracted

---

2. Visual inspection of a scree plot also confirms the presence of two dimensions.

TABLE C.1. Readability metrics and associated inputs in the *Abstract readability* measure

	Words	Sentences	Characters	Syllables
Anderson's Readability Index (RIX)		X	X	
Automated Readability Index (ARI)	X	X	X	
Coleman-Liau[a]	X	X		X
Danielson-Bryan[a]		X	X	
Dickes-Stewer-Handformel	X	X	X	
Fang's Easy Listening Formula		X		X
Farr-Jenkins-Paterson	X	X		X
Flesch	X	X		X
Flesch-Kincaid[a]	X	X		X
FORCAST[a]	X			X
Fucks's Stilcharakteristik[a]	X	X	X	
Gunning Frequency of Gobbledygook (FOG)	X	X		X
Kuntzsch's Text-Redundanz-Index				X
Linsear-Write[a]	X			X
LIX Score	X	X	X	
Neue Wiener Sachtextformeln (nWS)[a]	X		X	X
Simple Measure of Gobbledygook (SMOG)		X		X
Strain Index		X		X
Wheeler-Smith	X	X		X

Note: Adapted from figure 3.1 in Black et al. (2016, 50). See the koRpus documentation (https://reaktanz.de/?c=hacking s=koRpus, April 5, 2017) for more detail on each measure.

[a]Indicates readability measures with more than one associated metric included in the *Abstract readability* measure.

abstract using the readability metrics identified in table C.1, each of which draws on a unique algorithm based on some combination of the text's words, sentences, characters, and syllables.

Again following the lead of Black and colleagues (2016), I then use principal components analysis to reduce these twenty-eight measures into a single score for each proposed rule abstract.[3] *Abstract readability* is the first dimension of the PCA analysis; each of the component metrics loads with the expected sign and the resulting composite measure accounts for 74 percent of the observed variance. The mean of this variable is centered at 0 (s.d. = 4.58), and it ranges from −21.1 to 27.7.

For the *Preamble length* measure, for each XML document I extracted the preamble text. This is the text where the agency describes (supposedly in plain language) the proposal included in the language that will affect the *Code of Federal Regulations* (CFR). I capture all text between the <SUPLINF> and

3. Table C.1 includes nineteen distinct measures of text readability. However, some of these measures include more than one metric; for example, the Flesch-Kincaid measure offers both a grade-level and an age-level estimate for each text.

<LSTSUB> tags.[4] I then count (and subsequently log) the number of words included in this portion of the text.

D. Measuring Interest Group Opposition

To develop the *Group opposition* measure, I relied on industry campaign contribution data from the Center for Responsive Politics (CRP, at http://www .opensecrets.org/). I began by mapping agencies to policy areas using topic codes from the Policy Agendas Project's online database (Baumgartner et al. 2016). For example, the Office of Housing (HOUSING) in the Department of Housing and Urban Development (HUD) maps onto topic code 14, "community development and housing issues," in the Policy Agendas database. For the most part, this categorization was based on the Policy Agendas codebook, where many of the bureaus are specifically mentioned in the context of a particular topic area. When the bureau was not mentioned in the codebook, I relied on my best judgment.

Because the CRP organizes campaign contributions into industries, I then repeated this bridging exercise to match industries to policy areas. For example, "home builders" are a discrete industry in the CRP data, and I matched that with the "community development and housing issues" topic code (14). Here, my coding scheme largely followed the coding choices made by Curry (2015). However, while the mapping here is nearly identical to Curry's coding, the match is not exact, because I was unable to locate industry data for six of the "miscellaneous" categories (agriculture, business, energy, health, communication and electronics, and transport) that he includes in his table B3. For each policy area, I then aggregate the total industry spending in terms of money given to Democrats and money given to Republicans.

Table D.1 shows the resulting mapping of interest group campaign spending to bureaus. Because campaign spending data are reported biannually, I average between the reporting years to get estimates for the off years. The first column includes the relevant Policy Agendas major topic areas and codes. The second column includes the CRP industries that are matched with each policy area. Finally, the third column lists the agencies that are matched to each policy area.

---

4. In some cases, the signature line for the relevant agency authority was included in this section of the text, whereas in others it was excluded. Therefore, where appropriate, I excluded text from the <SIG> tag.

TABLE D.1. Mapping of bureaus to interest group spending by industry

Policy agendas topic	CRP industries	Bureaus
Agriculture (4)	Agricultural services and products; crop production & basic processing; dairy, food process and sales; forestry and forest products; livestock; poultry and eggs; tobacco	AMS, APHIS, ARS, DEPT (USDA), FAS, FNS, FS, FSA, FSIS, GRAIN, NIFA, NRCS, RBCS, RHS, RUS
Banking, finance, and domestic commerce (15)	Accountants; beer, wine and liquor; building materials and equipment; business associations; business services; casinos/gambling; chemical and related manufacturing; commercial banks; construction services; credit unions; finance/credit companies; food and beverage; general contractors; insurance; lodging/tourism; misc. finance; misc. manufacturing and distribution; misc. services; real estate; recreation/live entertainment; retail sales; savings and loans; securities and investment; special trade contractors; steel production textiles	ATTTB, BATF (TREAS), BEA, BIS, BPD, CDIF, CENSUS, COMP, CRF, DEPT (DOC), DEPT (TREAS), EDA, FCEN, FEMA (DHS), FEMA (IND), FISCAL, FMS, IRS, ITA, NIST, NOAA, NTIA, PTO, SBA, TA, THRIFT
Civil rights, minority issues, and civil liberties (2)	Abortion policy/pro–abortion rights; abortion policy/anti-abortion; clergy and religious organizations; gun rights, women's issues	CCR, EEOC
Community development and housing issues (14)	Home builders	DEPT (HUD), FHFA, GNMA, HOUSING, OCPD, OFHEO, OPIH, POLICY
Defense (16)	Defense aerospace; defense electronics; misc. defense	AF, ARMY, CBP, CG (DHS), CORPS, DARC, DEPT (DHS), DEPT (DOD), ICE, NAVY, OASEC, TSA, UCIS, VA
Education (6)	Education; teachers' unions	DEPT (ED), FSA, IES, OCR (ED), OELA, OESE, OII, OPE, OPEPD, OSDFS, OSERS
Energy (8)	Alternative energy production and services; electric utilities; mining, oil and gas; waste management	BSEE, DEPT (DOE), DSA, EERE, NNSA
Environment (7)	Environment	EPA
Government operations (20)	Civil servants/public officials, postal unions	GSA, NARA, OFCCP, OGE, OPM

(continued)

Policy agendas topic	CRP industries	Bureaus
Health (3)	Health professionals; health services/HMOs; hospitals and nursing homes; pharmaceuticals/health products	ACF, AHRQ, CDC, CMS, DEPT (HHS), FDA, IHS, HRSA, NIH, OASEC, OCR (HHS), PHS, SAMSHA
International affairs and foreign aid (19)	Foreign and defense policy; pro-Israel; trucking	AID, STATE
Labor, employment, and immigration (5)	Building trade unions; industrial unions; misc. unions; postal unions; public sector unions; teachers unions; transportation unions	DEPT (DOL), EBSA, ESA, ETA, MSHA, OAW, OLMS, OSHA, PBGC, VETS, WAGE, WCOMP
Law, crime and family issues (12)	Gun control	BATFE (DOJ), BOP, CIVIL, DEA, EOIR, FBI, INS, LEGAL, OJP, OSPC
Public lands and water management (21)	Forestry and forest products	BLM, BOEM, BOR, DEPT (DOI), FWS, NPS, ONRR, OSMRE, OST
Science, space, technology, and communications (17)	Electronics manufacturing and equipment; internet; printing and publishing; telecom services & equipment; telephone; utilities; TV/music/movies	NSF
Social welfare (13)	Human rights; retired	AGING, CNCS, SSA
Transportation (10)	Air transport; automotive; railroads; sea transport; transportation unions; trucking	CG (DOT), DEPT (DOT), FAA, FHA, FMCSA, FRA, FTA, MARI, NHTSA, PHMSA, RITA

References

Aberbach, Joel D. 1990. *Keeping a Watchful Eye: The Politics of Congressional Oversight*. Washington, DC: Brookings Institution Press.

Abramowitz, Alan I. 2010. *The Disappearing Center: Engaged Citizens, Polarization, and American Democracy*. New Haven, CT: Yale University Press.

Acs, Alex. 2015. "Presidents and Agencies in the Regulatory State: A Revealed Preference Approach to Measuring Policy Disagreement." Working paper, University of Pennsylvania.

Acs, Alex, and Charles M. Cameron. 2013. "Does White House Regulatory Review Produce a Chilling Effect and 'OIRA Avoidance' in the Agencies?" *Presidential Studies Quarterly* 43(3):443–67.

Adolph, Christopher. 2013. *Bankers, Bureaucrats, and Central Bank Politics: The Myth of Neutrality*. New York: Cambridge University Press.

Advisory Committee on Construction Safety and Health. 1998. "Minutes of the October 7–8, 1998, Meeting." https://www.osha.gov/doc/accsh/meetingminutes/oct98.html.

American Pizza Community. 2017. Comment on Docket No. FDA-2011-F-0172. August 1. https://www.regulations.gov/document?D=FDA-2011-F-0172-2717.

Ansolabehere, Stephen, Jonathan Rodden, and James M. Snyder. 2006. "Purple America." *Journal of Economic Perspectives* 20(2):97–118.

Armour, Stephanie. 2013. "Obama's Calorie Display Rules Delayed by Grocer Blowback." *Bloomberg News*, May 10. http://www.bloomberg.com/news/2013-05-09/obama-s-calorie-display-rules-delayed-by-grocer-blowback.html.

Ashley, Elizabeth M., Clark Nardinelli, and Rosemarie A. Lavaty. 2015. "Estimating the Benefits of Public Health Policies that Reduce Harmful Consumption." *Health Economics* 24(5):617–24.

Asimow, Michael. 1994. "On Pressing McNollgast to the Limits: The Problem of Regulatory Costs." *Law and Contemporary Problems* 57(1):127–37.

Associated Press. 2013. "FDA Head Says Menu Labeling 'Thorny' Issue." *Richmond (VA) Times-Dispatch*, March 13. http://www.timesdispatch.com/entertainment-life/food-dining/fda-head-says-menu-labeling-thorny-issue/article_6337c9cb-4268-5463-b510-401d0fa022ff.html.

Bachrach, Peter, and Morton S. Baratz. 1962. "Two Faces of Power." *American Political Science Review* 56(4):947–52.

Bafumi, Joseph, and Michael C. Herron. 2010. "Leapfrog Representation and Extremism: A Study of American Voters and Their Members in Congress." *American Political Science Review* 104(3):519–42.

Balla, Steven J. 2015. "Political Control, Bureaucratic Discretion, and Public Commenting on Agency Regulations." *Public Administration* 93(2):524–38.

Balla, Steven J., and John R. Wright. 2001. "Interest Groups, Advisory Committees, and Congressional Control of the Bureaucracy." *American Journal of Political Science* 45(4):799–812.

Barber, Michael, and Nolan McCarty. 2013. "Causes and Consequences of Polarization." In *Political Negotiation: A Handbook*, edited by Jane Mansbridge and Cathie Jo Martin, 37–90. Washington, DC: Brookings Institution Press.

Barney, Jay B., and Delwyn N. Clark. 2007. *Resource-Based Theory: Creating and Sustaining Competitive Advantage*. New York: Oxford University Press.

Baumgartner, Frank R., Bryan D. Jones, John Wilkerson, and E. Scott Adler. 2016. "Policy Agendas Project." Online database distributed by the Department of Government at the University of Texas at Austin. http://www.comparativeagendas.net.

Bawn, Kathleen. 1995. "Political Control versus Expertise: Congressional Choices about Administrative Procedures." *American Political Science Review* 89(1):62–73.

Beam, Christopher. 2009. "Recess in Name Only: What Happens in Congressional Offices When the Boss Is Gone?" *Slate*, August 26. http://www.slate.com/articles/news_and_politics/politics/2009/08/recess_in_name_only.html.

Beck, Leland E. 2013. "EPA Tier 3 Vehicle Emissions Standards: Too Little Time to Comment." *Federal Regulations Advisor*, May 21. http://www.fedregsadvisor.com/2013/05/21/epa-tier-3-vehicle-emissions-standards-too-little-time-to-comment/.

Becker, Nora V., and Daniel Polsky. 2015. "Women Saw Large Decrease in Out-of-Pocket Spending for Contraceptives after ACA Mandate Removed Cost Sharing." *Health Affairs* 34(7):1204–11.

Beckmann, Matthew N. 2010. *Pushing the Agenda: Presidential Leadership in US Lawmaking, 1953–2004*. New York: Cambridge University Press.

Begley, Sharon. 2014. "FDA Prices 'Lost Pleasure' of Junk Food into Calorie Count Rule." *Reuters*, December 8. http://www.reuters.com/article/us-usa-health-calories-exclusive-idUSKBN0JM0DU20141208.

———. 2015. "U.S. to Roll Back 'Lost Pleasure' Approach on Health Rules." *Reuters*, March 18. http://www.reuters.com/article/us-usa-health-lostpleasure-idUSKBN0ME0DD20150318.

Bernstein, Marver H. 1955. *Regulating Business by Independent Commission*. Princeton, NJ: Princeton University Press.

Berry, Michael J. 2016. *The Modern Legislative Veto: Macropolitical Conflict and the Legacy of Chadha*. Ann Arbor: University of Michigan Press.

Bertelli, Anthony M., and Christian R. Grose. 2009. "Secretaries of Pork? A New Theory of Distributive Public Policy." *Journal of Politics* 71(3):926–45.

———. 2011. "The Lengthened Shadow of Another Institution? Ideal Point Estimates for the Executive Branch and Congress." *American Journal of Political Science* 55(4):767–81.

Binder, Sarah A. 2003. *Stalemate: Causes and Consequences of Legislative Gridlock*. Washington, DC: Brookings Institution Press.

———. 2008. "Consequences for the Courts: Polarized Politics and the Judicial Branch." In *Red and Blue Nation*, edited by Pietro S. Nivola and David W. Brady, 2:107–33. Washington, DC: Brookings Institution Press.

Black, Ryan C., Ryan J. Owens, Justin Wedeking, and Patrick C. Wohlfarth. 2016. *US Supreme Court Opinions and Their Audiences.* New York: Cambridge University Press.

Bolton, Alexander. 2015. "Collegial Leadership Structures, Ideological Diversity, and Policymaking in the United States." Working paper, Duke University.

Bolton, Alexander, Rachel Augustine Potter, and Sharece Thrower. 2016. "Organizational Capacity, Regulatory Review, and the Limits of Political Control." *Journal of Law, Economics & Organization* 32(2):242–71.

Bonica, Adam. 2013. "Ideology and Interests in the Political Marketplace." *American Journal of Political Science* 57(2):294–311.

Boushey, Graeme T., and Robert J. McGrath. 2015. "The Gift of Gridlock: Divided Government, Bureaucratic Autonomy, and the Politics of Rulemaking in the American States." Working paper, George Mason University.

Box-Steffensmeier, Janet M., Laura W. Arnold, and Christopher J. W. Zorn. 1997. "The Strategic Timing of Position Taking in Congress: A Study of the North American Free Trade Agreement." *American Political Science Review* 91(2):324–38.

Brehm, John, and Scott Gates. 1993. "Donut Shops and Speed Traps: Evaluating Models of Supervision on Police Behavior." *American Journal of Political Science* 37(2):555–81.

Bressman, Lisa Schultz. 2007. "Procedures as Politics in Administrative Law." *Columbia Law Review* 107(8):1749–1821.

Brookings Institution. 2017. "Vital Statistics on Congress." Report. Washington, DC. https://www.brookings.edu/multi-chapter-report/vital-statistics-on-congress/.

Bruce, Bertram C., Ann D. Rubin, and Kathleen S. Starr. 1981. "Why Readability Formulas Fail." In *IEEE Transactions on Professional Communication*, PC-24, 50–52. Urbana: University of Illinois, Center for the Study of Reading.

Burford, Anne McGill, and John Greenya. 1986. *Are You Tough Enough?* New York: McGraw-Hill.

Bush, George Walker. 2010. *Decision Points.* New York: Crown Publishing.

Cameron, Charles M. 2000. *Veto Bargaining.* New York: Cambridge University Press.

Carnes, Nicholas. 2013. *White-Collar Government: The Hidden Role of Class in Economic Policy Making.* Chicago: University of Chicago Press.

Carpenter, Daniel P. 1996. "Adaptive Signal Processing, Hierarchy, and Budgetary Control in Federal Regulation." *American Political Science Review* 90(2):283–302.

———. 2001. *The Forging of Bureaucratic Autonomy: Reputations, Networks, and Policy Innovation in Executive Agencies, 1862–1928.* Princeton, NJ: Princeton University Press.

———. 2002. "Groups, the Media, Agency Waiting Costs, and FDA Drug Approval." *American Journal of Political Science* 46(3):490–505.

———. 2010. *Reputation and Power: Organizational Image and Pharmaceutical Regulation at the FDA.* Princeton, NJ: Princeton University Press.

Carpenter, Daniel P., and George A. Krause. 2012. "Reputation and Public Administration." *Public Administration Review* 72(1):26–32.

Center for Science in the Public Interest. 2011. "Comparison of Menu Labeling Policies." http://cspinet.org/new/pdf/comparison_of_ml_policies_6-9.pdf.

Centers for Disease Control and Prevention. 2014. "Facts about Obesity." http://www.cdc.gov/obesity/data/facts.html.

———. 2016. "Trends in Current Cigarette Smoking Among High School Students and Adults,

United States, 1965–2014." http://www.cdc.gov/tobacco/data_statistics/tables/trends/cig
_smoking/.

Central Intelligence Agency. 2017. "World Factbook: The United States." *CIA World Factbook.*
https://www.cia.gov/library/publications/the-world-factbook/geos/us.html.

Chaloupka, Frank J., Kenneth E. Warner, Daron Acemoglu, Jonathan Gruber, Fritz Laux,
Wendy Max, Joseph Newhouse, Thomas Schelling, and Jody Sindelar. 2014. "An Evaluation
of the FDA's Analysis of the Costs and Benefits of the Graphic Warning Label Regulation."
Tobacco Control 24(2):112–19.

Chamber of Commerce. 2013. "Sue and Settle: Regulating Behind Closed Doors." Report, May.
https://www.uschamber.com/sites/default/files/documents/files/SUEANDSETTLE
REPORT-Final.pdf.

Chen, Jowei, and Tim Johnson. 2014. "Federal Employee Unionization and Presidential Control
of the Bureaucracy: Estimating and Explaining Ideological Change in Executive Agencies."
Journal of Theoretical Politics 26(3):1–24.

Chong, Dennis, and James N. Druckman. 2007. "Framing Theory." *Annual Review of Political
Science* 10:103–26.

Chubb, John E. 1983. *Interest Groups and the Bureaucracy: The Politics of Energy.* Palo Alto, CA:
Stanford University Press.

Claims Journal. 2008. "Democrats Press Labor Department on OSHA Rule on Chemical Exposure." July 25. http://www.claimsjournal.com/news/national/2008/07/25/92208.htm.

Clark, Tom S. 2009. "The Separation of Powers, Court Curbing, and Judicial Legitimacy." *American Journal of Political Science* 53(4):971–89.

Clinton, Joshua D., Anthony Bertelli, Christian R. Grose, David E. Lewis and David C. Nixon.
2012. "Separated Powers in the United States: The Ideology of Agencies, Presidents, and
Congress." *American Journal of Political Science* 56(2):341–54.

Clinton, Joshua D., and David E. Lewis. 2008. "Expert Opinion, Agency Characteristics, and
Agency Preferences." *Political Analysis* 16(1):3–20.

Clinton, Joshua D., David E. Lewis, and Jennifer L. Selin. 2014. "Influencing the Bureaucracy:
The Irony of Congressional Oversight." *American Journal of Political Science* 58(2):387–401.

Clinton, William J. 1998. "Plain Language in Government Writing," Presidential Memorandum
for the Heads of Executive Departments and Agencies. June 1.

Coglianese, Cary. 1997. "Assessing Consensus: The Promise and Performance of Negotiated
Rulemaking." *Duke Law Journal* 46(6):1255–1349.

———. 2005. "The Internet and Citizen Participation in Rulemaking." *I/S Journal of Law and
Policy for the Information Society* 33(1):33–58.

Coglianese, Cary, and David Lazer. 2003. "Management-Based Regulation: Prescribing Private
Management to Achieve Public Goals." *Law & Society Review* 37(4):691–730.

Cohen, Jeffrey E. 1986. "The Dynamics of the 'Revolving Door' on the FCC." *American Journal
of Political Science* 30(4):689–708.

Congressional Research Service. 2018. "What Can the New President Do about the Effective
Date of Pending Regulations?" January 18. Washington, DC. https://fas.org/sgp/crs/misc/
dates.pdf.

Consortium for Citizens with Disabilities. 2005. "Letter to Secretary Margaret Spellings." May 4.
https://www.c-c-d.org/fichiers/EduTFLetter2Spellings.pdf.

Copeland, Curtis W. 2008. "Midnight Rulemaking: Considerations for Congress and a New
Administration." Washington, DC: Congressional Research Service.

Copeland, Curtis W., and Richard S. Beth. 2008. "Congressional Review Act: Disapproval of Rules in a Subsequent Session of Congress." Washington, DC: Congressional Research Service.

Cox, Gary W., and Mathew D. McCubbins. 1993. *Legislative Leviathan: Party Government in the House.* Berkeley: University of California Press.

———. 2005. *Setting the Agenda: Responsible Party Government in the U.S. House of Representatives.* Berkeley: University of California Press.

Croley, Steven. 2003. "White House Review of Agency Rulemaking: An Empirical Investigation." *University of Chicago Law Review* 70(3):821–85.

Curry, James M. 2015. *Legislating in the Dark: Information and Power in the House of Representatives.* Chicago: University of Chicago Press.

Davis, Kenneth Culp. 1969. "A New Approach to Delegation." *University of Chicago Law Review* 36(4):713–33.

Delli Carpini, Michael X., and Scott Keeter. 1997. *What Americans Know about Politics and Why It Matters.* New Haven, CT: Yale University Press.

Derthick, Martha A. 2011. *Up in Smoke: From Legislation to Litigation in Tobacco Politics.* Washington, DC: CQ Press.

Dewey, Caitlin. 2017. "Industry Is Counting on Trump to Back off Rules That Tell You What's in Your Food." *Washington Post,* April 27. https://www.washingtonpost.com/news/wonk/wp/2017/04/27/industry-is-counting-on-trump-to-back-off-rules-that-tell-you-whats-in-your-food/?utm_term=.4ef5cb367063.

Dilulio, John D. 1994. "Principled Agents: The Cultural Bases of Behavior in a Federal Government Bureaucracy." *Journal of Public Administration Research and Theory* 4(3):277–318.

Doherty, Kathleen M. 2013. "Generating Expertise or Exerting Political Control: The Use of Expert Advisory Committees in Bureaucratic Policymaking." Presentation at the annual meeting of the Midwest Political Science Association, Chicago.

Doherty, Kathleen M., and Jennifer L. Selin. 2014. "Letting the Sun In: Administrative Procedure, Information Gathering, and Congressional Control." Presentation at the annual meeting of the Midwest Political Science Association, Chicago.

Downs, Anthony. 1967. *Inside Bureaucracy.* Boston: Little, Brown.

Economist. 2011. "Heated but Hollow: The House Embarks on a Rhetorical Debate about Greenhouse Gases." *Economist,* February 11. http://www.economist.com/node/18114709.

ElBoghdady, Dina. 2012. "Pizza Chains Band Together over Proposed Menu-Labeling Plan." *Washington Post,* June 10. http://www.washingtonpost.com/business/economy/pizza-chains-band-together-over-proposed-menu-labeling-plan/2012/06/19/gJQAxcf3oV-story.html.

Elliott, Donald E. 1992. "Re-Inventing Rulemaking." *Duke Law Journal* 41(6):1490–96.

Entman, Robert M. 1993. "Framing: Toward Clarification of a Fractured Paradigm." *Journal of Communication* 43(4):51–58.

Epp, Derek A. 2018. *The Structure of Policy Change.* Chicago: University of Chicago Press.

Epstein, David, and Sharyn O'Halloran. 1999. *Delegating Powers: A Transaction Cost Politics Approach to Policy Making Under Separate Powers.* New York: Cambridge University Press.

Eskridge, William N., and Lauren E. Baer. 2007. "The Continuum of Deference: Supreme Court Treatment of Agency Statutory Interpretations from *Chevron* to *Hamdan.*" *Georgetown Law Journal* 96(2):1083–1226.

Farina, Cynthia R., Mary Newhart, and Cheryl L. Blake. 2015. "The Problem with Words:

Plain Language and Public Participation in Rulemaking." *George Washington Law Review* 83(4):1358–1409.

Farina, Cynthia R., Mary Newhart, Claire Cardie, and Dan Cosley. 2011. "Rulemaking 2.0." *University of Miami Law Review* 65(2):395–448.

Federal Motor Carrier Safety Administration. 2011. "Hours of Service Final Rule: Regulatory Impact Analysis." https://www.fmcsa.dot.gov/sites/fmcsa.dot.gov/files/docs/2011_HOS _Final_Rule_RIA.pdf.

———. 2012. "FMCSA Strategic Plan, FY 2012–2016." https://www.fmcsa.dot.gov/sites/fmcsa .dot.gov/files/docs/FMCSA_StrategicPlan_2012-2016_508CLN.pdf.

Feldman, Martha. 1989. *Order without Design: Information Production and Policymaking.* Palo Alto, CA: Stanford University Press.

Fenno, Richard F. 1978. *Home Style: House Members in Their Districts.* Boston: Little, Brown.

Ferejohn, John, and Charles Shipan. 1990. "Congressional Influence on Bureaucracy." *Journal of Law, Economics & Organization* 6(1):1–20.

Fiorina, Morris P. 1989. *Congress: Keystone of the Washington Establishment.* New Haven, CT: Yale University Press.

———. 2008. *Culture War? The Myth of a Polarized America.* 3rd ed. New York: Pearson Longman.

Food and Drug Administration. 2011. "Preliminary Regulatory Impact Analysis: Food Labeling: Nutrition Labeling of Standard Menu Items in Restaurants and Similar Retail Food Establishments Notice of Proposed Rulemaking." Center for Food Safety and Applied Nutrition, Docket No. FDA-2011-F-0172. https://www.fda.gov/downloads/Food/LabelingNutrition/UCM249276.pdf.

Fritschler, A. Lee. 1969. *Smoking and Politics: Policymaking and the Federal Bureaucracy.* New York: Appleton-Century-Crofts.

Furlong, Scott R., and Cornelius M. Kerwin. 2005. "Interest Group Participation in Rule-Making: A Decade of Change." *Journal of Public Administration Research and Theory* 15(3):353–70.

Gailmard, Sean, and John W. Patty. 2007. "Slackers and Zealots: Civil Service, Policy Discretion, and Bureaucratic Expertise." *American Journal of Political Science* 51(4):873–89.

———. 2013. *Learning While Governing: Expertise and Accountability in the Executive Branch.* Chicago: University of Chicago Press.

Garvey, John. 2011. "HHS's Birth-Control Rules Intrude on Catholic Values." *Washington Post*, September 30. https://www.washingtonpost.com/opinions/hhss-birth-control-rules -intrude-on-catholic-values/2011/09/27/gIQAOj8s9K_story.html.

Gellhorn, Walter. 1986. "The Administrative Procedure Act: The Beginnings." *Virginia Law Review* 72(2):219–33.

Gelman, Andrew, and Jennifer Hill. 2006. *Data Analysis Using Regression and Multilevel/Hierarchical Models.* New York: Cambridge University Press.

General Accounting Office. 1998. "Federal Rulemaking: Agencies Often Published Final Actions Without Proposed Rules." General Accountability Office Report, GGD-98-126. http://www .gao.gov/assets/230/226214.pdf.

Gersen, Jacob E., and Anne J. O'Connell. 2008. "Deadlines in Administrative Law." *University of Pennsylvania Law Review* 156(4):923–90.

———. 2009. "Hiding in Plain Sight? Timing and Transparency in the Administrative State." *University of Chicago Law Review* 76(3):1157–1214.

Gilmour, John B., and David E. Lewis. 2006. "Political Appointees and the Competence of Federal Program Management." *American Politics Research* 34(1):22–50.

Golden, Marissa Martino. 1998. "Interest Groups in the Rule-Making Process: Who Participates? Whose Voices Get Heard?" *Journal of Public Administration Research and Theory* 8(2):245–70.

———. 2000. *What Motivates Bureaucrats? Politics and Administration During the Reagan Years.* New York: Columbia University Press.

Goldstein, Amy, and Sarah Cohen. 2004. "Bush Forces a Shift in Regulatory Thrust." *Washington Post*, August 15. http://www.washingtonpost.com/wpdyn/articles/A1315-2004Aug14.html.

Goodwin, James. 2013. "Transparency Withdrawn: A New Tactic for Shielding OIRA's Regulatory Review Activities?" Center for Progressive Reform. http://www.progressivereform.org/CPRBlog.cfm?idBlog=31D6C986-C3A6-6822-D4F31AC111043A76.

Gormley, William T., Jr. 1983. *The Politics of Public Utility Regulation.* Pittsburgh, PA: University of Pittsburgh Press.

———. 1986. "Regulatory Issue Networks in a Federal System." *Polity* 18(4):595–620.

Government Accountability Office. 2015. "Letter to Sen. James Inhofe, 'Environmental Protection Agency—Application of Publicity or Propaganda and Anti-Lobbying Provisions.'" Government Accountability Office Legal Opinion, B-326944. December 14. http://www.gao.gov/assets/680/674163.pdf.

Haas, Peter M. 1992. "Epistemic Communities and International Policy Coordination." *International Organization* 46(1):1–35.

Hacker, Jacob S. 2004. "Privatizing Risk without Privatizing the Welfare State: The Hidden Politics of Social Policy Retrenchment in the United States." *American Political Science Review* 98(2):243–60.

Hacker, Jacob S., and Paul Pierson. 2006. *Off Center: The Republican Revolution and the Erosion of American Democracy.* New Haven, CT: Yale University Press.

Haeder, Simon F., Susan Webb Yackee, and Jason Webb Yackee. 2016. "The Shelf Life of a Statute: Congressional Accountability and Government Regulation, 1950–1987." Presentation at the annual meeting of the Midwest Political Science Association, Chicago.

Haleblian, Jerayr, and Sydney Finkelstein. 1993. "Top Management Team Size, CEO Dominance, and Firm Performance: The Moderating Roles of Environmental Turbulence and Discretion." *Academy of Management Journal* 36(4):844–63.

Harnack, Lisa J., and Simone A. French. 2008. "Effect of Point-of-Purchase Calorie Labeling on Restaurant and Cafeteria Food Choices: A Review of the Literature." *International Journal of Behavioral Nutrition and Physical Activity* 5(1):1–6.

Harris, Gardiner. 2012. "White House and the FDA. Often at Odds." *New York Times*, April 2. http://www.nytimes.com/2012/04/03/health/policy/white-house-and-fda-at-odds-on-regulatory-issues.html.

Harris, Richard A., and Sidney M. Milkis. 1989. *The Politics of Regulatory Change: A Tale of Two Agencies.* New York: Oxford University Press.

Hart, Peter D., and David Winston. 2005. "Ready for the Real World? Americans Speak on High School Reform." *Educational Testing Service.* https://www.ets.org/Media/Education_Topics/pdf/2005highschoolreform.pdf.

Harter, Philip J. 1982. "Negotiating Regulations: A Cure for the Malaise?" *Environmental Impact Assessment Review* 3(1):75–91.

Heinzerling, Lisa. 2014. "Inside EPA: A Former Insider's Reflections on the Relationship Between the Obama EPA and the Obama White House." *Pace Environmental Law Review* 31(1):325–69.

Hieke, Sophie, and Charles R. Taylor. 2011. "A Critical Review of the Literature on Nutritional Labeling." *Journal of Consumer Affairs* 46(1):120–56.

Hill, Gayle W. 1982. "Group Versus Individual Performance: Are $N + 1$ Heads Better Than One?" *Psychological Bulletin* 91(3):517–39.

Horn, Murray J. 1995. *The Political Economy of Public Administration: Institutional Choice in the Public Sector*. New York: Cambridge University Press.

Howell, William G., and Jon C. Pevehouse. 2011. *While Dangers Gather: Congressional Checks on Presidential War Powers*. Princeton, NJ: Princeton University Press.

Huber, Gregory A. 2007. *The Craft of Bureaucratic Neutrality: Interests and Influence in Governmental Regulation of Occupational Safety*. New York: Cambridge University Press.

Huber, John D., and Nolan McCarty. 2004. "Bureaucratic Capacity, Delegation, and Political Reform." *American Political Science Review* 98(3):481–94.

Huber, John D., and Charles R. Shipan. 2002. *Deliberate Discretion? The Institutional Foundations of Bureaucratic Autonomy*. New York: Cambridge University Press.

Hume, Robert J. 2009. *How Courts Impact Federal Administrative Behavior*. New York: Routledge Press.

Hurley, Patricia, David Brady, and Joseph Cooper. 1977. "Measuring Legislative Potential for Policy Change." *Legislative Studies Quarterly* 2(4):385–98.

Jacobs, Lawrence R., and Theda Skocpol. 2012. *Health Care Reform and American Politics: What Everyone Needs to Know*. New York: Oxford University Press.

Johnson, Jenna, and Ylan Q. Mui. 2017. "Trump to CEOs: Stay Here, and I'll Wipe Out 75 Percent of Regulations, Fast-Track Factories." *Washington Post*, January 23. https://www .washingtonpost.com/news/post-politics/wp/2017/ 01/23/trump-to-ceos-ill-wipe-out-75 -percent-of-regulations-fast-track-us-factories/?utm_term=.06db2f258990.

Jolliffe, Ian. 2002. *Principal Components Analysis*. Hoboken, NJ: Wiley Online Library.

Jones, Elise S., and Cameron P. Taylor. 1995. "Litigating Agency Change." *Policy Studies Journal* 23(2):310–36.

Jordan, William S., III. 1999. "Ossification Revisited: Does Arbitrary and Capricious Review Significantly Interfere with Agency Ability to Achieve Regulatory Goals through Informal Rulemaking." *Northwestern University Law Review* 94(2):393–450.

Kannan, Phillip M. 1996. "The Logical Outgrowth Doctrine in Rulemaking." *Administrative Law Review* 48(2):213–25.

Kaufman, Herbert. 1960. *The Forest Ranger: A Study in Administrative Behavior*. Washington, DC: Resources for the Future.

Kerrigan, Heather. 2012. "Civil Service Reform: Lessons from Georgia and Indiana." *Governing*, June 13. http://www.governing.com/topics/public-workforce/col-civil-service-reform -lessons-from-georgia-indiana.html.

Kerwin, Cornelius M., and Scott R. Furlong. 2011. *Rulemaking*. 4th ed. Washington, DC: CQ Press.

Kessler, David. 2001. *A Question of Intent: A Great American Battle with a Deadly Industry*. New York: PublicAffairs.

Kim, Doo-Rae. 2007. "Political Control and Bureaucratic Autonomy Revisited: A Multi-Institutional Analysis of OSHA Enforcement." *Journal of Public Administration Research and Theory* 18(1):33–55.

Kiszko, Kamila M., Olivia D. Martinez, Courtney Abrams, and Brian Elbel. 2014. "The Influence of Calorie Labeling on Food Orders and Consumption: A Review of the Literature." *Journal of Community Health* 39(6):1248–69.

Kolenikov, Stanislav, and Gustavo Angeles. 2009. "Socioeconomic Status Measurement with

Discrete Proxy Variables: Is Principal Component Analysis a Reliable Answer?" *Review of Income and Wealth* 55(1):128–65.

Kraft, Michael E., Mark Stephan and Troy D. Abel. 2011. *Coming Clean: Information Disclosure and Environmental Performance.* Cambridge, MA: MIT Press.

Krause, George A. 1999. *A Two Way Street: The Institutional Dynamics of the Modern Administrative State.* Pittsburgh, PA: University of Pittsburgh Press.

Krause, George A., and J. Kevin Corder. 2007. "Explaining Bureaucratic Optimism: Theory and Evidence from US Executive Agency Macroeconomic Forecasts." *American Political Science Review* 101(1):129–42.

Krause, George A., and James W. Douglas. 2005. "Institutional Design versus Reputational Effects on Bureaucratic Performance: Evidence from US Government Macroeconomic and Fiscal Projections." *Journal of Public Administration Research and Theory* 15(2):281–306.

Krehbiel, Keith. 2010. *Pivotal Politics: A Theory of US Lawmaking.* Chicago: University of Chicago Press.

Labaton, Stephen. 2004. "Agencies Postpone Issuing New Rules Until after Election." *New York Times*, September 27. http://www.nytimes.com/2004/09/27/business/agencies-postpone-issuing-new-rulesuntil-after-election.html?_r=1.

———. 2007. "OSHA Leaves Worker Safety in Hands of Industry." *New York Times*, April 25. http://www.nytimes.com/2007/04/25/washington/25osha.html.

Lavertu, Stéphane, and Susan Webb Yackee. 2012. "Regulatory Delay and Rulemaking Deadlines." *Journal of Public Administration Research and Theory* 24(1):185–207.

Lee, Frances E. 2015. "How Party Polarization Affects Governance." *Annual Review of Political Science* 18:261–82.

Lee, Soo-Young, and Andrew B. Whitford. 2012. "Assessing the Effects of Organizational Resources on Public Agency Performance: Evidence from the US Federal Government." *Journal of Public Administration Research and Theory* 23(3):687–712.

Leonnig, Carol D. 2008. "U.S. Rushes to Change Workplace Toxin Rules." *Washington Post*, July 23. http://www.washingtonpost.com/wp-dyn/content/article/2008/07/22/AR200807 2202838_pf.html.

Levin, Ronald R. 2016. "Testimony on H.R. 4768, the 'Separation of Powers Restoration Act of 2016.'" House Judiciary Committee Hearing, May 17, 2016. https://judiciary.house.gov/wp -content/uploads/2016/05/Levin-Testimony.pdf.

Levine, Linda. 2008. "Worker Safety in the Construction Industry: The Crane and Derrick Standard." Washington, DC: Congressional Research Service.

Levy, Helen, Edward C. Norton, and Jeffrey A. Smith. 2016. *Tobacco Regulation and Cost-Benefit Analysis: How Should We Value Foregone Consumer Surplus?* Technical Report No. 22471. Washington, DC: National Bureau of Economic Research.

Lewis, David E. 2008. *The Politics of Presidential Appointments: Political Control and Bureaucratic Performance.* Princeton, NJ: Princeton University Press.

Li, Feng. 2008. "Annual Report Readability, Current Earnings, and Earnings Persistence." *Journal of Accounting and Economics* 45(2–3):221–47.

Lichtblau, Eric. 2011. "Economic Downturn Took a Detour at Capitol Hill." *New York Times*, December 26. http://www.nytimes.com/2011/12/27/us/politics/economic-slide-took-a -detour-at-capitol-hill.html.

Lincoln, Taylor, and Negah Mouzoon. 2011. *Cranes & Derricks: The Prolonged Creation of a Key Public Safety Rule.* Washington, DC: Public Citizen. https://www.citizen.org/documents/ CranesAndDerricks.pdf.

Lipton, Eric, and Coral Davenport. 2015. "Critics Hear E.P.A.'s Voice in 'Public Comments.'" *New York Times*, May 19. https://www.nytimes.com/2015/05/19/us/critics-hear-epas-voice-in-public-comments.html?_r=0.

Lipton, Eric, and Michael D. Shear. 2015. "E.P.A. Broke Law with Social Media Push for Water Rule, Auditor Finds." *New York Times*, December 14. https://www.nytimes.com/2015/12/15/us/politics/epa-broke-the-law-by-using-social-media-to-push-water-rule-auditor-finds.html?_r=1.

Livermore, Michael A. 2007. "Reviving Environmental Protection: Preference-Directed Regulation and Regulatory Ossification." *Virginia Environmental Law Journal* 25:311–86.

———. 2014. "Cost-Benefit Analysis and Agency Independence." *University of Chicago Law Review* 81(2):609–88.

Lowande, Kenneth. 2018. "Politicization and Responsiveness in Executive Agencies." *Journal of Politics*.

———. Forthcoming. "Who Polices the Administrative State?" *American Political Science Review*.

Lowi, Theodore J. 1969. *The End of Liberalism: Ideology, Policy, and the Crisis of Public Authority*. New York: Norton.

Lubbers, Jeffrey S. 2012. *A Guide to Federal Agency Rulemaking*. 5th ed. Washington, DC: American Bar Association.

Lupia, Arthur. 2016. *Uninformed: Why People Know So Little about Politics and What We Can Do about It*. New York: Oxford University Press.

MacDonald, Jason A. 2010. "Limitation Riders and Congressional Influence over Bureaucratic Policy Decisions." *American Political Science Review* 104(4):766–82.

———. 2013. "Congressional Power over Executive Branch Policy Making: Limitations on Bureaucratic Regulations, 1989–2009." *Presidential Studies Quarterly* 43(3):523–37.

MacDonald, Jason A., and William W. Franko. 2007. "Bureaucratic Capacity and Bureaucratic Discretion: Does Congress Tie Policy Authority to Performance?" *American Politics Research* 35(6):790–807.

MacDonald, Jason A., and Robert J. McGrath. 2016. "A Race for the Regs: Unified Government, Statutory Deadlines, and Federal Agency Rulemaking." Working paper, George Mason University.

Magat, Wesley A., Alan J. Krupnick, and Winston Harrington. 1986. *Rules in the Making: A Statistical Analysis of Regulatory Agency Behavior*. Washington, DC: Resources for the Future.

Mann, Thomas E., and Norman J. Ornstein. 2012. *It's Even Worse Than It Looks: How the American Constitutional System Collided with the New Politics of Extremism*. New York: Basic Books.

Maor, Moshe, Sharon Gilad, and Pazit Ben-Nun Bloom. 2013. "Organizational Reputation, Regulatory Talk, and Strategic Silence." *Journal of Public Administration Research and Theory* 23(3):581–608.

Marvel, John D., and Robert J. McGrath. 2016. "Congress as Manager: Oversight Hearings and Agency Morale." *Journal of Public Policy* 36(3):489–520.

Mashaw, Jerry L. 1994. "Improving the Environment of Agency Rulemaking: An Essay on Management, Games, and Accountability." *Law and Contemporary Problems* 57(2):185–257.

Mashaw, Jerry L., and David L. Harfst. 1986. "Regulation and Legal Culture: The Case of Motor Vehicle Safety." *Yale Journal on Regulation* 4:257–316.

Mayhew, David R. 1974. *Congress: The Electoral Connection*. New Haven, CT: Yale University Press.

———. 2005. *Divided We Govern: Party Control, Lawmaking and Investigations, 1946–2002.* New Haven, CT: Yale University Press.

McCann, Pamela J., Charles R. Shipan, and Yuhua Wang. 2017. "Congress and Judicial Review of Agency Actions." Working paper, University of Michigan.

McCarty, Nolan, Keith T. Poole, and Howard Rosenthal. 2016. *Polarized America: The Dance of Ideology and Unequal Riches.* Cambridge, MA: MIT Press.

McCubbins, Mathew D., Roger G. Noll, and Barry R. Weingast. 1987. "Administrative Procedures as Instruments of Political Control." *Journal of Law, Economics & Organization* 3(2):243.

———. 1989. "Structure and Process, Politics and Policy: Administrative Arrangements and the Political Control of Agencies." *Virginia Law Review* 75(2):431–82.

———. 1999. "The Political Origins of the Administrative Procedure Act." *Journal of Law, Economics & Organization* 15(1):180–217.

McCubbins, Mathew, and Tom Schwartz. 1984. "Congressional Oversight Overlooked: Police Patrols versus Fire Alarms." *American Journal of Political Science* 28(1):165–79.

McGarity, Thomas O. 1991. "Some Thoughts on Deossifying the Rulemaking Process." *Duke Law Journal* 41(6):1385.

McGrath, Robert J. 2013. "Congressional Oversight Hearings and Policy Control." *Legislative Studies Quarterly* 38(3):349–76.

McMorris Rodgers, Cathy, and Loretta Sanchez. 2013. "Takeout Menus and the Specter of Red Tape." *Bloomberg News,* July 5. https://republicanwomenspolicycommittee-ellmers.house .gov/media-center/editorials/mcmorris-rodgers-takeout-menus-and-the-specter-of-red -tape.

Meier, Kenneth J., and Laurence J. O'Toole. 2006. *Bureaucracy in a Democratic State: A Governance Perspective.* Baltimore: Johns Hopkins University Press.

Melnick, R. Shep. 1983. *Regulation and the Courts: The Case of the Clean Air Act.* Washington, DC: Brookings Institution Press.

———. 2014. "The Odd Evolution of the Civil Rights State." *Harvard Journal of Law & Public Policy* 37(1):113–34.

Mendelson, Nina. 2011. "Foreword: Rulemaking, Democracy, and Torrents of E-mail." *Administrative Law Review* 79(5):1343–80.

Meredith, Marc. 2009. "The Strategic Timing of Direct Democracy." *Economics & Politics* 21(1):159–77.

Mettler, Suzanne. 2014. *Degrees of Inequality: How the Politics of Higher Education Sabotaged the American Dream.* New York: Basic Books.

Metzger, Gillian E. 2005. "The Story of *Vermont Yankee*: A Cautionary Tale of Judicial Review and Nuclear Waste." Research Paper No. 05-92, Columbia Law School. http://lsr.nellco.org/ cgi/viewcontent.cgi?article=1016&context=columbia_pllt.

Miller, Gary J., and Andrew B. Whitford. 2016. *Above Politics: Bureaucratic Discretion and Credible Commitment.* New York: Cambridge University Press.

Moe, Terry M. 1985. "The Politicized Presidency." In *The New Direction in American Politics,* edited by John Chubb and Paul Peterson, 235–70. Washington, DC: Brookings Institution Press.

———. 1989. "The Politics of Bureaucratic Structure." In *Can the Government Govern?*, edited by John E. Chubb and Paul E. Peterson, 285–323. Washington, DC: Brookings Institution Press.

———. 2006. "Political Control and the Power of the Agent." *Journal of Law, Economics & Organization* 22(1):1–29.

Moffitt, Susan L. 2010. "Promoting Agency Reputation through Public Advice: Advisory Committee Use in the FDA." *Journal of Politics* 72(3):880–93.

———. 2014. *Making Policy Public: Participatory Bureaucracy in American Democracy*. New York: Cambridge University Press.

Morgan, David. 2013. "U.S. Sets Birth Control Rule for Employers with Religious Ties." *Reuters*, June 28. http://www.reuters.com/article/us-usa-healthcare-contraceptives-idUSBRE 95R0QN20130628.

Morse, Susan C., and Leigh Osofsky. 2018. "Regulating by Example." *Yale Journal on Regulation* 35:127–80.

Moynihan, Donald, Pamela Herd, and Hope Harvey. 2014. "Administrative Burden: Learning, Psychological, and Compliance Costs in Citizen-State Interactions." *Journal of Public Administration Research and Theory* 25(1):43–69.

Muehlenbachs, Lucija, Elisabeth Newcomb Sinha, and Nitish Ranjan Sinha. 2011. "Strategic Release of the News at the EPA." Working Paper No. 11-45, Resources for the Future, Washington, DC.

Myers, Ben, and Peter Olsen-Phillips. 2017. "In Congress, Even Lawmakers' Degrees Are a Partisan Issue." *Chronicle of Higher Education*, May 5. http://www.chronicle.com/interactives/congress-education.

Naff, Katherine C., Norma M. Riccucci, and Siegrun Fox Freyss. 2013. *Personnel Management in Government: Politics and Process*. Boca Raton, FL: CRC Press.

Naughton, Keith, Celeste Schmid, Susan Webb Yackee, and Xueyong Zhan. 2009. "Understanding Commenter Influence during Agency Rule Development." *Journal of Policy Analysis and Management* 28(2):258–77.

Neistat, Casey. 2013. "Calorie Detective." *New York Times*, February 12. http://www.nytimes .com/2013/02/13/opinion/calorie-detective.html?_r=0.

Nelson, David, and Susan Webb Yackee. 2012. "Lobbying Coalitions and Government Policy Change: An Analysis of Federal Agency Rulemaking." *Journal of Politics* 74(2):339–53.

Nestle, Marion. 2013. "Rumor: The White House Is Holding Out for Weak Calorie Labeling." *Food Politics*, February 13. http://www.foodpolitics.com/2013/02/rumor-the-white-house -is-holding-out-for-weak-calorie-labeling/.

———. 2014. "The FDA's New Calorie Count Requirements." Interview with Evan Kleiman. KCRW (Los Angeles), December 14. https://kcrw.co/2L96zf6.

Neustadt, Richard. 1960. *Presidential Power and the Modern Presidents*. New York: Free Press.

Nicholson, Stephen P., and Robert M. Howard. 2003. "Framing Support for the Supreme Court in the Aftermath of *Bush v. Gore*." *Journal of Politics* 65(3):676–95.

Niskanen, William. 1971. *Bureaucracy and Representative Government*. Chicago: Aldine.

Nixon, David C. 2004. "Separation of Powers and Appointee Ideology." *Journal of Law, Economics & Organization* 20(2):438–57.

Nixon, David C., Robert M. Howard, and Jeff R. DeWitt. 2002. "With Friends Like These: Rule-Making Comment Submissions to the Securities and Exchange Commission." *Journal of Public Administration Research and Theory* 12(1):59–76.

Noll, Roger G. 1971. *Reforming Regulation: An Evaluation of the Ash Council Proposals; A Staff Paper*. Washington, DC: Brookings Institution Press.

Nou, Jennifer. 2013. "Agency Self-Insulation under Presidential Review." *Harvard Law Review* 126(7):1755–1837.

Nou, Jennifer, and Edward Stiglitz. 2016. "Strategic Rulemaking Disclosure." *Southern California Law Review* 89(4):733–92.

NYU Law. 2013. "OIRA Administrator Speaks at Institute for Policy Integrity's Fifth Annual Cost-Benefit Analysis and Issue Advocacy Workshop." IPI Workshop. http://www.law.nyu .edu/news/IPI-Workshop-2013.

O'Connell, Anne J. 2008. "Political Cycles of Rulemaking: An Empirical Portrait of the Modern Administrative State." *Virginia Law Review* 84(4):889–986.

———. 2011. "Agency Rulemaking and Political Transitions." *Northwestern Law Review* 105(2):471–534.

Office of Personnel Management. 2008. "Federal Human Capital Survey." https://www.opm .gov/fevs/reports/data-reports.

———. 2014. "FedScope Database." https://www.fedscope.opm.gov.

———. 2017. "Frequently Asked Questions: Employment." https://www.opm.gov/faqs/topic/ employment/?cid=5d9058d6-78fb-42a2-9d2a-9d14c22982f0&page=2.

Oleszek, Walter J. 1996. *Congressional Procedures and the Policy Process.* 4th ed. Washington, DC: CQ Press.

Olson, Mary K. 1996. "Substitution in Regulatory Agencies: FDA Enforcement Alternatives." *Journal of Law, Economics & Organization* 12(2):376–407.

O'Neill, Catherine, Amy Sinden, Rena Steinzor, James Goodwin, and Ling-Yee Huang. 2009. "The Hidden Human and Environmental Costs of Regulatory Delay." White Paper No. 907, Center for Progressive Reform. http://www.progressivereform.org/articles/costofdelay _907.pdf.

O'Quinn, Israel. 2015. "Testimony, Hearing on Restaurant and Fast Food Nutrition Labeling." House Energy and Commerce Subcommittee on Health. Food City, Strategic Initiatives Director. June 4. https://www.c-span.org/video/?3263891/hearing-menu-labeling -requirements.

Ostrander, Ian. 2016. "The Logic of Collective Inaction: Senatorial Delay in Executive Nominations." *American Journal of Political Science* 60(4):1063–76.

Owens, Ryan J., Justin Wedeking and Patrick C. Wohlfarth. 2013. "How the Supreme Court Alters Opinion Language to Evade Congressional Review." *Journal of Law and Courts* 1(1):35–59.

Papke, Leslie E., and Jeffrey M. Wooldridge. 1996. "Econometric Methods for Fractional Response Variables with an Application to 401(k) Plan Participation Rates." *Journal of Applied Econometrics* 11(6):619–32.

Parker, Richard W. 2006. "The Empirical Roots of the Regulatory Reform Movement: A Critical Appraisal." *Administrative Law Review* 58(2):359–400.

Pfeffer, Jeffrey, and Gerald R. Salancik. 2003. *The External Control of Organizations: A Resource Dependence Perspective.* Palo Alto, CA: Stanford University Press.

Picket, Kerry. 2013. "National Restaurant Association Urges Congress to Maintain Menu Labeling Regs for All." *Breitbart,* October 31. http://www.breitbart.com/Big-Government/2013/ 10/31/National-Restaurant-Association-Urges-Congress-To-Maintain-Menu-Labeling -Regs-For-All.

Pierce, Richard J. 1995. "Seven Ways to Deossify Agency Rulemaking." *Administrative Law Review* 47(1):59–95.

———. 2011. "Rulemaking Ossification Is Real: A Response to Testing the Ossification Thesis." *George Washington Law Review* 80(5):1493–1503.

Podziba, Susan. 2012. "Safety Starts at the Top." *New York Times,* June 12. http://www.nytimes .com/2008/06/12/opinion/12podziba.html.

Poletta, Francesca, and M. Kai Ho. 2006. "Frames and Their Consequences." In *The Oxford*

Handbook of Contextual Political Analysis, edited by Robert E. Goodin and Charles Tilly, 187–209. New York: Oxford University Press.

Poole, Keith, and Howard Rosenthal. 1997. *Congress: A Political-Economic History of Roll-Call Voting*. New York: Oxford University Press.

Portnoy, Jenna, and Lisa Rein. 2017. "House Republicans Revive Obscure Rule That Allows Them to Slash the Pay of Individual Federal Workers to $1." *Washington Post*, January 5. https:// www.washingtonpost.com/local/virginia-politics/house-republicans-revive-obscure-rule -that-could-allow-them-to-slash-the-pay-of-individual-federal-workers-to-1/2017/01/04/ 4e80c990-d2b2-11e6-945a-76f69a399dd5_story.html?utm_term=.8cb5b4e99910.

Posner, Eric A., and Adrian Vermeule. 2002. "Interring the Nondelegation Doctrine." *University of Chicago Law Review* 69(4):1721–62.

Potter, Rachel Augustine. 2017. "Slow-Rolling, Fast-Tracking, and the Pace of Bureaucratic Decisions in Rulemaking." *Journal of Politics* 79(3):841–55.

Potter, Rachel Augustine, and Charles R. Shipan. 2018. "Agency Rulemaking in a Separation of Powers System." *Journal of Public Policy*. https://doi.org/10.1017/S0143814X17000216.

Potter, Rachel Augustine, and Craig Volden. 2018. "Women's Leadership and Policymaking in the U.S. Federal Bureaucracy." Working paper, University of Virginia.

Rabe-Hesketh, Sophia, and Anders Skrondal. 2008. *Multilevel and Longitudinal Modeling Using Stata*. College Station, TX: Stata Press.

Raso, Connor N. 2010. "Strategic or Sincere? Analyzing Agency Use of Guidance Documents." *Yale Law Journal* 119(4):782–824.

———. 2015. "Agency Avoidance of Rulemaking Procedures." *Administrative Law Review* 67(1): 101–67.

———. 2017. "Congress May Tell Courts to Ignore Regulatory Agencies' Reasoning, but Will It Matter?" *Series on Regulatory Politics and Perspective* (blog). Center on Regulation and Markets, Brookings Institution. https://www.brookings.edu/research/congress-may-tell-courts -to-ignore-regulatory-agencies-reasoning-but-will-it-matter/.

Reynolds, Molly E. 2017. *Exceptions to the Rule: The Politics of Filibuster Limitations in the U.S. Senate*. Washington, DC: Brookings Institution Press.

Rice, Sabriya. 2011. "HHS OKs Birth Control with No Co-pay." *CNN*, August 1. http://www.cnn .com/2011/HEALTH/08/01/free.birth.control/.

Ringquist, Evan J. 1995. "Political Control and Policy Impact in EPA's Office of Water-Quality." *American Journal of Political Science* 39(2):336–63.

Ritchie, Melinda. 2018. "Back-Channel Representation: A Study of the Strategic Communication of Senators with the US Department of Labor." *Journal of Politics*. 80(1):240–53.

Rogowski, Jon C. 2015. "Presidential Influence in an Era of Congressional Dominance." *American Political Science Review* 110(2):325–41.

Rosenberg, Gerald N. 2008. *The Hollow Hope: Can Courts Bring about Social Change?* Chicago: University of Chicago Press.

Rosenbloom, David. 2008. "The Politics-Administration Dichotomy in US Historical Context." *Public Administration Review* 68(1):57–60.

Rothenberg, Lawrence and Matthew Sweeten. 2015. "Analyzing Agency Choice with Text Analysis: The Case of the NLRB." Presentation at the Annual Meeting of the American Political Science Association, San Francisco.

Rumsfeld, Donald. 2013. *Rumsfeld's Rules*. New York: HarperCollins.

Sage, William M. 1999. "Regulating through Information: Disclosure Laws and American Health Care." *Columbia Law Review* 99(7):1701–1829.

Savage, James D. 2005. *Making the EMU: The Politics of Budgetary Surveillance and the Enforcement of Maastricht.* New York: Oxford University Press.

Scalia, Antonin. 1978. "*Vermont Yankee*: The APA, the DC Circuit, and the Supreme Court." *Supreme Court Review* 1978:345–409.

———. 1989. "Judicial Deference to Administrative Interpretations of Law." *Duke Law Journal* 1989(3):511–21.

Scheufele, Dietram A., and Shanto Iyengar. 2017. "The State of Framing Research: A Call for New Directions." In *The Oxford Handbook of Political Communication*, edited by Kate Kenski and Kathleen Hall Jamieson, 619–32. New York: Oxford University Press.

Schmidt, Patrick E. 2002. "Pursuing Regulatory Relief: Strategic Participation and Litigation in U.S. OSHA Rulemaking." *Business and Politics* 4(1):71–89.

Schoenbrod, David. 2008. *Power without Responsibility: How Congress Abuses the People through Delegation.* New Haven, CT: Yale University Press.

Scholz, John T. 1991. "Cooperative Regulatory Enforcement and the Politics of Administrative Effectiveness." *American Political Science Review* 85(1):115–36.

Scholz, John T., Jim Twombly, and Barbara Headrick. 1991. "Street-Level Political Controls over Federal Bureaucracy." *American Political Science Review* 85(3):829–50.

Schriver, Karen A. 2000. "Readability Formulas in the New Millennium: What's the Use?" *ACM Journal of Computer Documentation* 24(3):138–40.

Schulman, Tamara. 2010. "Menu Labeling: Knowledge for a Healthier America." *Harvard Journal on Legislation* 47(2):587–610.

Sebelius, Kathleen. 2012. "Contraception Rule Respects Religion." *USA Today*, February 5. http://usatoday30.usatoday.com/news/opinion/editorials/story/2012-02-05/Kathleen-Sebelius-contraception-exemption/52975092/1.

Segal, Jeffrey A., and Albert D. Cover. 1989. "Ideological Values and the Votes of US Supreme Court Justices." *American Political Science Review* 83(2):557–65.

Seidenfeld, Mark. 1997. "Demystifying Deossification: Rethinking Recent Proposals to Modify Judicial Review of Notice and Comment Rulemaking." *Texas Law Review* 75(3):483–524.

Selin, Jennifer L. 2015. "What Makes an Agency Independent?" *American Journal of Political Science* 59(4):971–87.

Sferra-Bonistalli, Esa L. 2014. "'Ex Parte' Communications in Informal Rulemaking." Administrative Conference of the United States (ACUS), May 1. Recommendation No. 2014-4. https://www.acus.gov/sites/default/files/documents/Final%20Ex%20Parte%20Communications%20in%20Informal%20Rulemaking%20%5B5-1-14%5D_0.pdf.

Shapiro, Ari. 2011. "Obama Office Alters More Federal Rules Than Bush." *NPR News*, November 28. http://www.npr.org/2011/11/28/142721675/obama-office-alters-more-federal-rules-than-bush.

Shapiro, Martin M. 1988. *Who Guards the Guardians? Judicial Control of Administration.* Athens: University of Georgia Press.

Shapiro, Stuart. 2007. "The Role of Procedural Controls in OSHA's Ergonomics Rulemaking." *Public Administration Review* 67(4):688–701.

Shepherd, George B. 1996. "Fierce Compromise: The Administrative Procedure Act Emerges from New Deal Politics." *Northwestern University Law Review* 90(4):1557–1683.

Shipan, Charles R. 1997. *Designing Judicial Review: Interest Groups, Congress, and Communications Policy.* Ann Arbor: University of Michigan Press.

———. 2004. "Regulatory Regimes, Agency Actions, and the Conditional Nature of Congressional Influence." *American Political Science Review* 98(3):467–80.

Sinclair, Susan E., Marcia Cooper, and Elizabeth D. Mansfield. 2014. "The Influence of Menu Labeling on Calories Selected or Consumed: A Systematic Review and Meta-Analysis." *Journal of the Academy of Nutrition and Dietetics* 114(9):1375–88.

Sniderman, Paul M., and Sean M. Theriault. 2004. "The Structure of Political Argument and the Logic of Issue Framing." In *Studies in Public Opinion: Attitudes, Nonattitudes, Measurement Error, and Change*, edited by Willem E. Saris and Paul M. Sniderman. Princeton, NJ: Princeton University Press, 133–65.

Snyder, Susan K., and Barry R. Weingast. 2000. "The American System of Shared Powers: The President, Congress, and the NLRB." *Journal of Law, Economics & Organization* 16(2): 269–305.

Song, Anna V., Paul Brown, and Stanton A. Glantz. 2014. "When Health Policy and Empirical Evidence Collide: The Case of Cigarette Package Warning Labels and Economic Consumer Surplus." *American Journal of Public Health* 104(2):e42–e51.

Spaeth, Harold J., Lee Epstein, Andrew D. Martin, Jeffrey A. Segal, Theodore J. Ruger, and Sara C. Benesh. 2016. *Supreme Court Database.* Version 2015, Release 03. http://supreme courtdatabase.org.

Spriggs, James F., and Paul J. Wahlbeck. 1995. "Calling It Quits: Strategic Retirement on the Federal Courts of Appeals, 1893–1991." *Political Research Quarterly* 48(3):573–97.

Stack, Kevin M. 2016. "Preambles as Guidance." *George Washington Law Review* 84(1):1252–92.

Stein, Karen. 2011. "A National Approach to Restaurant Menu Labeling: the Patient Protection and Affordable Health Care Act, Section 4205." *Journal of the American Dietetic Association* 111(5):S19–S27.

Stephenson, Matthew C. 2008. "Evidentiary Standards and Information Acquisition in Public Law." *American Law and Economics Review* 10(2):351–87.

———. 2010. "Information Acquisition and Institutional Design." *Harvard Law Review* 124:1422–83.

Stewart, Richard B. 1975. "The Reformation of American Administrative Law." *Harvard Law Review* 8(8):1667–1813.

Stiglitz, Edward H. 2013. "Unaccountable Midnight Rulemaking—A Normatively Informative Assessment." *NYU Journal of Legislation & Public Policy* 17(1):137–92.

Stokes, Alan. 1978. "The Reliability of Readability Formulae." *Journal of Research in Reading* 1(1):21–34.

Strauss, Peter L. 1996. "From Expertise to Politics: The Transformation of American Rule-Making." *Wake Forest Law Review* 31:745–77.

Sunderman, Gail L., and James S. Kim. 2007. "The Expansion of Federal Power and the Politics of Implementing the No Child Left Behind Act." *Teachers College Record* 109(5):1057–85.

Sunstein, Cass R. 2013a. "The Office of Information and Regulatory Affairs: Myths and Realities." *Harvard Law Review* 126:1838–2139.

———. 2013b. *Simpler: the Future of Government.* New York: Simon and Schuster.

Swartz, Jonas J., Danielle Braxton, and Anthony J. Viera. 2011. "Calorie Menu Labeling on Quick-Service Restaurant Menus: An Updated Systematic Review of the Literature." *International Journal of Behavioral Nutrition and Physical Activity* 8(1):135–43.

Swedberg, Richard, and Ola Agevall. 2005. *The Max Weber Dictionary: Key Words and Central Concepts.* Stanford, CA: Stanford University Press.

Thaler, Richard H., and Cass R. Sunstein. 2008. *Nudge: Improving Decisions about Health, Wealth, and Happiness.* New Haven, CT: Yale University Press.

Thatcher, Liz. 2014. "Common Sense for Menu Labeling; New Requirements for Nutritional Content Signs Will Cost Americans Billions." *Washington Times,* January 30. http://www .washingtontimes.com/news/2014/jan/30/thatcher-common-sense-for-menu-labeling/.

Tiller, Emerson H., and Pablo T. Spiller. 1999. "Strategic Instruments: Legal Structure and Political Games in Administrative Law." *Journal of Law, Economics & Organization* 15(2):349–77.

Tocqueville, Alexis de. 1839. *Democracy in America.* Vol. 1. New York: George Adlard.

Tozzi, Jim. 2011. "OIRA's Formative Years: The Historical Record of Centralized Regulatory Review Preceding OIRA's Founding." *Administrative Law Review* 63:37–69.

Tsebelis, George. 2002. *Veto Players: How Political Institutions Work.* Princeton, NJ: Princeton University Press.

US Department of Agriculture. 2000. "Glickman Announces National Standards for Organic Food." USDA Press Release. December 20. https://web.archive.org/web/20011123030146/http://www.usda.gov/news/releases/2000/12/0425.htm.

Verkuil, Paul R. 1995. "Rulemaking Ossification? A Modest Proposal." *Administrative Law Review* 47(3):453–59.

Vinson, M. Scott, and Scott DeFife. 2011. "Letter to the FDA on Menu Labeling Proposed Rule." National Restaurant Association and National Council of Chain Restaurants, July 5. http://www.restaurant.org/Downloads/PDFs/advocacy/20110705_ml_fda_jointindustry.pdf.

Vogel, David. 2012. *The Politics of Precaution: Regulating Health, Safety, and Environmental Risks in Europe and the United States.* Princeton, NJ: Princeton University Press.

Volden, Craig. 2002. "A Formal Model of the Politics of Delegation in a Separation of Powers System." *American Journal of Political Science* 46(1):111–33.

Wade, James B., Joseph F. Porac, and Timothy G. Pollock. 1997. "Worth, Words, and the Justification of Executive Pay." *Journal of Organizational Behavior* 18(1):641–64.

Wagner, Wendy E. 2009. "The CAIR RIA: Advocacy Dressed up as Policy Analysis." In *Reforming Regulatory Impact Analysis*, edited by Winston Harrington, Lisa Heinzerling, and Richard D. Morgenstern, 56–81. Washington, DC: Resources for the Future.

———. 2010. "Administrative Law, Filter Failure, and Information Capture." *Duke Law Journal* 59(7):1321–1432.

———. 2012. "Revisiting the Impact of Judicial Review on Agency Rulemakings: An Empirical Investigation." *William & Mary Law Review* 53(5):1717–95.

Wagner, Wendy, Katherine Barnes, and Lisa Peters. 2011. "Rulemaking in the Shade: An Empirical Study of EPA's Air Toxic Emission Standards." *Administrative Law Review* 63(1):99–158.

Walker, Christopher J. 2014. "Chevron inside the Regulatory State: An Empirical Assessment." *Fordham Law Review* 83(2):703–29.

Walter, Laura. 2010. "OSHA Publishes Cranes and Derricks Final Rule." *EHS Today*, July 29. http://ehstoday.com/standards/osha/osha-publishes-cranes-derricks-final-rule-0729.

Warren, Elizabeth. 2016. "Corporate Capture of the Rulemaking Process." *Regulatory Review*, June 14. http://www.regblog.org/2016/06/14/warren-corporate-capture-of-the-rulemaking-process/.

Warren, Kenneth F. 2011. *Administrative Law in the Political System.* 5th ed. Boulder, CO: Westview.

Washington Post. 2010. *Landmark: The Inside Story of America's New Health-Care Law—the Affordable Care Act—and What It Means for Us All.* New York: Public Affairs Press.

Waterman, Richard W., Amelia A. Rouse, and Robert L. Wright. 2004. *Bureaucrats, Politics, and the Environment.* Pittsburgh, PA: University of Pittsburgh Press.

Weatherford, Katie. 2013. "Shelanski Lays Out Top Priorities If Confirmed as Next OIRA Administrator." Center for Effective Government. June 12. http://www.foreffectivegov.org/blog/shelanski-lays-out-top-priorities-if-confirmed-next-oira-administrator.

Wedeking, Justin. 2010. "Supreme Court Litigants and Strategic Framing." *American Journal of Political Science* 54(3):617–31.

Weingast, Barry R., and Mark J. Moran. 1983. "Bureaucratic Discretion or Congressional Control? Regulatory Policymaking by the Federal Trade Commission." *Journal of Political Economy* 91(5):765–800.

Wells, Jeff. 2017. "Food Industry Appeals to a Receptive Trump Administration for Regulation Delays." *Food Dive*, April 27. https://www.fooddive.com/news/grocery--food-industry-appeals-to-a-receptive-trump-administration-for-regulation-de/441507/.

Wernerfelt, Birger. 1984. "A Resource-Based View of the Firm." *Strategic Management Journal* 5(2):171–80.

West, William F. 2004. "Formal Procedures, Informal Processes, Accountability, and Responsiveness in Bureaucratic Policy Making: An Institutional Policy Analysis." *Public Administration Review* 64(1):66–80.

———. 2009. "Inside the Black Box: The Development of Proposed Rules and the Limits of Procedural Controls." *Administration and Society* 41(5):576–99.

West, William F., and Connor Raso. 2013. "Who Shapes the Rulemaking Agenda? Implications for Bureaucratic Responsiveness and Bureaucratic Control." *Journal of Public Administration Research and Theory* 23(3):495–519.

Wiley Rein. 2011. "FDA Postpones Enforcement of Menu Labeling Requirements." *News & Insights* (blog), February 24. http://www.wileyrein.com/newsroom-newsletters-item-3675.html.

Wilson, James Q. 1989. *Bureaucracy: What Government Agencies Do and Why They Do It.* New York: Basic Books.

Wilson, Woodrow. 1887. "The Study of Administration." *Political Science Quarterly* 2(2): 197–222.

Wiseman, Alan E., and Jack R. Wright. 2015. "Delegation and Bureaucratic Policymaking in the Presence of Binding Legal Constraints: Like a Good Neighbor, *State Farm* Is There?" Working paper, Vanderbilt University.

Wood, B. Dan. 1988. "Principals, Bureaucrats, and Responsiveness in Clean-Air Enforcements." *American Political Science Review* 82(1):214–34.

Wood, B. Dan, and Richard W. Waterman. 1991. "The Dynamics of Political Control of the Bureaucracy." *American Political Science Review* 85(3):801.

Woods, Neal D. 2013. "Regulatory Democracy Reconsidered: The Policy Impact of Public Participation Requirements." *Journal of Public Administration Research and Theory* 25(2):571–96.

Yackee, Jason Webb, and Susan Webb Yackee. 2006. "A Bias towards Business? Assessing Interest Group Influence on the US Bureaucracy." *Journal of Politics* 68(1):128–39.

———. 2009. "Divided Government and US Federal Rulemaking." *Regulation & Governance* 3(2):128–44.

———. 2010. "Administrative Procedures and Bureaucratic Performance: Is Federal Rule-Making 'Ossified'?" *Journal of Public Administration Research and Theory* 20(2):261–82.

———. 2011. "Testing the Ossification Thesis: An Empirical Examination of Federal Regulatory Volume and Speed, 1950–1990." *George Washington Law Review* 80:1414–92.

Yackee, Susan Webb. 2006. "Sweet-Talking the Fourth Branch: The Influence of Interest Group Comments on Federal Agency Rulemaking." *Journal of Public Administration Research and Theory* 16(1):103–24.

———. 2012. "The Politics of Ex Parte Lobbying: Pre-Proposal Agenda Building and Blocking during Agency Rulemaking." *Journal of Public Administration Research and Theory* 22(2):373–93.

Yehle, Emily, and Robin Bravender. 2014. "OIRA Chief's Buttoned-Down Image Belies Eccentric Roots." *Greenwire*, February 19. http://www.eenews.net/stories/1059994788.

Zellner, Arnold. 1962. "An Efficient Method of Estimating Seemingly Unrelated Regressions and Tests for Aggregation Bias." *Journal of the American Statistical Association* 57(298):348–68.

Index

Page numbers in italics refer to figures and tables.

administrative procedure, 8–9; public opinion and, 27, 45n65; reconciliation process and, 54; *Regulatory Proposals Dataset* and, 204, *208*; reputation and, 11, 18–19, 24, 31, 52, 56–57, 66–67, 77, 88, 116, 162; return letters and, 43; role of bureaucrats and, 64–68; as rote administrative activity, 5; separation-of-powers system and, 5, 12, 19; stakeholders and, 55, 58–59, 63, 65, 69–78; as strategic enterprise, 54–84; success in, 46, 51, 56–57, 59, 64–67, 68n35, 72n46, 84, 111, 127, 133; timing and, 132–36, 139, 143–44, 149–53; understanding, 6–12; *Unified Agenda* and, 90–91, 203–4; vetoes and, 55, 58, 61, 77, 81–82 (*see also* vetoes); writing as tool and, 31, 85–91, 95–97, 105, 111–12
rule-of-law, 27
rule text accessibility: abstract readability and, 211; analysis of, 210–12; *Federal Register* and, 210; koRpus package and, 210; principal component analysis (PCA) and, 210–11; Regulatory Identification Number and, 210; *Regulatory Proposals Dataset* and, 210
Rumsfeld, Donald, 131, 133

safety: Federal Motor Carrier Safety Administration and, *30*, 65–68, 72–73, 81n67, *138*, *206*, *214*; Food Safety and Modernization Act and, 175; National Highway Traffic Safety Administration and, *30*, 92, 96, *100*, *113*, *120*, 134, *138*, *207*, *214*; notice-and-comment and, 27, 34, 46; OSHA and, 11 (*see also* Occupational Safety and Health Administration); policy choice and, 61; public opinion and, 27, 132; *Regulatory Proposals Dataset* and, *205–8*
Same administrator variable, 146–48, *155*
sanctions, 5, 20, 40, 58, 116
saturated fat, 160
Savage, James, 181
Scalia, Antonin, 69, 80
Schwartz, Tom, 40, 58
Sebelius, Kathleen, 13, 38n49
seemingly unrelated regression (SUR) models, 105
Separation of Powers Restoration Act (SOPRA), 197–98
separation-of-powers system: notice-and-comment and, 23; power of procedure and, 5, 12, 19; rulemaking as strategic enterprise and, 61
Shapiro, Ari, 37n47
Shelanski, Howard, 145–46
Sierra Club, 115, 143
size-unity ratio, 101
Skidmore v. Swift & Co., 50n82
slow-rolling, 80–81, 84, 133–35, 145, 147, 152
Social Security Administration (SSA), 7n23, 92, *138*, *210*, *214*

sodium, 160
special education, 85–86, *207*
Spellings, Margaret, 86n3
stakeholders: consultation and, 20, 114–15, 118, 121, 123, 126–28, 216–18; feedback and, 11, 20, 75–78, 115, 118; menu labeling and, 173–78; notice-and-comment and, 27, 29, 32; power of participation and, 74–78; power of procedure and, 11–12, 14; rulemaking as strategic enterprise and, 55, 58–59, 63, 65, 69–78; writing as tool and, 86–87
standardized tests, 85–86
State of California v. Health and Human Services, 21n56
statutory deadline, 48n76, 104, *113*, 129–30, *140*, *142*, 143, *154–56*, 164
Strategic Timing Hypothesis, *83*, 84, 134–35, 139
Strategic Writing Hypothesis, *83*, 84, 88–90, 100, 105
Strauss, Peter L., 26
student aid, 3–4, *30*, 49, 93, 188, *206*
"Study of Administration, The" (Wilson), 23
Sunstein, Cass, 35–36, 43, 145–46
Supreme Court: agency deference and, 15n45; final rule and, 72n45; framing effects and, 71n43; Harlan and, 48n77; Marshall and, 5n19; notice-and-comment and, 25, 28, 34, 45n64, 48–51; obfuscated opinions and, 74n53; overturned decisions and, 74n53; power of procedure and, 3n10, 3n12, 15n45; Scalia and, 69, 80; USDA and, 25; writing as tool and, 90n10, 98n30, 102

Tea Party, 59
timing: advisory committees and, 131n4; agencies and, 133–53; bureaucrats and, 134, 137n17, 138n17, 150, 152; clock time and, 139–41, 150; connecting to theory and, 133–35; courts and, 134, 136, *140*, 142–44, 153, *154–56*; Cox proportional hazard model and, 141, *154–56*; delay effects and, 80; delay mechanisms and, 145–52; *Employment* variable and, 150–51; EPA and, *138*, 143; evaluating strategic, 139–44; event history models and, 139–41, 152–53; *Expertise* variable and, 150–51; fast-tracking and, 80–81, 84, 133, 152; FDA and, 137, *138*, 143; *Federal Register* and, 140–41; final rule and, 20, 80, 132, 135–43, 150–51; hazard rate and, 139–41; HHS and, *138*; *Impact* and *Complexity* scores and, *140*, *142*, 143, 149n31, *154–56*; interest groups and, 131–36, 143–44, 152; measuring effects of, 136–39; menu labeling and, 176–79; midnight rulemaking and, 80–81, 134; OIRA and, 35, 135–36, 139–53, *154–56*; OSHA and, 131–32, 143, 152; ossification and, 133–34; pacing and, 78–81, 143–45, 147, 150, 152, *155–56*; political climate and, 133, 141–42; political oversight